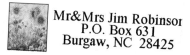
Mr&Mrs Jim Robinson
P.O. Box 631
Burgaw, NC 28425

D0327170

Heloise
Hints
for All
Occasions

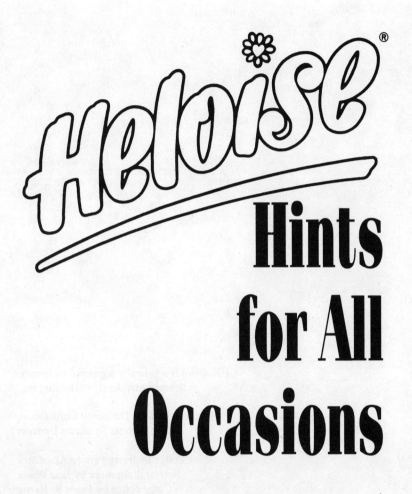

Heloise

Hints for All Occasions

A PERIGEE BOOK

Copyright © 1995 by The Hearst Corporation,
King Features Syndicate Division

Book design by Irving Perkins Associates
Interior illustrations by Jane Waski
Cover design by James R. Harris
Cover illustration by Stan Skardinski
Author photograph on back cover by Al Rendon

Published simultaneously in Canada.

ISBN 0-399-51893-2

Printed in the United States of America

To my mother, the original Heloise, who entertained with such flare, and who taught me it's not just the food, it's the atmosphere and company you remember!

Acknowledgments

So many people, so little space!

My thanks to one and all who helped work their magic and turn this into a book! Marcy Meffert, my faithful, fun and workaholic editor/writer/researcher/friend. My office "staff," who make what I do seem easy: Ruth, Joyce, Kelly, Angie and Janie. Merry Clark, editorial director of Heloise, Inc., and John Duff, publisher of Perigee Books, for directing me gently. Every author should have an editor as kind and wonderful as you. Judy New, registered dietitian, for all her help. And my special thanks to Jane Waski for her delightful and whimsical illustrations.

And, forever and ever, my unbelievably understanding husband, David, who probably wouldn't know what I looked like without "copy" in my hand.

Contents

Introduction

Hints for All Occasions sounds like such a broad topic at first, but when you think about it, it really means the Heloise approach to life.

You can spend months planning a big event, or you can throw together a quick meal on the spur of the moment, and both are entertaining! Hints on how to be a host and guest are both covered in this book.

My mother, who started the Heloise column in 1959 as a military housewife, taught me a lot. You don't have to spend a lot of money on food or decorations. Many times the simplest meals presented with flare are the ones that people remember the most. Even a plain old tuna fish sandwich, cut on a diagonal or in points, placed on a pretty plate with pickles, olives or coleslaw with a dash of paprika for color can look *wow*! Most chefs know that presentation is all important because that's your first impression of the food. I hope the little tricks and hints in this book I have learned from my mother and thousands of readers will help you.

And, when all else fails, put on a smile, make the best of what you can, and you will succeed.

If you would like to share a hint, I would love to hear from you! Please drop me a note or fax me a line.

Heloise
P.O. Box 795000
San Antonio, TX 78279
Fax # (210) H-E-L-O-I-S-E (435-6473)

Party Planning

Have you ever discovered, as you set the table shortly before a party, that the only candles in the house are burned-down stubs left over from Christmas? And your children have scratched smiley Santa faces into the wax?

Or have you ever looked into the refrigerator after all the guests have gone and found food that you forgot to serve? And, of course, it was a major-effort recipe! ("Major-effort" defined as time-consuming to prepare and with exotic and expensive ingredients.)

The situations above are distressing, but neither is as bad as finding unmailed party invitations in a coat pocket or briefcase the day before your party is scheduled! And it's worse if the party is catered and you've paid a nonrefundable deposit!

Checklists are the keys to stress-free, successful party planning. You can machine copy the lists in this section and then stick them on your fridge, where you can easily check off completed tasks and purchases. I've left some "white space" so that you can note your own reminders on the lists.

Do save party lists with your own "do-it-again" or "bad idea" comments on them to help you in the future. Also, make notes on recipes to help you the next time you make them. For example, write down how many people the casserole for eight actually serves and how much longer it took to bake four casseroles than it did when you baked only one, and so on.

Party Time Line—Who, What, When, Where, and How

WHO

Make a guest list as soon as you decide you will have a party, because the number of people involved governs the other decisions you will make about location, food and beverages.

WHAT

Determine the type of party you will have: Will it be a casual barbecue/picnic, a formal sit-down dinner, a catered buffet? Will it be a brunch, luncheon, dinner party or cocktails with heavy or light hors d'oeuvres?

WHEN

Set the date. The bigger the party, the greater the lead time you'll need to

✓ Get invitations printed and mailed
✓ Book party facilities, if it's not to be in your home or backyard
✓ Book a caterer, if you are hiring one

✓ Rent tables, chairs, or other equipment
✓ Arrange for music or other entertainment, if any will be provided

WHERE

Celebrations like weddings, reunions, and other large events, which require renting party rooms or facilities, may need to be booked as early as one year in advance. However, large and small hotels in most cities may be able to accommodate you with shorter notice.

Some city parks have outdoor party facilities which need to be reserved in advance if you want to use pavillions or barbecues for a party such as a family reunion; contact your city's Parks & Recreation Department.

AND HOW ...

Invitations: If invitations will be printed, you'll need to allow at least three weeks for printing. While some printers in larger cities may have faster service, it's still less stressful if you have the invitations printed early, as soon as you have all the information on date, time, and place.

❋ Invitations to large, catered events are usually mailed so that they are received four or five weeks prior to the event. Guests are requested to respond by a certain date so that hosts can make proper arrangements for food and beverages.

❋ At the other extreme, if you decide in the morning that you will have a casual backyard picnic for anyone who's not busy that night, a phone call that day is just fine.

NOTE: If you are a guest, please take the time to respond, yes or no. The host needs to know how many portions to order for a catered event and will be billed for all no-shows.

If You Hire a Caterer: Hire the caterer as soon as you know when you will have the party. Caterers can be helpful in finding a suitable party facility if you need one. If you are having the party catered in your home, the caterer will probably want to visit and check out how best to cook or heat food and prepare beverages, and determine the best "traffic flows" to serve your guests.

Finding a Caterer: Hire a caterer whose work you've seen and admired firsthand. Otherwise, get recommendations from friends or business associates whose taste is similar to yours. Watch the social section of your newspaper to find out who caters a lot of local parties. Ask the food editor of your newspaper or your florist to recommend good catering companies. If you are new in town, call the local convention or tourist bureau to find out who is popular.

✻ The most important hint: Whether the catered party is at a rented facility or in your home, don't assume anything about what the caterer will provide.

✓ Write down clearly in the contract all details about food, beverages, and serving them so that you and your caterer aren't saying to each other, "But I thought you were bringing that," as the guests are ringing your doorbell. You can use the food, beverage, and service checklist in this section.

✓ What is the price per person and how will the price change if you furnish the wine, a special dessert, cheeses, or whatever else you want to take responsibility for?

✓ When does the caterer need a final guest count? Can last minute guests be accommodated? Will you be billed for no-shows? (The answer is usually yes. It's customary because the caterer has prepared the number of portions ordered.)

✓ What are the fees for bartending and food service?

✓ Will tableware, serving dishes, punch bowl, ice buckets, serving utensils, warming trays, chafing dishes, etc. be yours or the caterer's?

✓ If you are using disposable plates, napkins, and cups, who will buy them, you or the caterer?

✓ Who will furnish table linens and centerpieces?

✓ What time will which foods on the menu be served?

✓ Who is responsible for how much of the cleanup after the party?

✓ Are the leftovers yours? Or does the caterer get to take them after the party is over?

NOTE: If you have booked a caterer many months or a year ahead, as you would for a wedding, it's a good idea to call about two months before the event to confirm that you are still on the books. And, of course, call when you have the number of guests who have responded.

Food and Food Service List

Whether or not you hire a caterer, you'll have peace of mind and better organization if you list and briefly describe each food item on the menu. Note the sauces, garnishes, or other kitchen and on-table flavor enhancers to be served with them, such as salt, pepper, salsa, mustard, mint jelly, etc.

✓ **Hors d'oeuvres**
   Hot
   Cold
   Crudité
   Serving dishes and utensils

If served "stand-up" and not at table, will small plates, forks, and napkins be needed?

✓ **Entrée(s)**
Casserole
Meat/fish
Sauces
Garnishes

✓ **Side Dishes**
Starch
Vegetable(s)
Salad

✓ **Rolls/breads**
Butter/margarine
Other bread toppings—roasted garlic, olive oil, etc.
Will the bread need to be heated before serving?

✓ **Desserts**
Garnishes such as whipped cream, fruits, mint leaves, chocolate shavings
Serving plates/bowls and utensils

✓ **Cheeses**
Crackers
Crisp breads
Garnish for cheese tray (grapes, parsley)
Cheese board, plate, spreaders, knife, toothpicks for cubes
Small dessert-size plates

✓ **Nuts**
Serving dish
Small spoon for scooping
Small napkins

✓ **Mints or chocolate treats**
Serving dish or plate

Food Serving Needs

Generally speaking, to "think green" means using disposable plates in areas where water conservation is a priority and using nondisposables in areas where limited landfill space requires people to decrease their trash output as much as possible.

NOTE: If you don't have enough china and flatware to serve the number of guests but you still want to "think green," buy sturdy plastic ware which can be washed and reused.

✓ Plates—hors d'oeuvres, dinner, salad, bread and butter, dessert
✓ Bowls for soups
✓ Bowls/platters or compotes for serving courses
✓ Flatware
✓ Serving utensils
✓ Warming trays, chafing dishes
  NOTE: Where will you plug in electrical warming trays, chafing dishes, coffeemakers? Cords should not dangle where they will trip people, and plugging too many appliances into one circuit can blow fuses or trip circuit breakers in some houses.
✓ Tablecloth(s) or placemats
✓ Napkins (include extras for bread baskets or when serving messy meals like barbecue)
✓ Centerpiece(s)
✓ Trivets to protect table from hot dishes

Beverages and Beverage Service

List all beverages, their garnishes, and serving needs.

✓ **Tea**
  Loose tea or tea bags
  Milk
  Lemon, mint leaves
  Sweeteners (sugar, honey, artificial sweetener)
  Teapot for hot tea
  Pitcher and ice for iced tea
  Tall spoons for stirring iced tea
  Cups or iced tea glasses

✓ **Coffee**
  Party coffeemaker
  Decaf and/or regular coffee
  Milk/coffee cream
  Sweetener (sugar or artificial sweetener)
  Spoons for stirring coffee
  Cups or mugs

✓ **Liquors to serve with coffee**
  Small glasses
  Crushed ice or ice cubes

✓ **Ice**
  Ice bucket and tongs for cubes
  Coolers for chilling canned beverages

✓ **Soft Drinks**
  (Include some decaffeinated and diet ones.)

✓ **Beer**
   (Include some nonalcoholic beers for designated drivers and
   others who don't drink alcohol.)

✓ **Wines/Champagne**
   Small knife for cutting seals on wine bottles
   Corkscrew
   Ice bucket or other means for keeping wine chilled
   Linen towel for opening and serving champagne

✓ **Mixed Drink Ingredients**
   Gin, vodka, whiskey, etc.
   Mixers (seltzer, ginger ale, others)
   Garnishes (limes/lemons, maraschino cherries, olives, cock-
   tail onions, pineapple slices, mint leaves, etc., appropriate
   to the drinks served)
   Shaker, pitcher or blender for mixing

✓ **Glasses, stemware, cups (disposable or not)**

✓ **Punch**
   Ingredients (juices, sparkling waters, liquors, etc.)
   Ice block with or without garnish frozen in it
   Garnishes (orange, lemon, or other fruit slices, maraschino
   cherries, nonpoisonous edible flowers, etc.)
   Punch bowl and ladle
   Punch cups or 4- to 6-ounce glasses

"Cook-It-Myself" Party

Make a "catering contract" with yourself that lists all the details
you would have in a regular catering contract and try to do as
much as possible ahead of time.

After you make menu and "to do" lists, put them on the fridge

9

door so that you can check off each task completed and each food purchased. Writing out a menu and posting it prevents forgetting to serve things that may be in the back of the refrigerator. If your guests help you in the kitchen, it's easier for them, too, if you have everything written down about what to serve and in what bowl, dish, etc. If you wish, you can write down on a piece of paper the name of the food that goes into a certain serving bowl or platter and just put the piece of paper into or on the dish. Then your helpers will know without asking.

❀ My most important hint for someone who is having a "cook-it-myself" party is: If someone asks, "What can I do or bring?" take the offer.

❀ If you have a specific menu planned, with only certain specialties, and you think the food or wine gift offered or brought by a guest may not fit in with your menu, you can always say, "I would love it if you'd bring me one of your delicious (banana breads, ginger cookies, whatever) so that I can enjoy a restful coffee break on the day after." If a guest brings wine that won't go with the food, you can either serve it as a cocktail beverage or say something like "I think I'll put this aside for tomorrow when I put my feet up to rest after this party."

❀ If you need help to prepare for and serve at a party in your home and can't afford to hire someone, trade off services with a friend in similar circumstances. The bonus is that you'll get invited to your friend's party for sure!

TWO WEEKS BEFORE A BIG "COOK-IT-MYSELF" PARTY

❀ If you have young children, admit that it's difficult to parent and host a big party at the same time, and either hire a sitter to entertain the children and put them to bed, or arrange to swap children's sleepovers with their friends. You can return the favor when they have a party or a night out.

❋ Plan your menu and make two shopping lists—one for perishables and one for nonperishables. Please see "How Much to Buy" in this section.

✓ Buy the nonperishables immediately. You can be almost certain that something on your list that is always on the shelf at your favorite store will suddenly become sold out and unavailable the day before your party.

✓ Nonperishables can include such items as:
   All bottled beverages and all bottled, canned, frozen food items and spices. Also disposable plates, cups, glasses, tableware and napkins if you are using them.

✓ Order all special cuts of meat from your butcher if you can, because Murphy's Law will prevail when a party is being planned. If you want a pork tenderloin, so will everyone in town!

✓ Make a list of the perishables to be bought the day before the party, such as salad veggies, coffee cream, and baked goods. Some, like French bread, must be bought the day of the party.

HOW MUCH SHOULD I BUY?

Beverages

Generally, people consume two or three drinks during the first two or so hours of the party and less after that. To prevent serving a lot of liquor without adequate amounts of food, it's best to wait no longer than one hour from the guests' arrival time to their being seated and/or served the dinner.

If you are on a tight budget, consider serving jug wines or punch (alcoholic or nonalcoholic) along with soft drinks. Be aware that nonalcoholic beverages are a must-serve for non-imbibers and for that designated driver in each group.

Hard Liquor: A liter-size bottle contains 33.8 ounces or about twenty-two 1½-ounce drinks. Do be sure that whoever is tending bar measures with a jigger of 1½ ounces per drink so that the amounts are uniform and guests don't get surprised by the kind of drink that melts their dental work!

NOTE: People from different areas of the country have different tastes in liquors, but you will be safe if you have:

✓ Red and white wine
✓ Vodka
✓ Gin
✓ Scotch
✓ A blended whiskey
✓ A Canadian whiskey
✓ Bourbon
✓ Rum
✓ Vermouth
✓ A cream sherry
✓ Port wine
✓ Beers: regular, light, and nonalcoholic
✓ Assorted after-dinner liquors

Mixers should include:
✓ Tomato and fruit juices
✓ Ginger ale
✓ Club soda

✓ Mineral water
✓ Tonic water
✓ Bitter lemon
✓ Soft drinks

Since many people drink the mixers with or without alcoholic additions, and you can drink the leftovers yourself after the party, stock up on a good supply, especially when they are on sale.

Wine: You will get about ten 3-ounce portions of wine from a 1-liter bottle. A 7- or 8-ounce tulip glass can be used to serve almost any wine, and the glasses are filled about halfway.

When calculating your dinner wine, expect a 750 ml. bottle of table wine to provide approximately eight 3-ounce servings, and you can count on an average of two servings per person. A 750 ml. bottle of dessert wine will provide approximately ten 2½-ounce servings, and you can expect two servings per person of this wine, too.

Most hosts offer white, red, or rosé wines as cocktail wines. You can usually get help on which wines to serve with what foods from a wine store or a liquor store that has a large wine selection. Very large stores often have party planners to help you make selections and buy the right amounts. Be aware that the old rules of white wine with fish and red wine with meat aren't rigidly observed anymore. Also, many books are available to help you make wine selections to go with different foods.

NOTE: Wines that come with a screw-on cap and not a cork are ready to drink when you buy them. If you plan to drink the wines soon, all bottles can be stored upright. Corked wine bottles should be stored on their sides. Store wines in a cool, dark place like a cellar, if you have one. Generally speaking, whites and rosés are chilled; reds are served at room temperature. Personal taste can enter into this, too. The quickest way to cool wine is to put it into an ice bucket containing two-thirds crushed ice and one-third water. It will take about 20 to 30 minutes. It takes 1½ to 2½ hours to chill wine in the refrigerator to 40 or 45 degrees.

Champagne: Champagne is generally meant to be consumed in a short time, not kept for 5 or 10 years, so don't buy an excessive amount. You may want to open a large bottle for the first round and bottles smaller than Magnum size for subsequent rounds of serving. Here are amounts and meanings of words in the "champagne language":

A split holds 18.7 centiliter
A half holds 37.5 centiliter
A bottle holds 75.0 centiliter
A Magnum is the equivalent of 2 bottles

A Double Magnum is the equivalent of 4 bottles
A Jeroboam is the equivalent of 4 bottles
A Rehoboam is the equivalent of 6 bottles
An Imperial is the equivalent of 8 bottles
A Methuselah is the equivalent of 8 bottles (different shape than the Imperial)
A Salmanazer is the equivalent of 12 bottles
A Balthazar is the equivalent of 16 bottles
A Nabuchadnezzar is the equivalent of 20 bottles
(Our thanks to Champagne Wines Information Bureau, New York, NY 212-682-6300)
NOTE: Champagne should be stored on its side in a cool, dark place. Some say that champagne stored in the refrigerator picks up odors. Chill champagne by putting it in the refrigerator or a bucket of ice water two hours before serving.

Punch: A gallon of punch makes about 40 punch-cup servings. Remember that a large block of ice frozen in a gelatin mold won't dilute the punch as much as fast-melting ice cubes.

Food Amounts

While it depends on the occasion, how early you serve the food, and how hungry your guests are, there are rules of thumb for estimating amounts of food to buy.

- A quart of dip, such as crab or broccoli, will make about 150 teaspoon-size servings.
- One pound of cooked lean meat provides about thirty-two ½-ounce slices for small sandwiches.
- A 3½- to 4-pound chicken makes chicken salad for about 70 small triangular sandwiches.
- A ½-ounce slice of cheese is enough for one small sandwich.
- A 20- to 24-ounce loaf of sandwich bread has about 25 slices and will make 52 small, triangular, closed sandwiches.

- A 6- to 8-pound ham with a bone will serve 18 to 24 people for a buffet or 12 to 16 people for dinner; an 8- to 10-pound ham with a bone will serve 24 to 30 people for a buffet and 16 to 20 people for dinner.
- Boneless meats, such as a rolled rib roast, are calculated at about ½ pound per person before cooking, yielding about 3 ounces per serving after they are cooked.
- Meats with a lot of bone, such as barbecue ribs, can vary greatly according to how meaty or bony the slab is; one slab of baby back ribs may serve only 3 people, and a regular slab of ribs may serve 4 to 6 people.
- Vegetables vary greatly, too, but ½ cup is usually one serving. For example, ¼ pound of fresh green beans or ½ cup of canned green beans equals one serving.
- Serve one medium baked potato per person, or if you are preparing creamed or mashed potatoes, plan on 6 to 8 pounds of potatoes serving 25 people at ½ cup per serving.
- Rice servings are estimated at about ¾ cup (cooked measure) per serving; noodles are usually about ½ cup (cooked) per serving.
- When making a green salad, one head of lettuce makes about 6 or so servings, not calculating the amount of other veggies you add to it.
- A 12-ounce can of nuts should serve 20 to 25 people.
- One-half pound of small candies serves about 25 people.
- A pound of coffee brews 50 cups.

NOTE: Do keep track of the vegetarians in your group and make sure you offer some meatless dishes. And, naturally, if you know that neither Jane nor Bill can eat shellfish, do tell them if that dip has minced clams in it. Too often well-meaning hosts urge guests to "just try" a food (or drink) that the guests may be allergic to or just don't like. Remember that fun means not being forced into things you don't want to or can't do, and you want your guests to have fun at your party!

Buy by the Pound, Measure in Cups

Since most recipe amounts are measured by the cup and most of the foods you buy are sold by the pound, here are a few approximate equivalents to help you avoid buying too much.

Apples: 1 pound equals about 3 medium or 3 cups sliced.

Bananas: 1 pound equals about 3 medium or 2½ cups sliced.

Butter or Other Fats: 1 pound equals 2 cups; or 1 stick (¼ pound) equals ½ cup.

Candied Fruit and Peels: ½ pound equals 1½ cups cut up.

Cheese, American Cheddar: 1 pound equals 4 cups grated.

Cheese, Cottage: 1 pound equals 2 cups.

Cheese, White Cream: 3-ounce package equals 6 tablespoons; ½-pound package equals 16 tablespoons or 1 cup.

Chocolate, Unsweetened: ½ pound equals 8 (1-ounce) squares.

Coconut, Shredded: 1 pound equals 5 cups.

Coffee, Ground: 1 pound equals 80 tablespoons.

Cream, Whipping: 1 pint equals 2 cups or 4 cups whipped.

Dates: 1 pound whole equals 2¼ cups; pitted equals 2 cups; cut-up equals 1¾ cups; finely cut equals 1½ cups.

Eggs: Sizes vary but usually 2 medium eggs equal ⅓ cup; 2 large eggs equal ½ cup; 3 medium eggs equal ½ cup; 3 large eggs equal ⅔ cup. Don't use less or more than the recipe calls for.

Figs: 1 pound whole equals 2¾ cups; cut-up equals 2¾ cups; finely cut equals 2½ cups.

Flour: 1 pound all-purpose equals 4 cups sifted; cake equals 4½ cups sifted; whole wheat equals 3½ cups sifted; rye equals 4½ to 5 cups sifted.

Lemon: 1 medium equals 2 to 3 tablespoons juice; 1½ to 3 teaspoons lightly grated rind

Marshmallows: ¼ pound equals 16

Nuts, Shelled (1 pound each, whole): almonds equals 3½ cups; pecans equals 4 cups; peanuts equals 3 cups; walnuts equals 4 cups.

    NOTE: 1 cup whole shelled nuts when coarsely chopped equals 1 cup minus 1 teaspoon; finely chopped equals ⅞ cup.

Oranges: 1 medium equals ⅓ to ½ cup juice; 1 to 2 tablespoons lightly grated rind.

Raisins: 15-ounce package whole equals 3 cups; cut-up equals 2¾ cups; finely cut equals 2½ cups.

Sugar: 1 pound granulated equals 2 cups; brown equals 2¼ cups, firmly packed; confectioners' equals 3½ cups, sifted.

ONE WEEK BEFORE THE PARTY

If you are going to do a heavy cleaning before a big, special party (scrub/wax floors, shampoo carpets, polish brass and silver, wash stored crystal or china), do it now. Then, the only cleaning you need to to just before a party is a quick feather dust, mop or vacuum, and bathroom wipe-down. You don't want to be too tired to enjoy your own party, and you need your energy to prepare the food if you will be cooking it yourself.

Pre-party House Cleaning: You can make a list of what to clean, but be realistic about how much and if serious major-effort cleaning is actually necessary. Some questions to ask yourself include:

✿ Will you wash windows for a party that will be held at night when nobody can see the windows?

✿ Do you need to scrub every nook, cranny, and crevice with a toothbrush even if you know that nobody who matters will care?

✳ Do you think surface cleaning is enough because you'd rather focus on the food?

NOTE: One of the best party-givers I know just flicks a feather duster over the furniture, pulls the shower curtain closed to hide the tiles, and replaces all bright light bulbs with lower wattage or colored bulbs so that nobody can see what's not clean even if they try. She does her major-effort cleaning *after* the party, since you have to clean after anyway. This was my mother's advice, too, and I do my darndest to follow it.

ON THE DAY BEFORE THE PARTY

1. Check all of your lists to make sure you have everything you need.
2. Get out your serving dishes, trays, and bowls to make sure they are clean and ready to use.

   NOTE: To avoid possible mess, pretest the capacity of serving casseroles or bowls by filling them with water measured according to the recipe's amount.
3. Arrange the serving dishes on the table to make sure they will all fit and that you will have enough trivets or other hot-dish protection for your table.
4. Look at your table linens to see if they need ironing or, with some permanent-press cloths, a spin in the dryer with a damp towel to fluff out wrinkles.

   NOTE: If you hang linens on pants hangers, you won't have so many creases in them, just the ones you need to center the cloth on the table.
5. Buy perishables if possible. (Some vegetables, meats, fruits, etc. will be suitable the next day, but some breads or rolls may not, such as French bread or specialty rolls.)

6. Cut, chop, slice, dice, marinate (meats), macerate (vegetables), cook, and do anything else to the food that can be done the day before.

ON THE DAY OF THE PARTY

1. If you haven't bought your perishables the previous day, do it in the morning while you are still calm and confident that everything will go on schedule.
2. Cook what needs cooking.
3. Set up what needs setting up.
4. Take a rest with your feet up so that you won't be too tired to have fun at your own party.
5. At the party, again, the most important hint is: *Do let guests help you if they ask!*

Kitchen Magic
with Heloise

This section has some of the most recent hints sent to me by readers and some classic Heloise hints that have been around since my mother first started the column. Since cutting and chopping recipe ingredients are major time-consumers when you are preparing party foods, I've tried to include as many shortcuts for these tedious tasks as I could find in my files. And since no matter how well you plan, you are still going to run out of, forget to buy, or just can't find that something you need, I've included a list of substitutions for ingredients and kitchen equipment.

Some kitchen errors can be corrected with my "food repair" hints. Kitchen errors due to food mishandling or storage can't always be corrected, and some can be dangerous since they can result in illness. That's why this section includes information on food storage and handling, to help you avoid having the kind of party everyone remembers for the wrong reason—everybody got sick!

Food Handling and Storage Safety

"When in doubt, throw it out" is the best rule if you're unsure that stored food is still safe to eat. This rule is even more important when you are having a party, because of the potential problems when handling and cooking larger amounts of food than you are accustomed to, because you may have food standing around longer than usual when it's on a buffet table and, not least, because the results will affect greater numbers of people.

Here are a few food handling and storage hints from the United States Department of Agriculture (USDA), which is your best source for how-to's on food care. If you have questions about food safety, you can call the USDA Meat and Poultry Hotline at 800-535-4555. The hours are Monday to Friday, 10 A.M. to 4 P.M. Eastern Time. Washington, D.C., area residents should call 202-720-3333.

According to the USDA, any perishable food can cause a foodborne illness. In addition to those problems caused by *E. coli,* there has been reported illness caused by salmonella in tomatoes, cantaloupes, and eggs; listeria in soft cheese; and botulism in baked potatoes and garlic bottled in oil. The mishandling of food that caused the reported illnesses occurred in both restaurants and homes.

The USDA says that, although there are many ways bacterial problems with food can develop as the food goes from farm to fork, there are many things you can do to prevent food-borne illness:

1. Most food-poisoning bacteria doesn't grow well or fast at refrigerator temperatures (below 40°F), so put meat and poultry into the refrigerator or freezer as soon as possible after buying it.

22

NOTE: Contrary to what some people think, *E. coli* bacteria are *not* killed by freezing, and that's why it's important to *cook food thoroughly*. *E. coli* can also appear in raw (unpasteurized) milk, unprocessed apple cider, and unchlorinated water. Other foods can "pick up" the bacteria from raw meat juices; for example, if you chop salad veggies on the same cutting board previously used for raw meat.

2. Never thaw food on the counter or let it sit out of the refrigerator for more than 2 hours. In high summer heat (85 degrees or more), food should not be out of the refrigerator for more than 1 hour.

NOTE: Refrigerated ground meat and patties should be used in 1 to 2 days; frozen meat and patties in 3 to 4 months.

4. Cooking kills most food-borne bacteria. Meat should be cooked to 160°F and poultry to 170°F to 180°F for doneness. Red meat is done when it's brown or gray inside; all meat, poultry, and fish juices should run clear and with no trace of pink.

5. Leftovers should be refrigerated immediately in small, shallow containers that allow them to cool quickly.

6. Beware of cross-contamination of foods from allowing raw meat, poultry, fish, or their juices to contact food that won't be cooked. Always prepare and serve foods on clean cutting boards, platters, and plates, and with clean utensils.

NOTE: Many people carry raw meat or fish to the backyard barbecue on a platter, and use the same platter to carry the cooked meat, which risks contamination. Use a clean platter for the cooked meat. The extra cleanup is worth the trouble.

7. Wash hands, utensils, and work areas with hot, soapy water after contact with raw chicken, fish, meat, and meat patties, to avoid cross-contamination. Follow good personal hygiene rules of hand washing, especially after using the bathroom.

Cutting Board Cleanliness

As this book is being written, there is a question about what types of cutting boards are safest. Some research has shown that for some as-yet-unknown reason bacteria did not survive overnight on wooden cutting boards but increased greatly on plastic ones. The USDA says that until the research is published and reviewed and fully substantiated, it still recommends use of nonporous material boards such as plastic or glass for cutting meat and poultry.

If you prefer wooden boards for cutting meat and poultry, reserve a board for this use exclusively. And, no matter what type of board you cut on, always wash with hot, soapy water *after each use*. Let the board air dry or pat it with fresh paper towels. Some nonporous material boards can be washed in the automatic dishwasher; laminated wood boards may split if washed in the dishwasher.

NOTE: The USDA recommends once-a-week sanitizing of all boards by flooding the surface with a solution of 2 teaspoons chlorine bleach to 1 quart of water. Let the board stand a few minutes, rinse well with clear water, and air dry or pat dry with fresh paper towels.

NOTE: Plastic boards that become excessively cut or grooved should be replaced.

In "Food News for Consumers" (Summer Supplement, 1993, by Joyce Johnston), the USDA gives the following hints especially for picnic food, but the information applies to party food and food you take to potluck events, too.

In the Kitchen: Start with clean preparation. Wash hands, work area, and utensils before preparing food. Do *not* thaw on the counter. Marinate foods in the refrigerator.

Menu Planning: When going on a summer outing, take only the amounts of food you'll use. Most foods are safe for short periods if kept in an insulated cooler with ice.

Salads and store-bought mayonnaise can be safe, if kept cold. Avoid custard-type foods. If you cannot take a cooler for the food, take fruits, fresh vegetables, hard cheese, canned or dried meats or fish, peanut butter, breads, crackers, dry cereal.

Packing Up Food-to-Go: Always use an insulated cooler and include a cold source in it such as block ice, frozen gel packs, or frozen water or juice in plastic or paper containers. (The bonus with frozen water in jugs is that when it melts, you can either drink it or wash your hands with it.)

HELOISE HINT: When packing for a picnic, do tuck in moist towelettes or washcloths. (Freeze wet washcloths in plastic zipper bags before going on a picnic, and you'll have a cool compress for stings and sprains or a nice brow-cooler to wipe your face.)

❋ Securely overwrap or bag foods that might drip or leak, especially raw meat, poultry and fish, to prevent raw juices from touching foods that are ready to eat.

❀ Avoid opening the cooler too often. Have one cooler for food, another for beverages and extra ice, to avoid opening the food container and warming the food each time you take a drink can out.

❀ Keep hot foods hot in a thermos or an insulated dish or put them into a foam cooler of their own.

❀ Keep the cooler in the passenger area of the car. When you go to a picnic, don't let the food just sit anywhere in the car; put it into the shade, cover it with a blanket, and avoid opening it too often. Try to replenish melted ice en route.

❀ At home or for a picnic, keep the food cold until the grill is heated. Plan to cook the food completely at the picnic site; no partial cooking ahead. *Do* cook thoroughly so that meat and poultry are not pink. Juices should run clear, and fish should flake with a fork.

CAUTION (for picnics or any other time): Do *not* allow raw meat, poultry, or fish juices to touch other foods. *Always* use a clean plate and utensils for serving cooked foods.

Serving Food: Food should never sit out for more than 1 hour at temperatures of 85 degrees or more. Pack and/or serve smaller portions in serving dishes so that you can replenish portions in clean dishes when necessary. Serve food quickly from a cooler when you are on a picnic and return it to the cooler as fast as possible.

Taking Food Home from a Picnic (or Party): When there are leftovers, put them back into the cooler or refrigerator immediately after eating. *Discard* all perishable foods left out at room temperature more than 2 hours, or more than 1 hour if the temperature is 85 degrees or more. If perishables have been on ice except while being cooked or served, and you were gone no more than 4 or 5 hours, you may be able to save picnic leftovers if you still have ice in the cooler or your gel pack is still solid.

26

FOOD STORAGE

If you have any doubt that people keep foods in storage for extraordinary periods of time, read on. When I asked my readers to write in and tell me about the oldest things in their refrigerators, the letters poured in. Here are the top ten letters published in my newspaper column. You can use this for a party game: Give a prize to the person who has the oldest "antique food" in the fridge!

1. A Michigan fridge had a fifty-three-year-old Christmas fruitcake.
2. A Texas fridge had a fifty-year-old jar of bread starter that still made wonderful sourdough bread and English muffins. (Sourdough "starters" traditionally have been "friendship" gifts from one woman to another, especially in the days of the Old West, when women moved away from family and friends and needed something from home to ease the loneliness.)
3. In Pennsylvania, a jar of canned blackberries from Mom was still in her daughter's fridge forty-five-plus years later.
4. A couple named, appropriately, Love in Connecticut still had a forty-five-year-old piece of their wedding cake in the refrigerator.
5. Another yeast starter was thriving in a Washington refrigerator for forty-three years, and it, too, was still being used.
6. A Massachusetts refrigerator had a bottle of forty-three-year-old soy sauce. Guess they didn't eat much Chinese food!
7. Another sentimental woman, from New York, still had the forty-three-year-old "small heart cakes" that surrounded her wedding cake.
8. An Indiana woman who apparently dislikes ironing still had her daughter's baby clothes in the fridge, dampened

and ready to iron. Her daughter was forty-two. She should get a procrastination award!

9. A Texas woman didn't have her wedding cake but did have a sugar bell from its top that was forty-two years old.

10. In New Hampshire, there was a forty-year-old jar of processed Limburger cheese spread in the fridge. I assume that people were afraid to open it for fear it would attack them and do bodily harm!

NOTE: If you keep such things in your fridge, you definitely won't have space for party foods when you need it!

FOOD STORAGE HINTS

Alcoholic Beverages in Lead Crystal: According to the Food and Drug Administration (FDA), lead crystal should not be used to store food or beverages for extended periods of time. If you wish to use lead crystal on special occasions, do so at your own discretion but do not leave the beverages or food in the crystalware for long periods. Studies show that small amounts of lead are leached from lead crystalware within minutes of contact and reach higher levels the longer the storage time.

Canned Foods: Although they may be safe to eat when stored for longer periods of time, commercially canned foods usually remain at their advertised quality for 18 to 24 months, if they've been stored properly. Not all canned foods have expiration dates on them that consumers can read; some of the dates are coded so that you would have to contact the manufacturer to find out if the food is outdated. Always follow the "when in doubt, throw it out" food safety rule.

Celery or Carrot Sticks: After you've washed and cut celery stalks or carrot sticks for a veggie platter, store them in a clean, recycled plastic two-liter soda bottle filled with one inch of water and cover with plastic wrap. Just cut off the top to make the bottom as tall as the veggie sticks. You can serve the veggies in your homemade container, too, at a picnic. The bonus is that, whether it's just for storage or picnic serving, the container is disposable and you have one less thing to wash after the party!

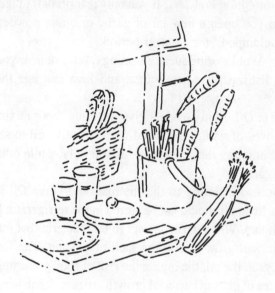

Cheese: If your guests didn't eat all of that expensive cheese you served at your party, you can store it so that it doesn't get moldy. Wrap the cheese in a vinegar-soaked paper towel or cheesecloth before putting it in a plastic bag or in plastic wrap. You won't taste the vinegar, I promise.

Freezer Storage: Line up the party foods, like fruits and vegetables, in shoe boxes, then stack them for storage in the freezer. No tops needed. Then you won't have to dig through all sorts of foods to find the party ones. If you don't have boxes, put your party foods together in a grocery bag and be sure to label it for easy identification so that you don't buy duplicates.

NOTE: Freezers can become warehouses for "antique food." Some people make a dated inventory list of foods in the freezer, checking off those that get used and adding new foods to the list as they are put in. Tape the list to the freezer door.

Fruit, Dried: Stored in a clean recycled mayonnaise jar with an airtight lid, dried fruit will keep up to a year.

Garlic or Onion Powders: If you only tear off half of the sealing foil when you open a new jar of garlic or onion powder, it will keep "unclumped" for a longer period.

NOTE: Avoid storing such seasonings above or near your stove, sink, or dishwasher, where steam and heat can age them prematurely.

Garlic in Oil: Many readers give me hints about mixing either whole cloves of garlic or minced garlic in olive oil to save until needed. Some say they cook with the oil only, while others cook with the garlic.

CAUTION: According to the International Olive Oil Institute, jars of garlic in oil should not be stored in the refrigerator for more than 24 hours. When garlic is kept in oil, bacteria that may be on the garlic will grow due to the lack of oxygen. The longer the garlic stays in the oil, the higher the risk of food poisoning. While the chances of getting bacterial growth are rare, it can happen, and this is a word to the wise!

For free information about olive oil, call the International Olive Oil Council's hotline at 1-800-232-6548, 9–5 Eastern standard time, Monday–Friday.

Luncheon Meats: When buying luncheon meats, check the expiration date on the package to get the freshest meat possible. Then, assuming that your refrigerator's constant temperature is about 40°F, luncheon meats will keep safely for three to five days after the package is opened.

Parsley: When you buy a bunch of parsley for a recipe, you seldom use all of it. So finely chop the whole bunch, spread it evenly on a cookie sheet, freeze, then store in freezer-safe plastic bags.

NOTE: If the parsley is to be cooked anyway, this is a chore you can do the week before a party so that all you need do when cooking is reach into the freezer for the amount you need. Cutting and chopping is always time-consuming when you cook for a crowd. This hint applies to any item that can be chopped and frozen so that it's ready when you are assembling a recipe, such as onions, chives, or bell peppers.

Spices: Always store in a pantry where it's cool, dark, and dry away from the stove, sink, or dishwasher. Replace the lid as soon as possible after each use, too.

NOTE: Spices don't usually spoil, but they do lose potency. The best way to check them is by smell and taste; if they don't smell or taste as they ought to, toss them out and buy new. Why take a chance on ruining expensive party foods?

FOOD "REPAIR"

Obviously, if food is spoiled, you have to throw it out so that nobody gets sick. However, many culinary mistakes can be corrected and/or disguised. Also, some foods that have a tendency to dry out in storage can be "repaired" and safely eaten.

This old turkey tale is a classic correction story: A hostess emerges from her kitchen proudly presenting her Thanksgiving turkey to a tableful of eager diners. But she trips and the turkey slips off its garnished platter, careening across the dining room floor. Totally poised, she picks up the turkey, returns it to its platter, and totes it back to the kitchen, cheerfully exclaiming, "Thank heavens I've prepared two of them!" She then returns with the same turkey on the same platter after a good cleanup, and the feast continues.

Brown Sugar: When brown sugar becomes a brick, you can

soften it quickly by zapping it a few seconds in the microwave or soften it gradually by putting a slice of bread or a slice of apple or a prune in with it for a day or so. Usually, you can leave the prune in with the sugar permanently.

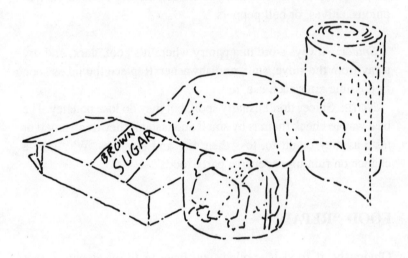

LETTER OF LAUGHTER: I received a letter from a reader who said that when she advised a new bride "to put a slice of bread on top of her brown sugar" to soften it, the bride called her to say that the trick didn't work. Then she learned that the young woman had put the bread on top of the closed canister of brown sugar! The idea is to put the bread directly *on* the sugar, she explained; there's no remote-control factor here!

Cake Break: If the cake comes out of the pan in pieces and baking another is out of the question, it's time to be creative. Cake pieces can be mixed or layered with custard, pudding, softened ice cream, whipped topping, or canned fruit-pie filling, and then garnished with dollops of whipped topping or whipped cream, shredded coconut, nuts, or fruit.

Cookies: When soft cookies become too crispy, place a slice of fresh bread on a piece of aluminum foil in the cookie container. The bread will get dry and the cookies will get a bit softer.

Dates: When pitted dates become dried pellets, they can be softened by putting a slice of apple in with them for a day or so.

Salt: If you accidentally add too much salt to a soup or stew, add peeled raw potatoes to the pot and they will help absorb some of the salt as they cook. You can remove them before serving or just leave them in as one of the ingredients.

Scorched Food: You may be able to salvage scorched food if you act quickly. Immediately take the pan of food to the sink and set it in cool water. Do not attempt to scrape out any of the scorched food that sticks to the pan. Carefully transfer the unstuck, unscorched food into another pan.

NOTE: You've heard that "a watched pot never boils," but be aware that a "watched pot" is less likely to scorch! Creamy, cheesy sauces and gravies especially need constant supervision to prevent scorching.

NOTE: Sometimes, liquid smoke, liquid bouillon, Worcestershire or soy sauce will cover up scorched meats. Taste test a bit of the meat with the cover-up before you "doctor" a whole recipe, because there's always the possibility of making matters worse!

Takeout Solution: If you are cooking for a party and totally ruin a course, consider calling a nearby restaurant or deli and buying whatever you need ready-made; such is the price of peace of mind, and when you need help, it's worth paying that price! And you don't have to tell if you don't want to!

Yogurt, Watery: If you are substituting low-fat or nonfat yogurt for sour cream in cooked foods, it sometimes separates or gets watery. Solve the problem by pouring off the liquid or stirring a bit of flour into the yogurt before cooking. If possible, add the yogurt to the food after it's removed from the heat.

Cooking and Kitchen Safety

Accidents are more likely to happen when we are in a rush or dither. The most important safety rule is to prepare as much as you can ahead of time so that you aren't rushed and don't get in a dither.

Barbecue and Grill "Nevers" and "Don'ts":

1. Never attempt to cook on an outdoor grill indoors.
2. Don't put your barbecue grill on dry grass or near other combustibles.

34

3. Never add starter fluid to warm or hot coals.
4. Never start coals with gasoline, kerosene, or other volatile fuels; they can cause explosions!
5. Don't wear loose-fitting clothing or shirts with droopy sleeves when cooking on a grill.
6. Close house windows near the barbecue.
7. Don't forget to keep a spray bottle filled with water nearby to spritz at the fire and keep it under control.

Boil-overs, Splattering: To avoid splattering burns and boil-over mess from boiling cereal, potatoes, pasta, or hot chocolate, grease the inside of the pot about one inch down on the inside with a stick of margarine. The boiling food will "contain and control" itself.

Cans, Handling and Recycling: To prevent cuts from can lids, put the lids into the can as soon as the contents are removed. For added safety for recycling, when you have time you can flatten the cans and squeeze up each end with pliers to keep the lids inside, so they won't harm the trash collectors.

Fondue Oil Trick: When beef fondue is being cooked at the table in oil, you can prevent the oil from spattering if you put two or three cubes of raw potato (about ½-inch square) into the oil. As the cubes get fried, remove and replace them with fresh ones. The bonus is you can eat the French-fry cube if you wish!

Popcorn: Don't attempt to make microwave popcorn in brown paper bags. Because popcorn has so little moisture in it, the bags receive most of the microwave energy and can catch fire easily! Instead, pop corn in poppers that have been specifically designed for microwaves or buy prepackaged microwave popcorn packets.

Tomato Sauce, No-Splatter Cooking: To avoid a mess on your stove (and burns from the splatters) when cooking tomato/spaghetti sauce, put a large metal spoon in the kettle while it cooks and it will help keep down splatters.

CAUTION: Be careful not to grab the hot spoon handle with a bare hand.

Kitcheneering Tricks

Apron: Need a quick cover-up? Scrunch the top of a large plastic trash bag to make long loops from the handle-ties and then slip the handle-ties over your head. Tie the rest of the bag around your waist with a piece of string or an old belt and you have an instant apron. And it's waterproof, too, in case it's an apron for a volunteer dishwasher!

Apple Sweetener: When baking apples, add apple juice instead of water to the pan for extra flavor.

Asparagus (Money Saver): Instead of discarding the cut-off ends from expensive fresh asparagus spears served to your guests, save them to cook the next day, and add to a cream sauce or soup. Or add them to a can of mushroom soup with sliced hard-boiled eggs and bits of leftover ham, then serve over toast or patty shells as a delicious lunch dish.

Bagels (and English Muffins) (Shortcut): It's handy to keep bagels and English muffins in the freezer for expected or unexpected overnight guests' breakfasts. If you cut them and put them back together before freezing them, they'll be ready to split and toast anytime you need them. No more gymnastics and endangered fingers from trying to cut frozen ones!

Baking Instructions: When following a recipe, look for instructions that say on which shelf the food should be baked. Temperatures vary inside the oven. For example, pizza bakes best on the lowest rack.

Baking Powder/Soda Power: If you bake only when it's a birthday, you may find that your baking powder or soda is too old to work properly. To avoid a cake flop, here's how to check the potency of each. Baking powder: Pour ½ cup of hot tap water over ½ teaspoon of baking powder. If the powder is fresh, it will bubble actively. The less active the bubbling, the less likely it is that your baked goods will rise well. Better buy new; you don't want to have to bake the cake twice! Baking soda: Add a teaspoon of vinegar or lemon juice to a pinch of baking soda. If it bubbles, the baking soda is still effective.

Beets (Shortcut Peeling Technique): After boiling beets, run cold water over them and rub the skins off with your hands.

Beets (Shortcut Pickling Technique): Save the juice from sweet pickles. Drain canned, sliced beets and put them into the juice. Leave them in the refrigerator for 24 hours before serving.

Bread Crumbs (Shortcut): Put pieces or slices of very dry bread in a sturdy plastic bag and mash with the side of a meat mallet or with a rolling pin.

NOTE: When wearing wooden clogs was a fad, you could quickly crush a bag of dried bread into fine crumbs by stomping on it while wearing clogs. It actually was fun!

Broth Freezing: When you will be adding only a portion of a can of broth to a recipe, you can freeze the remainder in ice cube trays so that you can add a cube or two to flavor other dishes. When planning for a party, make "broth cubes" the day (or week!) before so they'll be ready to pop into whatever you're cooking. Each cube is 1 ounce.

Cake Baking: When you bake a birthday or any other cake, normally you don't grease and flour the sides of a cake pan before pouring in the batter. But when some cake recipe directions say grease and flour the pan bottom and line it with wax paper, the wax paper will stay put when you place it into the pan if you also coat the sides of the pan with shortening, because the wax paper will then stick to the sides, too. Your cake will come out neatly, and frosting it won't be a crumby job.

Cake, Birthday: Double your flavors. Here's how a reader solved the problem of two people sharing a birthday celebration but not cake preferences. When one birthday person likes chocolate cake and the other likes white cake, prepare a 9-by-13-inch sheet cake pan. Mix a batch of each flavor of cake and then separately pour the chocolate mix on one end of the pan and the white on the other end. Bake as usual.

Cake, Chocolate: To avoid the white film left by flour sticking to the sides and bottom of chocolate cake layers, grease the pan as usual and sprinkle with cocoa instead of flour.

Cake Cooling: To prevent the top of a cake layer from sticking to the rack when you dump the cake out of the pan, spray the rack with nonstick vegetable spray before you use it; the layer won't stick and put crumb bits into the frosting.

Cake, Greasing Pan (No-Mess Shortcut): To flour and grease baking pans in one operation, make a mixture of ½ cup shortening, ½ cup vegetable oil, and ½ cup flour. Blend well and put into a jar with a tight lid. This mixture will keep in the fridge up to six weeks. Before baking, brush the mixture on the pans with a pastry brush. You won't have to clean messy flour from the sink or countertops.

Cake Mixing: If you only bake cakes at birthday time, remember to beat cake mixes exactly as directed on the box; overbeating or underbeating can result in a cake flop.

Cake, Removing Bundt Cake from Pan: If you lightly grease the pan and sprinkle it with sugar instead of flour, the cake will slide right out without sticking at all.

Cake, Stuck in Pan: This is a "Grandma's Day" hint that still works. When you remove the cake from the oven, place the cake pan on a wet towel. This allows it to steam away from the sides and bottom of the pan. The cake will pop out in one piece every time.

HINT 2: If a cooled cake won't come out of the pan, put the pan back into the warm oven for a couple of minutes. When the pan gets warm, remove it and try again. The cake should pop right out.

Casserole with Baked-On Gunk: When a casserole has baked-on gunk, soak it overnight in automatic-dishwasher detergent and water. When a glass casserole has burned-on gunk, and soaking as noted above doesn't work, place the casserole on newspapers inside a plastic garbage bag, spray with oven cleaner, let set, and wash as directed by the cleaner.

CAUTION: Sensitive skin can become irritated by automatic-dishwasher detergent or oven cleaner; wear gloves for protection. Also be aware that such harsh cleaners can damage kitchen counter, cabinet, or floor surfaces if they are not protected.

Cherry Tricks (with Canned Cherries): Add drained canned tart cherries to a fruit salad; spread warm cherry-pie filling instead of syrup on pancakes or waffles.

Chicken Skin (Shortcut Removing): Rub *uncooked* chicken with a clean, dry terry washcloth, and the skin will pull right off.

Chives: If you buy a pot of chives at a nursery or supermarket a week or so before your party, you'll be able to cut them fresh for your salad or other dish. The bonus is that a pot of chives on your kitchen windowsill is a nice decoration, too!

Chocolate Drizzle (No Mess): When you need to melt semi-sweet chocolate chips to drizzle-decorate cookies or a frosted cake, place the chips, *still in the bag,* into a bowl of hot water. Knead gently every few minutes until all the chips are melted. Then, cut across one corner of the bag to make a hole from which you can drizzle the chocolate—right out of the bag. No need for a pastry bag; no need to clean up a chocolate mess!

Chocolate Syrup (No Mess): If you plan to drizzle canned or bottled chocolate syrup over your company dessert, put the syrup into a clean "squirt" bottle from ketchup, etc., so that you can aim the syrup neatly.

Coffee Filters: When you are cooking for guests, do you get afflicted with the clumsies, especially when you try to separate paper coffee filters? The day before your party, wrap a quarter with transparent tape, sticky side out, and put it in with the filters. When you're ready to pick up a filter, just touch the side of it with the taped quarter and it will pop right up.

Coffee, Gourmet: If your budget won't accommodate your gourmet tastes, experiment until you've created your own "house blend" to serve at your party. Start by mixing one scoop gourmet coffee to three scoops regular coffee; if that ratio is not to your taste, adjust it until you get the right blend.

Cookie Baking (Decorating Trick): Those tiny, brightly colored candy balls for cookie decorating tend to roll off raw cookie dough and then make a mess when they burn onto the pan during the baking process. Try this trick to make them stick: Spritz the raw cookies lightly with plain water mist from a clean spray bottle and then sprinkle on the balls. It works best if you spritz just four or five cookies at a time and then decorate, instead of misting the whole pan at once. Or, lightly press them in.

Cookie Designs: Empty plastic thread spools with slots on the ends can be pressed into sugar-cookie dough to make interesting designs.

Cookie Sheets (Less Mess): Line cookie sheets with foil to avoid messy pan cleanups.

Corn on the Cob: When you are preparing corn on the cob for a large picnic gathering, getting all of the silks off the cob is a chore. Brush a clean toothbrush back and forth on the ears while holding them under running water. The silks will slip away!

Corn, Cutting from Cob (Less-Mess Shortcut): Put the small end of the ear of corn into the hole of an angel-food cake pan. Then, with an electric knife, cut the corn kernels off. As you cut, the kernels will fall into the pan and you'll have no mess!

Counter Space (Making Extra): When you don't have enough kitchen counter space for those extra party items, open a drawer, place a heavy cookie sheet over it, then close the drawer until the sheet fits tightly.

CAUTION: Remember that you've done this so you don't bump into your "emergency counter" and knock everything onto the floor!

Cracker Crumbs (Shortcut): Put crackers in a flat-bottomed bowl or pan and crush them with a hand-held potato masher. See Bread Crumbs in this section.

Cream (Low-Fat for Coffee): If you need coffee cream that's low-fat or you just forgot to buy cream for your party, you can make this low-fat, home-style coffee cream in a jiffy. Mix nonfat powdered milk into skim or evaporated skim milk in a small jar and store in the refrigerator. Shake up a bit before pouring into a cream pitcher for serving.

Cream (No-Splatter Whipping): Pour the cream into the bowl, cover the bowl with plastic wrap, cut a hole in the middle of the plastic that's big enough to insert the beaters, and whip away. Because the plastic wrap catches 80 to 90 percent of the splatters, you can increase the beater speed and get the cream whipped faster.

HINT 2: Put the bowl in the sink and the splatters stay where they can easily be rinsed off.

HINT 3: You will have less splattering if you start by running the mixer on Slow until the ingredients are blended, then gradually increase to the correct beating speed.

Cupcakes or Muffins (No-Mess Shortcut): An ice cream dipper will scoop up just the right amount of batter for each cupcake or muffin so that you don't dribble batter all over the tins. You can also scoop up batter with a gravy ladle. Or avoid scooping altogether—mix the batter in a large (2-quart) measuring cup or bowl that has a spout so that you can pour the batter into the cups.

Cutting Board (Renewing): After you scrub and sanitize a wooden cutting board with a mild bleach-and-water solution, reseason it by rubbing with mineral oil.

NOTE: Do not season wooden cutting boards, utensils, or salad bowls with vegetable oil, because it tends to turn rancid and the smell or taste will be very difficult, if not impossible, to remove.

Dishes and Crystal (Lead Tests): If you have antique plates and platters or crystal decanters that you like to use for serving at parties, and you are concerned about the dangers of lead leaching into foods or beverages, you can buy two- and four-pack lead-test kits at discount, hardware, and home improvement stores. You can also send a self-addressed, stamped, business-size envelope to Environmental Defense Fund, 257 Park Avenue South, 16th Floor, New York, NY 10010, to get a six-page comprehensive report on the different lead kits available and the "Shopper's Guide to Low-Lead China." Or call the Environmental Protection Agency's National Lead Information Center on its twenty-four-hour-a-day, seven-days-a-week 800-LEAD-FYI line. You will be asked to leave your name and address so you can be sent information about lead poisoning.

NOTE: The test packs can be carried in your pocket or purse so that you can test tableware before you buy it at flea markets and garage sales.

Eggs (Boiling): You'll get better results and more easily peeled eggs if you begin with older eggs (those that have been refrigerated for 7 to 10 days). Hard-boiled fresh eggs are almost impossible to peel.

1. Put the eggs into a deep pot in a single layer. Add enough water to cover by at least one inch. Cover the pot; bring to boil.
2. When the eggs begin to boil, let them cook for about three to four minutes, then remove them from the stove. Keep covered and let stand for 15 to 17 minutes.
3. Drain the hot water away, shake the pan to crack the shells, and run cold water over the eggs in the pot until the eggs are cool—about five minutes.
4. To peel easily, roll each egg between your hands to help loosen the shell. Hold the egg under cool, running water, starting with the large end. The shell should fall away.

Eggs (Preventing Cracks When Boiling): The old standby is to carefully pierce the large end of the egg with a sterilized pin before boiling.

NOTE: Don't push the pin in too far or it will puncture the egg sac. Don't cook the eggs on a high rolling boil; instead, cook them with a lower heat so that they won't be as likely to crack.

Fat Disposal: Avoid clogging drains with cooking fat, and feed birds at the same time. Wipe cooking fat from pans with leftover bread hunks and set them outside for the birds. Or pour the fat into a non-plastic container to throw away in the garbage bag.

Fresh Fruit Stains (Removing from Hands): When your hands get stained from handling fresh fruit, pour on a little lemon juice, rub, and rinse.

NOTE: Next time, get a pair of food-handling or other rubber gloves for this chore, to be kind to your hands and your manicure!

Frozen Treat (No Mess, Self-Defense): When you give visiting children frozen treats, poke the stick through a coffee filter or a slit in a margarine tub or other plastic lid. The drips won't be on your furniture and carpets!

LETTER OF LAUGHTER: A reader said that when she made her first pie crust, the recipe said to bake it for 15 to 20 minutes. She thought it was supposed to brown and so she baked it at least an hour. She said "you needed a hammer and chisel" to break up the crust. Needless to say, pie crust became a family joke in her house!

Frying Pan: When you are frying certain foods, such as eggs, they won't stick to the spatula (or a fork) if you spray the utensil with nonstick spray while you are spraying the pan.

Garbage Disposal (Odors): If you've been squeezing citrus fruits, such as lemon, orange, or lime, for your party recipes, toss the peels into the garbage disposal, and then after you've got all the food organized, run the disposal so that you won't have strange odors coming up from your sink drains. Always run lots of cold water through a disposal after grinding. But then you knew that!

Gelatin (No-Mess Serving): If a gelatin dessert or salad has a mind of its own and wobbles off the serving spoon when you try to dish it out, try an ice-cream scoop; it's neat!

Gelatin Shapes (No-Waste Method): When making gelatin shapes for children's church and school parties, you usually have lots of "scrap" pieces left over after you've cut the first batch with the cookie cutters. To avoid wasting the scraps, you can melt them in the microwave, re-refrigerate them in a dish that will allow the desired thickness, and when they are firm again, you can cut more shapes!

Grater (No-Mess Great Grating): Spray your grater liberally with vegetable-oil spray to keep cheese and other gratables from sticking.

Gravy Boat (Less Mess): You can serve extra tomato or spaghetti sauce in a gravy boat for less mess and fewer spills on the party tablecloth.

Greasing Pans (No-Mess Shortcut): Put your hand into a plastic sandwich bag, grab the grease, and rub it on the pans. Then turn the bag inside out as you remove it and throw it away with the mess all wrapped up.

Ham Broth: Save the broth left over from a baked ham and freeze it in an ice cube tray. Store the broth cubes in a container or zipper bag after they are frozen, so that you can add them to flavor vegetables, eggs, or casseroles.

Hamburger Patties: When you make hamburger patties for the freezer, put the meat into small plastic bags before shaping it. Your hands will stay clean and the bags will keep the patties separated. Stack the patties in a large round oatmeal box, which will hold about 12 patties. Then you can remove only the number of patties that you need. For long-term storage, you may want to put the oatmeal box into a freezer-safe plastic bag to protect the meat from freezer burn.

Ice Cream (Scooping Easily): Run the scoop under very hot water and it will cut through the ice cream more quickly and make neat smooth scoops, too.

Ice Cream (Serving Shortcut): Put individual portions (a scoop or so) of ice cream into transparent 6- to 8-ounce squatty plastic drink cups, cover with plastic wrap and store in the freezer if you have the space. It's ready to serve for a party dessert. You can top the ice cream with a liquor or fruit sauce (or canned pie filling) when it's served, or put foil cupcake liners into a cupcake pan and put a scoop of ice cream in each. Optional: Sprinkle with chocolate or colored sprinkles to decorate. You can place the foil cups on serving plates with cake, too. For a children's party, you could use clean, recycled 8-ounce yogurt cups for serving.

HINT 2: When you're scooping it, layer the ice cream with frozen fruit or freezable sauce to make a parfait.

Ice Cube Trays (No Mess): To prevent the freezer door from swinging shut just in time to spill some of the water out of the ice cube trays you are trying to freeze, try this hint. Grab a package or container of food that's already in the freezer, wedge it near the hinge so that it holds the door open, and then bring the cube tray to the freezer.

NOTE: This is one of those so-simple hints that makes you say, "Why didn't I think of that?"

Ice Cubes: Every day for several days before your party, you can empty your ice cube trays (or ice cube bin if you have an automatic ice maker) into plastic bags and store them in the freezer. Then you'll have enough ice without having to buy those cold, heavy bags of ice and carry them from the store.

NOTE: One of my readers prefers to store ice for parties in paper lunch bags. The ice doesn't stick together or pick up freezer odors, even when kept for several weeks.

Ice for Punch: Just about any food-grade plastic container can be used to get an ice hunk to float in punch—a margarine tub, whipped topping tub, pie tin, or gelatin mold. To make giant ice cubes, freeze water in clean individual applesauce or pudding containers, yogurt cups, measuring cups, etc.

Lasagna (Shortcut): Lasagna is a favorite crowd-server, and this is one of the best shortcuts ever because it saves all sorts of time and mess. You don't have to cook the noodles before assembling a lasagna. Layer the hard, uncooked lasagna noodles in the pan and increase the amount of sauce and cheese slightly to provide more liquid; bake as usual. You may want to experiment a time or two before you do this for guests, to find out how much more sauce is needed for this method; sauce amounts in individual recipes can vary.

Leftover Party Food: Is there anyone who never overestimates how much food to cook for guests? I can't count the times I added "just a little more" and that "just a little more" was the "just too much" that was left over. However, party leftovers can be a bonus, especially if, after you cook for a bunch, you are burned out on cooking for anyone. Here are some ways you can enjoy leftover meats and veggies:

1. Slice leftover meat for sandwiches or grind it to make sandwich spreads. To make a spread, add mayo, chopped celery, carrots, or mushrooms for filler.
2. Cut meat into slices or cubes to serve over rice or noodles. (You can add canned gravy or sauce if it's too dry.)
3. Freeze leftover veggies and their cooking water in a tightly covered container. When you have enough veggies, make vegetable soup by adding browned onions (or dry onion soup mix), bouillon or stock, and your favorite herbs and spices to the mix. Simmer in a pot for at least 20 to 30 minutes.
4. Add leftover cooked vegetables to salads and sandwich spreads for delicious, nutritious lunches.
5. Cut up leftover vegetables such as corn, potatoes, peas, and beans to make a vegetable hash. Fry in a skillet with some onions and garlic and add other favorite seasonings.
6. Leftover sweet potato casserole and other similar foods can be frozen in cupcake papers placed in a cupcake tin, so that you'll have lots of individual portions for days when you don't want to cook, which is usually several days after you've done some major-effort cooking for a party!
7. If you make too many pancakes or waffles for your brunch, freeze the extras for another day, when you can sit down to enjoy them. Heat them in the microwave or toaster.

Lemon Peel or Zest: When a recipe calls for lemon peel or zest, grate carefully so that none of the white spongy part of the peel gets grated as well; it can cause a bitter taste.

Marshmallows (Shortcut When They're Stuck): To unstick marshmallows, put some powdered sugar or cornstarch in the bag and work it in with the marshmallows. You may have to separate some of them by hand. But they shouldn't be sticky after they are well coated.

NOTE: Next time, prevent sticking by storing marshmallows in the freezer in an airtight, freezer-safe plastic bag or container.

Measuring (No Mess): When mixing baked goods that require sticky liquids such as honey, molasses, corn syrup, or oil, measure the oil first and then use the same cup to measure the sticky stuff, which will slip easily out of the oiled measuring cup (or spoon, too). Or spray the measuring cup with nonstick spray.

Meat Loaf Muffins: Bake individual meat loaves in muffin tins for children's parties; they are easier for children to eat and cook faster, too.

Meat Marinading: Place the meat into a self-sealing plastic bag, add all the ingredients, and place it in a cake pan in the refrigerator. Turning the meat so that the marinade gets on all of it is then easier.

Melons (Serving Shortcut): Instead of slicing watermelon, cantaloupe, or honeydew melons, scoop out pieces with a "melon baller," a large spoon, or an ice cream scoop and pile them into dessert dishes. They look pretty, and you'll have no rinds to deal with at the table.

Mushrooms (Quick-Slice Shortcut): A wire-type egg slicer will give you neat, evenly sliced mushrooms in half a jiffy.

Nuts (Baking): If the pieces are too big, nut bits may sink to the bottoms of cakes and nutbreads as they are baking. To prevent nuts from sinking in batters, chop them into smaller pieces. Some say that mixing nut bits with the dry ingredients before adding the dry to the moist ingredients helps suspend the nut bits better in the baking batter. (Try saying "bits better in the baking batter" five times quickly! Whew!)

Olive Oil (No-Mess Pouring): If you buy olive oil in large cans because you cook with it a lot, put it in a clean recycled plastic ketchup squeeze container so that you can squeeze out as much oil as you need without having to deal with a clumsy can on your counter when you need all the space possible to cook for guests.

Onions (Chopping): Chopping onions in large quantities can be hazardous if rushing makes you careless. You won't nick your fingers if, as you cut, you hold the onion with a corncob holder (tiny forks that stick in the ends of the cobs).

Onions (No-Tears Peeling and Chopping): People have sent me all sorts of methods to keep eyes from watering when peeling onions. Many say they hold a match or a cracker between their lips or teeth while they work. Others say that refrigerating onions before peeling and chopping prevents tears. But few went as far as the reader who wears snorkling goggles when she peels or chops onions. Wouldn't that startle your guests if they walked in early!

Onion (and Other) Odors on Hands: Wet hands and sprinkle a bit of baking soda on them, rub, and rinse.

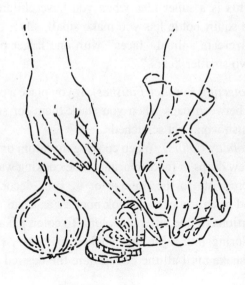

HINT 2: Sprinkle some lemon or lime juice on your hands, rub, and rinse.

HINT 3: My readers, and my mother's readers, swore that, for some mysterious reason, rubbing your hands on a stainless-steel sink, faucet, or utensil also removes onion odors. It works for me!

Oranges (Peeling Shortcut): Cut a small slice from the end, just enough to show the pulp. Invert a large tablespoon, work it under the skin, and go around the orange. In a few seconds, the orange will be ready to section and put into that fruit salad. This technique also works with grapefruit and lemons.

Organized Cooking: Put all the ingredients required by the recipe out on the counter and then return them to the cupboard as you add them to the food. Then you will know if you missed anything, even if you get interrupted by phone calls and people.

Pancake Batter (Shortcut): If you are serving pancakes to overnight guests and you want more time to visit with them in the morning, make the pancake batter the night before and store it in a thoroughly washed, clean plastic squeeze bottle, such as a ketchup bottle. Then you can just squirt the batter on the pan.

NOTE: This is a super idea when you have children visiting because the squirt bottle lets you make small, silver dollar–size pancakes or create animal "faces" with one larger pancake attached to two smaller "ears."

Pans (Protecting Nonstick Finishes): If you place a paper towel or plate in between pans when you stack them for storage, the nonstick finish won't get scratched.

Pasta (Holiday Colors): When cooking macaroni or other noodles, put a few drops of food coloring in the cooking water. Colors can be appropriate to the holiday or to your decor. To make multicolored pasta for a salad, cook noodles as usual, then separate into portions for the different colors. To color, put a few drops of food coloring into a jar, add cooked macaroni, shells, etc., cover, and shake until all the noodles are the desired color. You can also buy colored pasta, but it won't be in bright colors or colors of your choice.

Pastry Blender (Cutting Shortcut): A pastry blender breaks up hunks of browned ground meat for Sloppy Joes or spaghetti sauce and will also break up whole canned tomatoes for sauces.

NOTE: Before you attack the tomatoes with the pastry blender, poke holes in them with a fork to prevent splatters.

Peaches (Slicing Shortcut): To slice lots of peaches in very little time, cut in half (remove pits and skin, if fresh), place in wire egg slicer, and push the wires down. As you lift the wires, the slicer will bring the peach up and over into the bowl.

Picnic Cooler: Fill plastic soda bottles with water to about 2 inches from the top and freeze until the water is solid. Then put them in your picnic cooler instead of ice cubes. Food will keep cold without getting soggy, and as the ice thaws, you'll have ice water to drink.

Picnic Utensils: Put forks, knives, spoons, and other utensils into an empty paper towel or gift-wrap roll and fold in the ends to keep the utensils inside. They'll stay clean and won't poke holes in anything.

Pie Dough (Easy Rolling): Freezer paper, placed waxed-side-up, works better than wax paper for rolling out pie dough. It's wider, easier to pick up, and doesn't fall apart as wax paper does.

NOTE: If you dampen the counter beneath the paper, it won't slip as you roll the dough.

Pie Tin Size (Measuring Shortcut): If the recipe says to bake in a 9-inch pie tin and you don't know the dimensions of your pie tin, measure 4 cups of water and pour into the tin; a 9-inch pie tin will hold four cups of water.

Pies, Oven Spillovers (Quick Fix): When pie filling boils over and begins to burn in the oven and you can't stop because the pie's not baked yet, pour a thick layer of table salt on the spill. It will stop smoking and you'll be able to scoop out the mess with a spatula.

NOTE: Next time, put a cookie sheet or foil beneath the pan to catch those inevitable spills.

NOTE: When making pumpkin or custard pies, instead of filling the shell with all of the custard, keep out a cup or so of it in a measuring cup or pitcher. Then when you have the pie safely on the oven rack, pour in the remainder to the pie shell's capacity.

Plastic Wrap (Finding the End): Wrap transparent tape around your three middle fingers, with the sticky side out, and pat the tape along the roll until the edge sticks to it and pulls free. Some people say storing plastic wrap in the fridge helps, too.

Plastic Wrap (When It Won't Stick): Moisten the edges of the bowl and the wrap will stick.

Potatoes (Keeping White): Peel and cut up potatoes as needed for the recipe, place them in a bowl with enough water to cover and a teaspoon or so of vinegar (more or less, depending on amount of potatoes). They will stay white until you are ready to cook them.

Potatoes (Shortcut for Baking a Bunch): Instead of handling each potato to butter or oil the skin before baking, line up the potatoes on paper towels and spray them with vegetable-oil spray. Butter-flavored spray adds taste, too.

Potatoes (Mashed): Keep mashed potatoes at serving temperature until you are ready to serve dinner by putting them into a slow cooker. Then you won't have to mess around with mashing potatoes when you have meat to carve and sauce to make.

Recipe (Doubling Baked Goods): Use exactly two times the amount of each ingredient. To help you with tablespoon measurements:

    4 tablespoons = ¼ cup
    8 tablespoons = ½ cup
    12 tablespoons = ¾ cup

When doubling a cake recipe, add an extra minute to beating the batter. Also use twice as many pans of the same size called for by the recipe. To bake properly, the batter has to be the same depth in the pan as required by the original amount if it's to bake at the same temperature and for the same amount of time.

When making half of a recipe for baked goods, use exactly ½ of the amount of each ingredient. If the original recipe calls for 1 egg, beat up a whole egg and measure off half with a tablespoon. Baking pans for half recipes need to measure half the area of pans for whole recipes; again, it's necessary to have the same depth of batter in the pan as the original amount if it's to bake at the same temperature and for the same amount of time.

Recipe Cards (Recycling): Cut old greeting cards with plain white backs and use as recipe cards.

Recipe Cards (Keeping Handy): Put the recipe cards for the dishes you will serve at your party in a see-through plastic bag and tack the bag inside on a cupboard door. You will be able to look at it as you work without getting splatters on it. The bonus is that if a guest asks for the recipe, you need only reach into the cupboard for it.

Salad Bar Economy: If you are making a recipe that requires small amounts of fresh veggies, such as ¼ cup celery, 4 ounces sliced mushrooms, 1 cut tomato, etc., check out the supermarket salad bar for ingredients. They'll be already cut or chopped, and you won't have to buy whole packages of celery or carrots, if you don't need that amount. You'll be saving money, and you won't be using up refrigerator space for nonparty food.

Salad Dressings (Removing from Jar): A reader says that the best way to get the last bit of salad dressing (or jelly) out of the jar is with a long-handled wooden spoon. I like to scoop out that last bit with a narrow rubber spatula, too.

Scrapers and Spatulas (Shortcut Repair): When plastic spatulas and scrapers are frayed (or chopped in a blender?) so they won't scoop cleanly, grab a pair of kitchen shears and cut off the bad parts so they'll still do the job, at least for the duration of party cooking.

Shrimp (Less-Mess Serving): When you serve peel-your-own shrimp, give each person a coffee filter for discarded shells. Or serve shrimp Gulf-Coast tavern style piled on a table that has been covered with several layers of newspapers. After the shrimp feast is over, you can just roll up the mess inside the newspapers and toss it into the garbage.

NOTE: Don't make the mistake of leaving the shrimp shells in your inside garbage can overnight. The smell the next morning is more offensive than you can imagine! Do put them in a sealed plastic garbage bag *outside*!

Slow Cooker Cooking: Many party dishes can be prepared in and served from a slow cooker. Some good examples are baked or pinto beans and New Year's Day black-eyed peas (a Southern U.S. good luck custom). The trick is not to lift the lid too often. Each time you do, you may be adding as much as 20 minutes to the total cooking time. Also, if you fill the pot to its capacity, food won't dry out during the cooking process as it sometimes does with too-small amounts.

Soups (Thick, Condensed): A fork or wire whisk is the best implement to stir thick, condensed canned soups.

Spices: When you buy certain spices, such as saffron, chili powder, cumin, coriander, cardamom, cinnamon, and tumeric, my readers say that they will cost only about one-half to one-third of the supermarket or gourmet-shop price if you buy them in Asian-Indian grocery stores.

Sugar (Coloring It): Put a cup of granulated sugar in a glass bowl and add a few drops of food coloring. Mix well until the coloring is distributed evenly. To darken the color, add a drop or two more of the food coloring. Let dry. Store in a sprinkle-top bottle that's handy for decorating cookies and cakes.

NOTE: You can also color salt. Pastel-colored salt helps people with low vision tell how much they've put on foods and makes plain potatoes or rice look festive.

Sugar Shaker: Keep granulated sugar in a saltshaker so that it's handy for sprinkling on pie crust tops before baking, when you fry plantains, or even for sprinkling on cereal or freshly fried home-made doughnuts (made from canned biscuits that have had holes poked through their middles before frying in hot oil). If you mix the sugar with cinnamon, you can quickly make cinnamon-sugar toast or sweeten canned biscuits before baking them to make quickie sweet rolls.

Powdered sugar in a shaker is handy for sugaring funnel cakes, doughnuts, or French toast.

Tea for a Crowd: An electric coffeemaker can also be an instant hot water maker for tea. Put the proper number of tea bags in the carafe and you'll have brewed tea in a jiffy.

Or put the tea bags in a teapot or into the serving pitcher if you are making iced tea, and just use the coffeemaker to heat the water quickly. As the tea brews in the teapot or pitcher, you can make a pot of coffee for the non-tea-drinking guests.

Tomato Sauce (Freezing): When a recipe requires only 2 ounces of tomato sauce, or only a portion of a can of tomatoes, freeze the remainder in covered ice cube trays so that you will have individual cube portions ready the next time you need them.

NOTE: You may want to open a can of tomato sauce or canned tomatoes and freeze a cube tray full on the day before your party, so that you have premeasured ingredients for your party recipe and also fewer cans to deal with on party day.

Vegetables (Scrubbing): A Heloise nylon-net puff will clean mushrooms without bruising them and will get all the dirt out of celery "ribs," too. (To make a nylon-net puff, cut a large piece of nylon net into 5- to 6-inch strips. Fold the pieces together accordian style. Gather at the center, secure with a rubber band, and fluff.)

Watermelon (Seeding Shortcut): Fresh melon balls or chunks served in a hollowed-out watermelon can be the centerpiece as well as one of the courses at any party meal. Try digging out the watermelon seeds with an apple corer. It's neat and fast.

Zest (Shortcut): When a recipe requires lemon or orange zest and the skin is too soft to grate easily, put the fruit into the freezer for 10 minutes or so and it will be firm and easy to grate, with just a few swipes across the grater.

Zucchini (Scooping to Stuff Shortcut): Slice the zucchini lengthwise and scoop out the pulp with a melon baller, using long strokes. Then you can chop the zucchini flesh, add onion and spaghetti sauce, and stuff it all back into the zucchini shell. Top with mozzarella and cook until done. Your luncheon guests will think you worked all day!

Substitutions

In this section, I've listed the "out of" ingredient, then the substitute. I've also noted some cooking equipment substitutes for those times when you just can't find anything and don't have time to look. I hope it prevents panic when you are cooking for a party and find your cupboard is bare or just mixed up!

Alcoholic Beverages: If you don't keep alcoholic beverages in your home or cook with them, you can still use the recipes that require them as the ingredients. If the recipe calls for one or two tablespoons, you can usually consider the wine, sherry, etc. as an optional ingredient and omit it. If more than two tablespoons are required, you need to substitute because of the liquid component of the recipe.

For savory dishes, substitute chicken broth for white wine. For a fruity flavor or for sweet foods or desserts, you may be able to substitute apple, pineapple, or orange juice for alcoholic beverages. You can also use nonalcoholic wines in recipes. If you substitute extracts, try combining the number of drops recommended on the bottle with enough water to match the amount of water required by the recipe.

NOTE: If you are cooking for someone who must not have alcohol, be aware that the latest research shows that, contrary to traditional belief, all of the alcohol in wine (or liquors) does *not* evaporate in the cooking process; some remains in the food or sauce whether it's baked, stewed, roasted, boiled, flambéed, or whatever.

Buttermilk: A reader who found herself out of buttermilk when making corn muffins added a couple of heaping tablespoons of cottage cheese to her recipe and found the taste was richer and the leftover muffins stayed moist when they were reheated.

To make 1 cup of sour milk or buttermilk substitute, add 1 tablespoon lemon juice or vinegar to enough sweet milk to make 1 cup.

NOTE: You will need to do a little extra mixing to break down the curds in the batter.

Cake (Convert Microwave Directions to Conventional Oven): To bake a microwave cake mix in a conventional oven, follow the directions on the box, but mix the ingredients in a bowl and pour them into a regular cake pan that is near in size to the original cardboard cake pan that came with the mix.

Bake in a 325–350°F oven for three to four times the time recommended for microwave baking. For example, if the box directions say bake 10 minutes in the microwave, bake the cake 30 to 40 minutes in a conventional oven. Test the cake for doneness by inserting a toothpick or fork in the center. If it comes out dry, the cake is done.

Cake Frosting (Shortcut): Break milk chocolate candy bars into squares and place them immediately on the hot, just-out-of-the-oven cake. You'll have instant "magic" chocolate frosting.

Cheesecloth: When a stew or soup recipe says to tie spices (bay leaf, peppercorns, whole cloves) in a cheesecloth so that they can be removed later, and you don't have any cheesecloth, put the spices in a metal tea ball or tie them up in a coffee filter. One reader even removed the staples and tea from a large flow-through tea bag, put in the spices, and restapled the bag before tossing it into the stew.

CAUTION: It's especially important to put broken pieces of bay leaf in a tea ball or cheesecloth bag. They can get stuck in a person's throat very easily and be difficult to dislodge.

Chocolate Squares (Unsweetened): Three tablespoons cocoa plus ½ teaspoon shortening.

COFFEE CAKE LETTER OF LAUGHTER: It's a good idea always to read directions when you experiment with a new recipe. A reader said that her sister served a new coffee cake recipe at a family gathering and it sure was a nitty-gritty learning experience! She thought she'd followed the recipe exactly when she added a cup of coffee, but after checking, she learned that she hadn't been all that "exact." She had added a cup of coffee grounds instead of a cup of brewed coffee! Fortunately everyone had a good sense of humor, including the baker of the gritty cake!

Confectioners' Sugar: Slowly pour 1 to 1½ cups of granulated sugar in a blender and run at full power, stopping to stir once or twice to make sure that the sugar granules at the bottom get ground up. The trick is to grind only a small amount of sugar at one time.

Cookies from Cake Mix: To a boxed cake mix, add 2 eggs and ½ cup of vegetable cooking oil. You can also add raisins, nuts, or coconut. Mix well. With a teaspoon, drop spoonfuls of batter on an ungreased cookie sheet, 2 inches apart. Bake at 350°F for 8 to 10 minutes. Cool and enjoy!

Cornstarch: One tablespoon cornstarch for thickening equals about 2 tablespoons flour.

Cream for Coffee: Substitute a teaspoon of vanilla ice cream or add skim milk powder to taste for coffee cream in a cup of coffee. It's almost as scrumptious as Seattle's famous caffè latte!

Cutter for Homemade Noodles and Pancakes: When cutting pasta strips or pancakes for toddlers, a pizza cutter works better than a knife.

Dip Dish: Instead of a small bowl, substitute hollowed-out vegetables for dip containers. Tomatoes, green or red bell peppers, and red or green cabbage will work well and look delicious, too. If the dip is very thick, forming a "bowl" from cup-shaped lettuce leaves will do. Place the foodie dip dish in the center of a plate filled with what's to be dipped into it.

Egg: For 1 whole egg, substitute 2 egg yolks, left over from meringue or other recipes, plus 1 tablespoon water for baking cookies, or, for custards and similar mixtures, substitute 2 egg yolks.

Egg, Sunny Side Up: One reader certainly was creative in making a fried egg. He dropped two egg whites into a frying pan sprayed with some cooking spray. Then he added a tablespoon or two of egg substitute on top to replace the yolk and cooked without stirring. With a little pepper and salt to taste, there it was—a sunny-side-up fried egg that met his low cholesterol diet requirement.

Fines Herbes: When a recipe calls for "fines herbes," as many soups and stews do, and you can't find it in your supermarket or just don't have any, make your own. "Fines herbes" is a blend of equal parts of parsley, tarragon, chives, and chervil.

Fire Extinguisher: If you have a small grease fire on the stove, turn off the stove and douse the fire with baking soda.

Flour, Self-Rising: If a recipe requires self-rising flour and you don't have any, you can make your own.

Self-Rising Flour 1: Add 1 tablespoon baking powder to 1 cup of either all-purpose or regular flour.

Self-Rising Flour 2: Add 1 teaspoon bicarbonate of soda, 2 teaspoons cream of tartar, and ½ teaspoon salt to 1 cup of regular flour. If you use all-purpose flour, omit the salt.

Flour Thickener (for Gravies and Sauces): Both cornstarch and arrowroot can thicken sauces, gravies, casseroles, and stews. You can substitute either one for flour, but when you do, you'll need only half as much. For example, if a recipe requires 2 tablespoons of flour, substitute 1 tablespoon of arrowroot or cornstarch.

❀ Cornstarch is a starchy flour made from corn. It is especially good and quick for thickening stir-fry sauce. (Mix cornstarch and water in a cup, add soy sauce to taste, add to stir-fry pan, and boil quickly while stirring, until sauce is translucent and thickened.)

❀ Arrowroot is a starch made from a tropical plant found on St. Vincent Island in the Caribbean. It is good for thickening fruit and fruit juices because it results in a clearer sauce. But it doesn't brown, so it's not a good gravy base.

Funnel: Cut the top off any plastic bottle or jug, turn it upside down, and you have a funnel. The bonus is that it's disposable, too, if you don't want to wash and keep it.

Garlic Press: A reader who needed to crush two garlic cloves couldn't find her press, so she cleaned a pair of pliers, put the cloves in a plastic bag, and squeezed. Then she opened the bag and removed the outer skin. She said the pliers actually worked better than her garlic press.

Gelatin Liquid: You'll get more nutrition and better flavor, too, if you substitute 100 percent fruit juice (no sugar added) for water when you make gelatin. You will still need some water to dissolve the gelatin, but add the juice instead of ice cubes or cold water in the second step of preparation.

Honey: Mix ¾ cup sugar with ¼ cup liquid to make a honey substitute.

Hot Pad for Frying Pan: Substitute an old heavy cloth eyeglass case for a hot pad on the handle of a pot or frying pan.

CAUTION: Be sure it's well padded to prevent burns and don't use plastic or synthetic material.

Jar Lid Opener: Stuck lid on a small-neck sauce bottle or juice jar? Try twisting the lid off with a nutcracker.

Lemon for Iced or Hot Tea: Drop one lemon-drop candy into the glass before pouring in iced tea. It will dissolve and give the tea a hint of lemon while sweetening it as well.

Marshmallows: One large marshmallow equals 10 small ones.

Mayonnaise in Potato Salad: If you don't have or don't like mayonnaise in potato salad (or other salads), substitute vinegar and oil or some other favorite bottled salad dressing.

Meat Roasting Racks: If you don't have a rack for roasting meat, substitute an aluminum pie pan from a frozen pie. Place the pan on a cutting board and punch a few holes in the bottom with an ice pick. Then turn it upside down and place it into the roaster. You can bend it to an oval shape if it doesn't fit the roaster bottom as a round "rack." The bonus is that it's disposable if it gets too crusty to wash easily.

HINT 2: You can also roll up into an S a strip of aluminum foil that's too short to wrap anything and place the S foil "rack" in a roaster.

HINT 3: Crumpled heavy-duty foil can also be a "rack" for lighter pieces of meat, such as chicken parts.

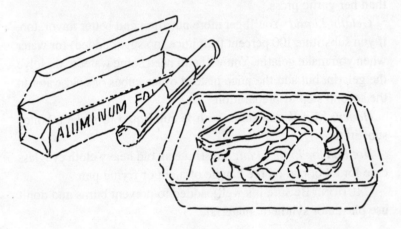

Milk: The recipe calls for milk and you are out of it?

1. Mix nondairy coffee creamer with water and add it to the recipe. The reader who sent in this hint has made pancakes, desserts, and many other dishes with this substitute and says she's never had bad results.
2. One-half cup evaporated milk plus ½ cup water equals 1 cup fresh sweet milk.
3. Make 1 cup sweet milk with powdered milk and water according to the directions on the container.

Nut Chopper: Put shelled nuts into a plastic bag and crush them with a meat mallet.

NOTE: Whomp on the nuts with the side of the mallet; otherwise the "tenderizing" teeth will poke holes in the plastic bag and you'll have a mess.

Nuts (Substitute in Recipe): If you or a guest can't eat nuts or you don't have any, substitute the same amount of rice cereal in the recipe.

Pies, Pecan and Walnut: You can substitute walnuts for pecans in a pecan pie recipe, with just a bit of difference in the flavor.

Saffron: You can substitute tumeric for saffron in many recipes.

Steak Sauce: Mix together equal parts of Worcestershire sauce and tomato ketchup to make steak sauce. If you have the time and inclination, you can spice it by adding a dash or so of whatever spice or spices suit your taste buds and go with the rest of the meal.

Taco Sauce (No-Mess Serving): When serving salsa or taco sauce picnic-style, having everyone spoon it out of a large jar can get messy, especially as you get to the bottom of the jar. Instead, pour the sauce into a clean salad-dressing bottle so that it can be poured out neatly.

Tomatoes: One cup of canned tomatoes is equal to about $1\frac{1}{3}$ cups of cut-up fresh tomatoes, simmered 10 minutes.

Toppings for Ice Cream or Waffles: Canned prepared pie fillings make delicious toppings for ice cream, waffles, or pound cake. Try peach, blueberry, apple, strawberry, or cherry.

Yogurt "Cheese" (Home-style Spread): Put plain, low-fat yogurt in a strainer lined with paper towels or a coffee filter, place the strainer in a bowl, refrigerate overnight or longer, and you'll have a thick creamy, spreadable "cheese." You can top it with fruit, honey, or preserves if you wish, or use it as a base for a dip.

NOTE: Wash and save the yogurt container so that you can return your yogurt spread to it for storage.

"Portable" Foods

Avoiding Spills in Your Car: A flat carton, such as the bottom of a case of soft drinks, lined with newspapers will keep a casserole from sliding around or spilling over in the car. The bonus is that if you are holding a hot dish on your lap, the carton will be a good insulator and the newspapers will absorb spills! Put a cake or pie dish into a cake box saved from the bakery or into another suitable carton that keeps the plate from moving, so that you don't mess up the cake frosting or spill pie juice.

Baked Goods Plates (Taking to Friends or Bake Sales): Buy cheap plates at garage sales so that you won't care if they don't get returned. One of my readers reports that since she started this practice, people think her plates are special and have been faithfully returning them!

HINT 2: Cover a clean foam meat tray with foil to make a plate for pound cake and nut bread or cookies. Plastic wrap over all will keep the goodies fresh and prevent their falling off.

HINT 3: Collect boxes of different shapes and sizes which can be lined with heavy-duty aluminum foil to hold different kinds of food. This includes carry-out boxes from fast-food restaurants, salad bars, or pizza places, if they are clean or can be washed.

Dishes: You can get rid of and recycle your chipped dishes by putting donations to bake sales and bazaars on them. If they look too bad, cover them with foil and/or a doily! You can use this hint for bowls of foods taken to potluck church or club events, too. Some of my readers keep a box of chipped dishes—their own and ones from bazaar purchases—just for this purpose. It means never having to worry about losing a good dish, and it's thinking "green," too, because you don't put more disposables into landfills.

Disposables: If you are taking food to someone's home to help out when there's a new baby, a sick person, or a funeral, do put the food in a disposable container, preferably one in which the food can be frozen and saved for another day, when it can be heated in the oven in its same container. Often families get more food than they can immediately eat, and it would be a big help if they could freeze the extra casseroles, cakes, or whatever for a later date. You might even wrap the food well and put a label on it describing the contents and giving reheating instructions. Check your supermarket for the different sizes of aluminum pans.

Jars for Bits and Bites: Any size jar can hold nuts, small candies, or cereal snack mixes. Save especially those with colorful plastic lids, so that all you need is a bow tied around the jar's girth or stuck to the top/lid.

Vegetables (Keeping Them Hot): One reader assigned to bring Brussels sprouts to a potluck dinner party knew that the host's stove would be busy, so she put the hot vegetables into a widemouth half-gallon thermos. They were still steaming several hours later when poured into her serving dish.

Decorating and Cleaning

Party decorating is determined by your budget as well as your taste, and pre-party cleaning is determined by your time and energy as well as your personal standards. In the case of cleaning, it may be better to lower your usual standards a little than to work yourself into a state of exhaustion. The idea is to have at least some fun at your own party.

I think decorating can be fun instead of one more pre-party chore if you know a few shortcuts and tricks and if you can let your imagination take over. For example, I've always thought it would be fun to have a butler, so, for one party, I dressed a mannequin in a tux and placed my "butler" at the door to greet my guests. Everyone walked into the party laughing, and you can be sure the ice was broken, because people who hadn't known each other previously had something to talk about—the butler did it!

Decorating and Table Setting

Ashtrays: Now that so few people smoke, most of us have pretty ashtrays sitting around looking for a function. Here are a few ways to decorate with them:

1. Fill ashtrays with different sizes, shapes, and colors of soaps to decorate a bathroom or kitchen.
2. Fill with assorted wrapped hard candies, especially mints for after dinner.
3. Fill with potpourri so that they freshen up a bathroom or other room.

NOTE: If your ashtrays are filled with something, those who still smoke will know that the presence of an ashtray is not unspoken permission to smoke in your house. Do put something outdoors in the designated smoking area to hold ashes and cigarette butts, such as a container filled halfway with sand or cat-box litter. (Perhaps an unbreakable old ashtray or metal bowl? A tuna can or coffee tin seems a bit inhospitable.)

Bar Stools: If the upholstered seats on your backless bar stools are worn or soiled, and it didn't bother you until you decided to have a party, buy some thick, large, patterned shower caps. While this isn't a permanent solution, it's a pretty good quick cover-up.

Bathroom Magazine Holder: A small wine bottle rack can hold rolled magazines neatly in your guest bathroom "library."

Candelabra: If you don't have sets, a grouping of crystal or pressed-glass candle holders of different designs and heights can be an unusual centerpiece. Or small votive candle holders or small decorative glasses or saucers can substitute for candlesticks.

Candles: When candles wobble in their holders, wrap a 1-inch-wide strip of clear plastic wrap or tape around the bottom of the candle. The candles will fit snugly, and the wrap is invisible if the candlesticks are glass.

Candles (Shortcut): When candles are dusty, you can wipe them with a soft cloth dipped in rubbing alcohol.

Centerpiece: Fill a large crystal bowl with water and float a couple of large flowers on the surface. If you live in the South and have a magnolia tree, one magnolia in a bowl might do it!

Centerpiece (Quick Fix): Forget a centerpiece? Cut flowers or just greenery from the yard and arrange them on the table. Or adapt silk flowers or greenery to be a table decoration. A single strand of ivy (silk or real) running the length of a table and a single candelabra or two candles in holders can do the trick.

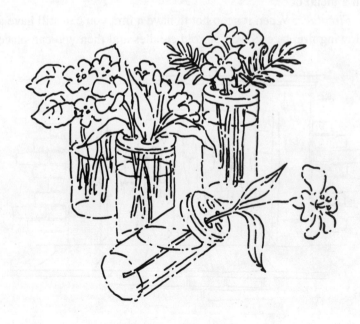

Directions to the Party:

1. Tie a bunch of inflated balloons to a porch, mailbox, or whatever will hold them without breaking them, so that guests can easily find the party house.
2. If everyone is outside in the backyard, do lock the front door and put a sign on the door telling everyone to go to the backyard. Don't just put a sign on the door that says "Come In" because you might be inviting unwelcome strangers into the house!
3. Inside the house, place small signs directing people to bathrooms so they won't always have to be asking directions.

Door Decorations on Metal Door: Buy a magnetized heavy-duty hook at a hardware store or in the hardware section of a department store, and you can hang wreaths and other decorations on a metal door.

Fireplace: When it's too hot to have a fire, you can still have a glowing fireplace. Save your old candles and then you can place

larger ones on the grate and stick smaller ones into the grate. Then, light them, close the screen, and enjoy the warmth of a flickering fire without the heat. The drips will burn up when you have a real fire in cooler weather.

Floral Arrangements: When flower stems are too short for the vase, pour in the water, then insert a piece of scrunched-up clear plastic wrap. The plastic will hold the flowers in place, and if the vase is clear glass, the scrunched wrap will look like bubbles in the water.

Floral Arranging: When arranging dried or silk flowers in a large vase, you can put sand or cat-box filler into the vase to hold the foliage in place. The bonus with cat-box filler is that it is also a hidden room deodorizer!

HINT 2: Marbles placed in the bottom of a vase or bowl will substitute for a floral arrangement holder "frog."

Flowers (Transporting): When you have to drive a potted plant home or deliver it to a party or gift recipient, lock it in the seat belt to prevent it from falling over and breaking blossoms.

Fun-House Mirror: For a casual party, hang a shiny, silver-backed erasable wall calendar with the calendar side facing the wall and the shiny reflective side facing the room. It will give distorted images like a fun-house mirror and serve as an ice-breaker conversation starter.

Party Favors: If you are giving a thank-you party for people who have helped you with a project, serve coffee or beverages in mugs or cups that guests can take home as a thank-you gift. Or if guests are seated at tables, fill small glass or ceramic vases with mints or gourmet jelly beans, set one at each place, and tell guests to take them home.

Party Favors (Centerpieces for Small Tables): Decorate plastic strawberry baskets by threading ribbon through the top holes and tying a bow, then fill them with goodies.

Pots for Plants: When clay flowerpots get chipped and discolored, clean them with soap and water, rinse well, and let dry. Then, put craft glue on the pots and wrap them with twine, starting at the bottom and working up to the top until they are completely covered. This technique will work on some types of plastic pots, too.

Small Table: A single candleholder and candle, a single flower in a bud vase, or a single flower head floating in a large brandy snifter can be the centerpiece on a small table.

"Crafty" Decorating Ideas

Not everyone has time to stay home and "play" creatively before a party, but if you do, here are some ideas for you. When possible, I've also added some shortcut substitutes for people who don't have time to create anything but time-savers. Also, holiday decorating ideas are included with the hints for the specific holiday in Section V.

Candle Holders for Outdoors: Wash tuna cans and spray paint them to match your outdoor furniture, then insert a candle when dry.

HINT 2: If you are feeling particularly ambitious, cut the whole top off large juice cans, fill with water, and freeze so that you can pound nail holes into the sides of the cans without bending or squashing them. After you put nail holes in the sides, in designs or just randomly, dump the ice, let dry, and paint the cans black or a color to match the season or your decor. Put some sand in the bottom to support old candle stubs and you have made a "luminaria," one of the lights placed along walkways at Christmastime in the Southwest. Luminarias can light patios and outdoor tables all year round.

Candles (Making Your Own): Save your used candles and candle stubs until you have a bunch. Put the pieces into a coffee can and place the can in a large pan of water. Heat the water on a low temperature.

CAUTION: Placing the can directly on a flame or stove coils or heating to high temperatures can cause paraffin to ignite.

Continue heating until all of the pieces have melted. If you need to remove some unmelted candle bits, you can do it with a disposable plastic fork.

To make a candlewick, tie one end of an appropriate length of cotton string to a pencil so that you can balance the pencil across the top of the mold as it holds the wick dangling down the mold's center. (A tall cylindrical potato-chip can makes a good mold.) After you have the wick suspended in the mold, pour in the melted wax and let cool. When the candle is cool, remove the mold and trim the wick.

Child's Booster Seat: If you frequently have children as guests, you can make booster seats to place on regular dining room chairs by sewing covers for telephone books. Make pillowcase-style covers from terry cloth or other washable fabrics in colors that match your decor, or wrap outdated phone books with adhesive shelf paper.

HINT 2 *(Shortcut):* Wrap outdated phone books with duct or masking tape, or, if you still need to use the books, put several thick rubber bands around them to hold them together and keep them from slipping off the chair.

Napkin Rings: After you use up a roll of transparent tape, save the plastic circle that held the tape and when you get enough, wrap/cover them with sticky paper, colored tape, florist's tape, heavy yarn, or some other cover-up to make napkin rings that match your linens or china.

HINT 2: Cut paper towel or toilet tissue rolls into about 2-inch lengths, then papier-mâché and paint them to match your decor.

You can also glue small dried flowers, seashells, or other decorations to the napkin rings after the paint dries.

NOTE: To paint the rings easily, first spray paint the insides of the rolls while they stand on end, let dry, and then thread the rolls on a piece of dowling or other stick, support the stick on the upper edges of a box, and spray.

HINT 3 *(Recycling Shortcut):* For a picnic or barbecue, save plastic milk jug rings (from some types of milk jugs, not the kind that unwind to break the seal). Then you can roll plastic tableware in a napkin and hold the roll shut with a "napkin ring." You can also buy small colored rubber bands for this purpose. If the "napkin rings" get disposed of with the other disposables, it won't matter.

Pot Holders and Hot Pads: Cut old quilted mattress covers into hot mitt or hot pad shapes and cover them with fabric scraps to make pot holders. Try making at least one of your hot pads about 6 to 8 inches wide by about 24 inches (or so) long. You can place a casserole on the center of this "super hot pad," bring up the "arms" of the pad to the sides, and carry it to your table or to someone's house. Since the bottom is covered, you can set it down without damaging surfaces with the heat. (Your lap is one of those surfaces!)

NOTE: If you really want to protect your lap or car floor from casserole spills, put the casserole in a foil-and-newspaper-lined flat box, such as those from a case of soft drinks, when you have to transport it to another house.

Sugar Starch for Crocheted Items: This old-fashioned "starch" is still popular because it's so easy to use and perfect when you want to make crocheted items such as Christmas tree ornaments, Easter baskets, small place-setting nut dishes, or doily ruffles very, very stiff and/or molded into a desired shape. Stir ¼ cup water and ¾ cup sugar together in a small pan over low heat until all of the sugar has melted and the solution looks clear. *Do not* boil. Wet crocheted items in warm water, roll in absorbent bath towels to remove as much water as possible, then dip each piece in the sugar starch. Let items air dry on an absorbent towel. You can press and arrange parts of flat items with your hands or place items to dry on measuring cups, bowls, shot glasses, or other objects to shape them as desired.

Tablecloth, Vinyl (Wrinkle Remover): Hang the tablecloth over the shower curtain rod, then turn on the hot water and keep the bathroom door closed so that steam builds up. Spray the cloth several times with very hot water and allow it to "steam" for several hours. Warm vinyl stretches out, and creases usually fall out at the same time.

NOTE: You can also iron the damp cloth on the flannel side with very low heat.

Table Linens (Substitutes):

1. Jazz up your table setting by substituting a pretty shawl for a table runner or cloth.
2. If you don't have a large enough tablecloth, try a twin-size bed sheet. If the look is too bland, you can perk up the table's appearance by placing a smaller tablecloth of a complimentary-colored solid or print over the center of the table. A small square can be placed catty-cornered and then you can put the centerpiece in the middle.

   NOTE: One reader places a small cutwork-embroidery 36-by-36-inch cloth, which is a "good linen" heirloom, over the center of different-colored plain poly-cotton tablecloths chosen according to her party color scheme or in holiday colors. This way, she gets to enjoy displaying her heirloom "good linen" even if it doesn't fit her table.

   My mother always advised readers to use and enjoy all of their "good" china, linens, and silver instead of just keeping them in a drawer. Her philosophy was "If you don't use them, the second spouse will."

3. A serape makes a good tablecloth if you are serving Mexican food.
4. Fringed terry-cloth fingertip towels in bright colors can substitute for place mats, especially when children are at the table—they absorb spills!
5. Cheap washcloths, the kind that come in stacks, can be wet with water to which you've added a squirt or so of lemon juice and heated *slightly (no burns!)* in the microwave. Then you can provide hot towels to cleanse hands in the Asian fashion. It's a terrific idea for barbecue, too!
6. Look for linen sales at discount houses. You can mix and match sale washcloths with tablecloths and place mats to vary your color scheme.
7. If you discover a stain on your good tablecloth on the day of the party, don't panic. Get creative! Can you cover the stain by placing a doily, a place mat, or a nice dinner napkin over it so that it looks like a decorating idea?

❋ You can place three complimentary-colored napkins (or a place mat and two napkins, or doilies) in a row down the center of a rectangular table and then place candlesticks and the centerpiece on them.

❋ You can place a small tablecloth over the center of the large one as described above.

❋ Scatter silk flowers or greenery as part of the table decorations, taking care to "decorate" over the stain(s); keep them in place with double-stick tape or stick-on self-gripping tape pieces.

❋ Place trivets or hot mats over the stain, and then when you bring the food to the table, place serving dishes on those mats or trivets.

❊ Be sure to turn lights low and dine by candlelight; everyone at the table will look better in the glow of the candles, and then nobody will think about stains even if they can see them.

Throw Pillows (Stuffing): Recycle plastic dry cleaner bags as stuffing for throw pillows.

CAUTION: Do sew pillow openings securely closed for safety's sake.

Wallpaper Samples and Leftover Scraps: Cover tissue boxes, wastebaskets, kitchen canisters, bread boxes, shelves, and anything else you want to match your walls or just cover up to make them look new.

NOTE: You can also cut out designs from remnants to make border trim for a wall, a border around a window, a mat for a framed picture, or, with some patterns, just frame the wallpaper as the picture.

Wastebaskets (Painting): When you are planning a party, you may look around the house and decide that wastebaskets, tissue boxes, and toothbrush holders either look nasty or just don't match the way you wish they did.

Don't throw them out! You can spray paint them to match the rest of your decor and look new. If you want to spray paint hard-molded plastic accessories, sand the surfaces lightly before spraying, to make the paint adhere better. To spray paint an outdoor galvanized trash can, apply vinegar to the whole surface to remove the protective coating, let dry, and then spray paint.

Wreath: Buy a plain straw wreath at a craft store. Cut fabric scraps into 1-inch squares. With a Phillips screwdriver placed at the center of the squares, poke the squares into the wreath at random intervals or in a circular pattern. The fabric can be of a color or print that matches your decor, season, or holiday. Finish off the wreath with a bow made from the same or matching fabric, if you wish.

Classic Heloise Cleaning Hints
(From Shortest Shortcuts to Major-Effort Methods)

The easiest way to clean is to hire someone else to do it, if you can afford to do so. One reader decided that instead of hiring people to do her yard work, she would do it, which she enjoyed, and use the money to hire someone to clean her house, which she did not enjoy. She discovered that her lawn care, which took thirty minutes, cost as much as housecleaning services charge for two hours of work. So, instead of a more costly commercial cleaning service, she hired a reliable homemaker to come in one day a week. Before the cleaner would come, she'd make a list of what needed doing and then pare down the number of jobs to what could reasonably be expected of one person in the time allotted. She would assemble all of the equipment and products needed to do the work, and when her helper arrived, she'd just explain what should be done and get out of the way.

THE BASICS

Whether you hire someone to clean or not, home-style cleaning solutions have been around for decades and are less expensive as well as less harmful to the environment. Heloise readers know that baking soda and vinegar are my favorites.

HELOISE HOME-STYLE CLEANING SOLUTIONS

Baking Soda: It's a gentle scouring powder that doesn't scratch. Baking soda removes many types of stains from many types of surfaces and also freshens drains, carpets, and laundry.

Vinegar: Plain white vinegar removes hard-water buildup and cleans mirrors and fixtures. Use it either diluted or full-strength, right from the bottle.

Ammonia-Based Cleaning Solution (for Heavy Duty Cleaning): Mix ½ cup of sudsy ammonia with enough water to make 1 gallon. This solution is an excellent grease cutter for cleaning the areas near the stove, oven, or microwave. It's also a good floor cleaner.

CAUTION: Ammonia products must *always* be used in well-ventilated areas, and *never* mix them with anything that contains bleach.

HELOISE HOW-TO HINTS FOR CLEANING

Some of these hints are classics, and others are the newest hints from my readers and columns.

Bathtub, Fiberglass (Shortcut): When the bottom of a fiberglass tub or shower stall is dirty, it's usually a combination of soap scum and body oils. Try scrubbing with hair shampoo, the cheapest brand will do, since shampoo is designed to remove body oils.

NOTE: Never use any type of abrasive cleanser on fiberglass. It could scratch the surface, which will make cleaning it nearly impossible. Look in hardware stores or plumbing supply stores for products that are made specifically for fiberglass tubs and showers.

Bed Freshener: To keep a guest room's bedding smelling fresh between guest visits, sprinkle underneath the bottom sheet with a bit of baby powder or tuck some fabric softener sheets beneath the bed sheet when you make the bed.

Blender (Classic Shortcut): Fill the blender partially with water, add a drop of regular dishwashing detergent, put the top on and blend a few seconds, or just add some warm sudsy water and blend. Rinse well and dry.

Brass or Copper Cleaner (Shortcut): Pour some full-strength vinegar on a sponge, sprinkle the sponge with salt, scrub brass (or copper), and then rinse well. Polish with soft cloth.

HINT 2 *(Major Effort):* Dissolve 1 teaspoon of salt in 1 cup of white vinegar and add enough flour to make a paste. Apply the paste to the brass, let stand about 10 minutes, then rinse the item very well with warm water and polish dry.

HINT 3: Many commercial metal cleaners have anti-tarnish ingredients, and when you plan a major-effort polishing job, you may want to use them so that you don't have to clean metals as often.

NOTE: Add a coat of protective wax to the decorative brass or copper items after cleaning them so that they will stay shiny longer.

Candle Wax (on Kitchen Cabinets): Wrap an ice cube in a cotton cloth or plastic and rub it over the wax until it hardens. Then, flick off as much wax as you can with a *plastic* spatula. After removing the wax, dissolve remaining residue by applying furniture cleaner (not polish) with a soft cloth and buffing the area with a dry cotton cloth. If some waxy residue still remains, repeat applications of furniture cleaner as noted above until it's gone.

Candle Wax (Removing from Candlesticks): My readers have two ways to remove candle wax—with heat or with cold.

COLD HINT: Put candlesticks in the freezer overnight; wax pops right off.

HOT HINT: With wood or metal holders, heat with hair dryer held about 6 inches from the candlestick and wipe away any melted wax with paper towels.

CAUTION: Hold metal candlesticks with hot pad or cloth to prevent getting burned.

HOT HINT 2: Take candlesticks outdoors and pour boiling water from the kettle on them.

CAUTION: Boiling water might crack some glass or china, and water also damages wood, so this hint is best for metal candlesticks.

Candle Wax (Votive Candles): When you need to remove used votive candles from their holders, store the holder in the freezer until it's chilled. The candle will come out easily.

Carpets (Freshening, Removing Odors): Sprinkle good ol' baking soda and/or a few sprinkles of your favorite potpourri on the carpet before you vacuum.

Cleaning (General): If you color-code rags—for example, white rags for cleaning windows, glass, and mirrors, and colored ones for dusting or polishing furniture—you'll never grab the wrong rag and smear oily furniture cleaner on windows, etc., especially when you are in a rush.

Coffeepot (White Plastic): Remove built-up coffee (or tea) stains by shaking some baking soda on a damp sponge, wiping it on the stained area, and letting it sit awhile. Rub again until clean, rinse well, and enjoy better-tasting coffee from a better-looking pot. Baking soda on a damp sponge will also clean the outside of the pot, and the heating plate, too. Rinse off the sponge after scrubbing and wipe to remove remaining baking soda residue.

Coffee (Tea) Cups (Shortcut): Drop a denture tablet into the stained coffee or tea cup or pot, let sit for a while, wash, and rinse.

Commode (Cleaning Off Mineral Deposits, Shortcut): Toss in a couple of denture tablets and let them fizz away.

HINT 2 *(Major Effort)*: Pour a bucketful of water (not hot) all at once into the commode. Most of the water will then empty out, making cleaning easier. Then, with either a commercial mineral-deposit remover or full-strength vinegar, scrub away at the mineral deposits. If they are very stubborn, soak paper towels in vinegar and place them on the deposits, and let sit several hours before scrubbing.

NOTE: If the commode is cleaned with vinegar or commercial cleaners regularly, at least once weekly, you won't get as much buildup and cleaning will take less time.

Countertop Stains (Kitchen and Bath, Shortcut): Scrub rust or other stains with a paste of baking soda and water; rinse well and buff dry.

Decanter, Crystal (Removing Lime Deposits): Pour full-strength vinegar into the decanter and allow to sit overnight. Add raw rice and shake to let the rice "scrub" the inside. If the deposit is very thick, you may have to repeat the "soak and shake" process several times.

HINT 2: Foaming toilet bowl cleaner will also remove lime deposits. But you must be certain to thoroughly wash and rinse the decanter after using this chemical. Also, take care to protect your hands from the bowl cleaner.

Decanter, Crystal (Removing Stains): Fill the decanter with hot water and drop in a couple of denture tablets. Let sit overnight, then vigorously brush the inside of the decanter with a bottle brush. Rinse well and dry. If stains remain, repeat the soaking process. When this method doesn't remove stains, they may be etched into the glass and impossible to remove.

Drain (Classic, Clearing a Slow One): Pour ½ cup of baking soda into the drain, followed by 1 cup of vinegar. (This mixture will boil up—don't panic . . . at least not yet!) Wait a minute and pour a quart of hot water down the drain, then run hot tap water for a good minute or two. The drain should flow better and will smell better, too.

NOTE: If you can't clear a drain with this drain cleaner or with a plumber's helper (plunger), call the plumber. If the plumber can't come and it's one hour before the party, it's time to panic! But don't "lose it" totally, just do the best you can, even if it means putting dirty dishes into the bathtub and pulling the shower curtain shut. The world won't end just because the sink is plugged, and your guests will marvel at your resourcefulness and composure! (So will you!)

NOTE: Next time, keep the drain clear with the above method so you won't have to show your forbearance with emergencies!

Dusting (Shortcut): Put a sock on each hand and wipe every dusty thing in sight.

NOTE: Terry sport socks work well for this hint, and they work even better if spritzed with a furniture dusting spray.

Dusting (Shortcut for Lampshades, Knicknacks, etc.): Aim your blow dryer, set on "air" or "cold," at anything with detailed, dust-catching surfaces, and you'll blow the dust away in a jiffy!

Fireplace Ash (Less Mess): Spritz the ashes with a plant mister so they don't fly around, then you can neatly scoop them from the fireplace with a dustpan.

Fireplace Odor: Sprinkle candle-making scents on pinecones and toss them into the fireplace to counter sooty odors.

Garbage Disposal (Odor, Shortcut): Drop some citrus peels

into the disposal, grind them up, and rinse. The whole kitchen will smell nice. Or pour some baking soda down the drain and leave it there until the next time you need to grind something down the disposal.

HINT 2 *(Major Effort):* When food particle buildup under the rubber gasket or in the blades causes a bad odor, you'll need to clean the gasket. If it won't come out, run hot water into the sink, add a few drops of liquid dishwashing detergent, and then brush up and down and around the gasket to clean out food particles and other gunk. Be sure to get up under the gasket. Rinse well.

NOTE: Buy an extra commode brush for this chore; it really works well!

Lamp Shade, Pleated (Dusting): A clean, good quality paint-brush will brush away dust from pleated lamp shades. It's also good for dusting anything else with crevices that collect grit, such as knicknacks, windowsills, or carved furniture.

Marble (Cultured, Maintenance) (Major Effort): Cultured (manmade) marble, such as is used for bathroom sinks and counters, benefits from periodic application of paste wax to keep its original luster; buff with a soft chamois cloth.

CAUTION: According to manufacturers referred to me by the Cultured Marble Institute, abrasive cleaners should never be used, even if they are advertised as safe for all surfaces.

HINT 2: A gel-type cleaner sold in hardware stores is recommended for cleaning and polishing cultured marble.

HINT 3 *(Shortcuts):* Vinegar will not harm *man-made* or *synthetic* marble (NOTE: It will damage real marble!) so you can quick-clean with vinegar. You can also clean it with a mild liquid soap, water, and a sponge.

HINT 4 *(Major Effort):* Car-polishing compound and baking soda can remove simple scratches and stains.

Microwave (Freshener): Pour the juice of 1 large or 2 small lemons and 2 cups of water into a microwave-safe glass container and place the container in the center of the microwave. After you cook the liquid on High for 12 minutes, carefully remove the container and wipe the microwave out with a clean, soap-free sponge.

Plastic Containers: To avoid cleaning tomato stains or slimy grease from plastic containers, line them with plastic foil before you add the foods. If they are already stained or greasy, try scrubbing them with baking soda sprinkled on a sponge. After they are clean, rinse well and dry.

Room Scents for Cents: Pour salt into the peel of an orange or lemon after you've removed the pulp, to put a pleasant citrus scent in a room.

HINT 2: Put the perfume card samples from magazines or some leftover potpourri in the bottom of the wastebasket before you put a plastic bag liner in it, so that the room smells nice.

HINT 3: Dab some of your favorite perfume on the light bulbs. The heat will disperse the fragrance.

HINT 4: Put some baking soda into several jar lids and place the lids out of sight under furniture and in closets to prevent odors and freshen the air without adding a scent or costing too many cents! Baking soda is especially effective in deodorizing a room that smells of cigar smoke.

Scuff Marks on Kitchen Floor (Shortcut): Rub with a dry paper napkin or paper towel and they'll be gone. You can also scrub them off with baking soda, but try the paper trick first—it's amazing how well this works!

Shower Curtain (Rinse): If you dunk a plastic shower curtain in a bucket of water to which you've added a bit of dishwasher rinsing agent, it will dry without water spots.

Shower Curtain (Washing Off Water Spots and Mildew from Plastic Curtains) (Easy Major Cleaning): Launder in machine with towels, add a cup of vinegar to the rinse water, let spin a few minutes in the dryer with the towels (not for the full cycle), remove while still warm, and hang immediately. Although this works so quickly a second curtain isn't really necessary, some people like to keep a second shower curtain on hand to hang when one curtain is in the laundry.

HINT 2 *(Shortcut):* Spray with full-strength vinegar from top to bottom, let set about 30 minutes, and scrub remaining spots, if there are any, with a soft brush.

NOTE: Some people cut off the hem and side seams of plastic shower curtains to eliminate convenient places for mildew to grow. Try to remember to stretch the curtain open after a shower so that it has a better chance to dry quickly, and you may not have to do a major-effort cleaning as often.

NOTE: Be aware that fabric shower curtains also keep water in the tub and, if you sew, you can make 12 buttonholes at the top of a twin-size, permanent-press sheet (to match your bedroom, if you wish), and hang it up as you would a plastic shower curtain. Water won't splash through it, and it's easy to maintain by laundering as you would any other bedding.

Shower Doors (Cleaning Off Water Spots Shortcut): While you're in the shower, wash your shower doors with shampoo poured on a sponge, plastic scrubbie or washcloth, rinse, and wipe dry with a used towel.

HINT 2 *(Major Effort):* Apply full-strength white vinegar, let set for about 30 minutes, and rinse.

Shower Doors (Keeping Clean): Put up a spring shower curtain rod *inside* the shower to hold a shower curtain *inside* the glass shower doors. Then the curtain will get all the splashes and soap scum. After the last shower before the party, you can pull the curtain to the side and the shower door will still be sparkling clean.

BONUS HINT: An extra spring shower curtain rod can be placed at the back wall of a shower to hold towels if you don't have enough towel bars in the bathroom when you have guests.

Shower Tiles (Major Effort, Removing Yellow from White Tiles): When white tiles become yellowed, it's usually soap scum, and commercial products will remove it well. Follow the directions on the label. A commercial product used for cleaning swimming pool tiles removes scum easily, but, as with all commercial products, *do* make sure the room is well ventilated.

HINT 2: Spray a solution of 1 part bleach to 1 part water on the tiles, let sit awhile, and then scrub with a sponge and rinse well. Heavy, scummy buildup may require you to repeat the process several times.

CAUTION: Test a small area first to make sure the bleach won't damage the tiles.

NOTE: Train the people in your house to wipe off the tiles with a used bath towel whenever they shower or bathe, and you won't have to do a major-effort cleaning very often.

Shower Walls (Rinsing Shortcut): Rinse shower and tub walls after scrubbing with a houseplant watering can. It's neat and fast.

Silk Flowers and Plants (Dusting Shortcut): Toss a handful of salt or cornmeal into a paper bag. Put the flowers, blossom end down, into the sack, gather it around the stems, hold tightly, and shake. Remove flowers and brush away remaining residue.

HINT 2 *(Major Effort):* When grime won't come off with the shortcut method, you may have to wash the flowers in cool, soapy water, if they are washable. Fill a sink with water, swish in a drop

or two of regular liquid dishwashing detergent, then swish the flowers in the water. Rinse well. Place the flowers or greenery on several thicknesses of paper towels to absorb color drips and moisture. Let air dry, and they should look bright and fresh again.

Silver (Foil Method): This method is quick, but it's not for all silver pieces and should only be used occasionally.

Place aluminum foil in the bottom of a cooking pot. (Aluminum pots may get darkened if used for this process.) Add enough water to cover the silver pieces. For each quart of water, add 1 teaspoon of salt and 1 teaspoon of baking soda. Bring the solution to a boil. Add silver. Boil 2 to 3 minutes or until the tarnish is removed. Remove silver, rinse, and buff dry with a soft cloth.

A second way to quickly clean silver with this method is to put a piece of aluminum foil at the bottom of the kitchen sink, fill the sink with hot, hot tap water, and then proceed as above, adding salt and baking soda to the water as directed. After tarnish is removed, rinse and buff as noted above.

Silver (Quick Fix): Sometimes, if you're in a hurry, just washing silver with regular mild liquid dishwashing detergent, rinsing well, and buffing with a soft cloth will remove minor tarnish enough to use the piece. If you have a jar of paste-type silver polish, you can poke those blackened tips of fork tines into it, wipe with a sponge, rinse, and dry for a quick cleaning. (Silverware polishing is one of those chores you really need to do a week or two before a party, because it can be time-consuming, and therefore nerve-wracking, on party day.)

CAUTION: The above methods may leave a dull white luster and remove the dark accents in design crevices, which many people find desirable. They may also soften the cement of hollow-handled flatware.

Sink (Kitchen): Sprinkle baking soda into the sink and pour a bit of vinegar over the soda. As it starts to bubble, scrub the sink with a brush and then rinse well. The sink will be clean with ease.

Sinks and Fixtures (Kitchen or Bath): In kitchen or bath, spray sinks and fixtures (and glass shower doors and their tracks and frames) with a petroleum-based pre-wash spray and wipe off with a soft cloth or old towel. It removes soap scum and water spots and makes everything shine at the same time.

HINT 2: Spray bathroom mirrors, sinks, fixtures, commode seats, and even floor tiles with window cleaner and wipe with paper towels.

HINT 3: Wipe sink fixtures with rubbing alcohol on a facial tissue or toilet paper to remove water spots and to shine.

Soap Dish: To clean a scummy soap dish, scrub with a nylon-net scrubbie and lots of hot water.

NOTE: Save yourself from this chore. Keep a sponge on or in the dish and put the soap on the sponge. You can quick-clean the sink with the soapy sponge, too.

Soap Dispenser: If you drop a few marbles into your liquid hand-soap dispenser, it will raise the level of the liquid so that the dispenser will work even when the level is getting low. Also, the marbles tend to stablize the dispenser by making it bottom-heavy.

Stainless Steel Sink (Shortcut): Put a few drops of baby or mineral oil on a paper towel or sponge and wipe your stainless steel sink. Water spots will disappear and the sink will shine!

Stickers, Price Tags (Shortcut): When you have children's stickers on the refrigerator or price tags on serving dishes, apply enough petroleum-based pre-wash spray or baby oil to the sticky area to saturate it, and wait for it to soak in. Then gently scrub the area with a nylon-net or plastic-mesh scrubbie until all of the sticker or sticker goo is gone. Sometimes you have to repeat the process. After the sticker is removed, wash as usual to remove remaining residue.

Vacuum Odor: Put some of your favorite potpourri, a fabric softener sheet, a few whole cloves, or a cotton ball moistened with your favorite cologne or peppermint extract into the dust bag before you vacuum, to freshen the air and to avoid that dusty, musty vacuum odor.

Window Blinds (Dusting): Vacuum with a brush attachment with the blinds closed—first with the blades closed toward the window and then with them closed toward you.

NOTE: If you dust blinds by hand, try dusting with felt squares (sold in craft or sewing supply stores); they pick up dust like a magnet!

HINT 2 *(Shortcut):* If you just noticed that the top side of the blinds' slats are dirty and it's the day of the party, close the blinds so that you can see only the slats' undersides (which are usually cleaner) from inside the house. Or, if the windows are clean, pull the blinds up!

Windows (Classic, Major Effort, Cleaning Hard Water Spots): Spray full-strength white vinegar on the glass and let it sit. Then scrub with nylon net or a plastic scrubbie. Heavy deposits may need repeats of this cleaning process. After you remove the deposits, you can buff the window with clean paper or cloth towels.

NOTE: The other classic Heloise window cleaner is a solution made by adding a couple of "glugs" of nonsudsy ammonia to a gallon of water.

Pre- or Post-Party Repairs and Cover-Ups

I don't know why, but when you decide to have a party, you suddenly see all the things that are wrong or worn out in your house. If you can't do repairs a week before the party, it may be a better idea just to cover up the damage or ignore it.

Before you make post-party repairs, you may want to contact your insurance company to find out if the damage by a guest is covered. For example, repair of a broken chair or reweaving the hole from a cigarette burn in a sofa (or reupholstering the sofa, if repair is not possible) could be covered by some homeowner policies.

NOTE: Your insurance company may require a representative to see the damage before authorizing repairs.

Barbecue (Cover-Up Rust): Sand rusted areas and paint with heat-resistant paint that is made especially for barbecues.

NOTE: Heat-resistant barbecue paint, usually black, is also a good super-durable paint to use on mailboxes, walkway lights, or other metal objects that get full, hot sun most of the day. One reader says her mailbox didn't need repainting for about ten years after she spray painted it with black, heat-resistant barbecue paint. It costs more, but she says her time is money.

Candle Wax from Fabric: Let set until hard. Scrape wax off with the back side of a knife. Place a couple of paper towels over and under the wax and press lightly with a warm but not too hot iron. The towels will absorb the wax. Repeat with clean towels until all wax is gone. If a spot remains, rub liquid detergent directly into the area and wash as usual.

Carpet Cleaning (Professional): If your carpet is professionally cleaned, it will dry faster if you set the air conditioner on 72° and turn on fans for air circulation.

Carpet Stains

CAUTION: Test all cleaning solutions on an inconspicuous place to make sure they are compatible with the fibers and dyes in your carpet.

HINT 1 *(Shortcut):* Dab at stain with a clean cloth moistened with club soda and then blot as dry as you can with a dry, clean cloth. Then finish the job after the guests are gone.

HINT 2 *(Major Effort):* To remove red stains or other hard-to-remove stains from carpet (such as mustard) with a commercial cleaner that contains sodium bisulfate, available at supermarkets, saturate the spot, cover with a cloth diaper or white towel, and iron with a steam iron. You may have to repeat the process two or three times until the stain is gone.

IMPORTANT CAUTIONS: Do not let the iron touch the carpet directly and use heat *only* with cleaners that contain sodium bisulfate, or you could damage the fibers in your carpet.

HINT 3 *(Major Effort):* Color remover (found with fabric dyes in supermarkets) can remove stains from some carpets if your test on an inconspicuous place shows that it won't remove the dye from your particular carpet. However, the Association of Specialists in Cleaning and Restoration (ASCR) does not recommend using this method on Olefin carpeting or expensive Oriental rugs. *Also,* protect your hands with rubber gloves and keep windows open for ventilation. Mix ¼ teaspoon of color remover with ½ cup of water. Saturate the stain with the solution, put a white towel over it, and with your steam iron, steam over it. To prevent crushing the pile, don't press the iron, just hold it close to the towel. Blot up, wet again with the solution, then steam until the stain is gone.

Rinse very well several times with clear water and blot dry. It's very important to rinse out all of the solution because it can damage the carpet fibers if allowed to remain in them.

Carpet (Chewing Gum): Put ice in a plastic bag and put the ice bag on the gum to harden it. Scrape gently with a dull table knife to get off as much gum as possible. Remove the remaining stain with a dry-cleaning solvent, which can be found in most shoe or grocery stores. *Follow the solvent's package directions exactly.*

Carpet (Pet Urine Stains and Odors): If you've ignored your puppy while cooking party foods and it has an "accident," you can quickly remove urine odor and stain from carpeting as follows: Soak up the area with paper towels or a rag you can throw away; rinse the spot with water and again soak up the moisture with more clean paper towels. Dab the spot with a solution of ⅔ cup vinegar and ½ cup water, let sit a few minutes, then soak up all moisture with clean paper towels until you remove as much as possible. The mild vinegar odor will evaporate in a short time.

NOTE: Next time remember to take puppy out!

Cigarette Burn on White Painted Furniture (Shortcut): Remove the black burn mark with extra-fine steel wool and then touch up the area with matching paint; let dry. If the burned area is indented, you may have to build it up with thin layers of paint, letting each dry between coats until the surface is level.

HINT 2 *(Major Effort):* To make the furniture look like new, you'll have to refinish the whole piece. Remove all paint with a paint remover, then sand the burned area to remove black areas and to reduce the "dented" appearance, so the surface is smooth. Then either repaint the piece to its original color or, if the wood is suitable, apply a polyurethane finish for a natural wood look.

Coffee and Tea Stains: Treat as promptly as possible before they set. Rinse in cold water first. Mix a detergent solution of 1 teaspoon mild liquid detergent in 1 cup of water. Dab it on the area, with paper towels under the stain to absorb the liquid. Rinse well in cold water. If the stain remains, apply a vinegar solution of ⅓ cup vinegar in ⅔ cup water, blot, and rinse.

Curtain Wrinkles: When curtain panels come out of the drier so wrinkled that rewashing doesn't take the wrinkles out, you can try thoroughly wetting the curtains and hanging them where they can drip without making a mess. Drape them over clotheslines or a shower rod and slide heavy butter knives into the hems and rod openings to see if the weight of the knives will pull the wrinkles out. If this fails, it would be best to take the curtains to your dry cleaners to see if they can remove the wrinkles with steam pressing. You might want to let them try with one panel first before you give them a roomful of curtains. However, if the curtains are already ruined, what more could happen?

Driveway Oil Stains: Spray on engine degreaser, sold at most auto supply stores; let stay on stain for 10 to 20 minutes. You may need to scrub a bit with an old broom, then rinse the area with a garden hose.

HINT 2 *(Classic):* Sprinkle cat-box litter on the stain, allow it to remain overnight to absorb stain, and sweep up the litter in the morning.

LETTER OF LAUGHTER: My favorite driveway grease-removal story is the one from the reader who poured a thick layer of cat litter over the grease stains in his driveway, and overnight, all the cats in the neighborhood thought he'd provided a giant litter pan for their use!

Gravy Stains on Table Linens: Treat immediately by blotting the stains with paper towels. When the cloth is removed, soak in a detergent solution of one teaspoon of colorless, mild detergent to each cup of lukewarm water. If this does not remove the stain, apply full-strength liquid laundry detergent to the stain. Then rub well and wash as usual. If the stain persists, dab with a vinegar solution of ⅓ cup vinegar in ⅔ cup water. If the item is expensive or an heirloom, take it to the cleaners and tell them what the stain is and what you have used to treat it, so that they can do the best possible job of removing it.

Lipstick on Napkins: Place a cloth or paper towel under the area. Using rubbing alcohol, dab and blot and then gently rub as you manipulate the cloth so that you are using clean areas as you blot up the stain.

Marble (Stain from Drinking Glass): To remove moisture rings caused when drinking glasses are allowed to stay on marble, rub the area with a commercial marble-polishing powder exactly as directed on the label.

You can buy marble cleaning and repair products at hardware stores or home-improvement centers. If these products don't work, you may have to give the job to a marble restorer. Look in the yellow pages or call several antiques dealers in your city to find out who does their marble restoration work.

NOTE: Contrary to popular opinion, marble surfaces are *not* like glass. Marble absorbs moisture; spills need to be wiped up as soon as possible. When placing glasses on marble, always protect the marble from moisture by keeping a coaster, paper towel, or napkin beneath the glass.

Nail Holes in Walls (Shortcuts): Cover and/or fill nail holes in walls with matching colored toothpaste, bar soap, chalk, or typewriter correction fluid. Rub toothpaste, soap, or chalk across the hole and wipe off the excess. "Paint" holes or repair holes with typewriter correction fluid; it will fill small nail holes all by itself.

NOTE: Typewriter correction fluid in a color to match your wall can also cover up scuffs, chips, and other marks.

Oil Stains on Fabric (Grease Spills on Tablecloth, etc.): Rub in baby powder or rub a piece of chalk on the stain. Shake off powder or chalk before laundering.

Potpourri (Making a Room Smell Fresher): If you don't have any more potpourri and you want to keep your pot a-boilin' with a homey, comfy scent, you can put your used potpourri in a colander or strainer, rinse it off with cold water, pour a bit of concentrated bottled scent (or that gift perfume that smells good but not when it's on you) on it, and reuse it in the potpourri crock.

HINT 2: Grab a handful of whole cloves, stick cinnamon, and other spices that you have on the shelf, toss them into the potpourri pot, add some water, and you'll have homemade potpourri.

HINT 3: Dab some of the perfume described above on cotton balls, put the cotton balls on a saucer or anything that will protect surfaces from damage, and place your "room scents" where you think they are needed.

Sink (Chipped Enamel Shortcut): Touch up a porcelain sink basin with matching colored typewriter correction fluid.

Sofa and Chair Cushions: Have previous guests had their derrieres wedged between the seat cushion and the back of your chair or sofa because the cushion has a mind of its own and keeps trying to escape being sat upon? Look for craft foam that's ½ inch thick, 24 inches wide, and several feet long. Tuck in the foam securely at the ends and back of the seat, then replace the cushions. The reader who sent in this hint said it stopped her cushions from sliding forward and it stopped her guests from having those odd, startled looks that they got when they sat down and got wedged into her sofa!

Table Linen Stains (General Hint): If you circle the spots that need pretreating before laundering with a water-soluble pen sold at fabric shops, you won't have to search for the stains when you are ready to launder the linens. The water-soluble pen marks will wash out with the stains.

Table Pad Stuck on Wood: If a foam-rubber-backed plastic table pad gets stuck to the table surface, you can try applying vegetable oil and scrubbing with a nylon net or plastic scrubbie.

CAUTION: *Do* test on an inconspicuous place before applying the oil or anything else to furniture, to make sure it won't damage the finish. If the oil doesn't work, you may have to refinish the whole table.

NOTE: Isn't it ironic that these pads, which are designed to prevent heat damage and scratches when placed beneath a tablecloth, can cause damage all by themselves? Fabric may be a better choice for a table pad! And *always* put a trivet beneath warm or hot dishes!

Tomato-Based Stains on Table Linens: Dab or scrape off excess liquid as soon as possible. Soak the item in cold water for about 30 minutes, then rub straight liquid laundry detergent directly into the remaining stain on the wet fabric. Launder in warm water and detergent.

Upholstery Stains on Chair Arm: Antimacassars were popular in Victorian times to protect chair and sofa upholstery from the "Macassar" hair oils used at that time, hence the name. You can use them, too, to cover up chair arms or headrest areas that are soiled. Some place mats or fancy hand towels will work if you don't have Victorian doilies in your linen collection. To keep them in place, buy twist pins with clear plastic heads where upholstery and slipcover supplies are sold. You just twist in the pins and they hold the "antimacassars" in place.

NOTE: If it's the last minute, either ignore the problem, assuming that you are the only one who notices it, or pin the cover-ups in place with colored ball-topped sewing or craft pins. Be sure to bury the pinpoint in the upholstery stuffing so you don't scratch your guests. You can also stick pieces of self-gripping tape on the cover-up and the chair; it comes in both light and dark colors.

White Rings from Hot Dishes on Wood Furniture: Make a paste of half baking soda and half toothpaste (any toothpaste is OK), and then, with a damp cotton cloth, apply some of the mixture to the ring in a gentle, circular motion until the ring disappears. Restore the shine by buffing with a dry cotton cloth.

NOTE: If the white ring remains, you may have to refinish the whole piece of furniture.

Wine on Tablecloth or Other Fabric: While the cloth is on the table, pour salt on the stain to absorb the liquid. When you remove the tablecloth, let it soak in cold water. After it soaks, if the stain is still visible, rub the area with a detergent solution of 1 teaspoon mild liquid detergent in 1 cup of water. Rinse and wash as usual. This should remove the stain. If it still persists, mix an ammonia solution of 1 tablespoon ammonia in ½ cup of water and then rub it on the stain.

Storing Party Things

Chairs (Folding): To keep extra folding chairs clean between uses, cover them with either cheap or on-sale king-size pillowcases, or large plastic garbage or dry cleaning bags.

China, Glassware (Safe Storage): Put a flat-bottomed coffee filter between stacked plates, bowls, and cups to prevent chipping. Cheap paper plates can also cushion plates and serving dishes. To make a paper plate fit into a bowl-shaped piece, cut several "rays" about three inches or so inward from the edge, toward the center, all around the paper plate.

Coffee Cups: When you have too many cups for the storage space, place one cup upside down with a second one right-side up on top of it. Then you can stack cups without them getting stuck together, broken, or scratched.

Glassware: You can get more glassware of all shapes and types in less space if you place it in rows with one glass or goblet upside down alternated with one right-side up; be sure to start each new row by placing the first glass the opposite-side up or down from the first glass of the previous row.

Decorations (Seasonal): Store in the zippered bags in which blankets and comforters are sold. They'll stay clean, and any parts that fall off will be saved in the bag.

Linens: If you hang tablecloths on dry cleaners' pants hangers, the kind with the sticky cardboard tube, you won't have to iron them before setting the table, because the only creases will be those that help you center the cloth on the table. You can also cut gift-wrap tubes down their lengths and then put them on sturdy hangers to make even fewer creases in tablecloths.

Silverware: Silverware and silver serving pieces can be stored in special cloth bags that are impregnated with anti-tarnish products, to avoid polishing silver every time it's used.

Quick Fixes for Unplanned Guests and Other Emergencies

Beds, Extra (Classic): My mother would make two beds from one by removing the mattress from the box spring and placing it in another room for the guest. Then she would sleep on the box spring. It's not really super comfy for the person on the box spring, but it will do for a night or two. You can pad the box spring with extra blankets or a comforter.

HINT 2: Store extra twin-bed mattresses beneath a double or king-size bed; you'll have extra beds for guests. They'll be low but will do, especially for small children, who will be safer since they won't be in danger of falling out of a strange bed if they wake up during the night.

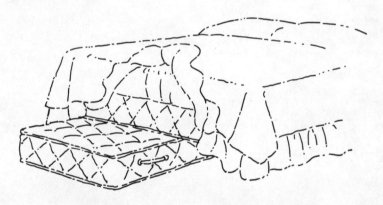

HINT 3: Invest in an inflatable mattress if you have frequent guests in a small apartment, and do get an auto-pump to make blowing up the mattress easier. They aren't expensive and save all sorts of energy!

HINT 4: A baby can sleep in a padded dresser drawer—removed from the dresser, of course! A toddler can sleep in a padded plastic wading pool.

Linens: Fold matching towels and washcloths or matching pillowcases and sheets into "packs" instead of placing them on shelves individually. Then you can just grab a complete set of bedding or bath towel/washcloth from the shelf when you are getting ready for guests.

Mattress Protection for Child: Protect your mattress from nighttime "accidents" by covering it with an old plastic shower curtain, shower curtain liner, or plastic tablecloth, before you put on the mattress pad and other bedding. Do check to be certain there are no cuts or holes to let moisture through.

Soap for Dispenser: Soap dispenser empty and you have no replacement? Substitute shampoo. It smells good, too!

The Big Event

So you've planned everything ahead, you've made your list and checked it twice, what else should you think about?

Some General Party Hints

❋ If you've hired a caterer, let the catering service help do the job and don't hover over them and get in the way. A good caterer—and would you hire one that's not good?—should be able to do the job and allow you to spend your time greeting and visiting with your guests.

❋ If you're doing it yourself, it can't be repeated too often: If someone offers to help, *accept!*

❋ If your house is too small to accommodate all of the people you owe or want to have at a party, try having two parties two days in a row. The house will be clean, you can prepare foods that will keep a day, and then, after your two days of entertaining, you need to perform only one real post-party cleanup.

❊ Take a hint from commercial party rooms during summer parties: Get the house somewhat cooler than you want it. Lots of people at a big party tend to warm up the room. (You could say it's all that "hot air" from cocktail party talk . . . You could . . . but I won't!) Run ceiling fans on Low if you have them, to keep air circulating.

Damage Control
(Also See "Food 'Repair,' " Section II)

Boiling-Over Liquids: Contain and absorb the spill as best you can with a kitchen towel. Worry about how you've totally ruined the towel tomorrow.

Burning Fat on Stove:

CAUTION: *Never* try to put out an oil or fat fire with water; it will splatter and cause you to get burned.

1. Salt or dry baking soda tossed at the fire will usually do the job on a small fire.
2. If it's possible to do it without burning yourself, put a lid on the pot to smother the flame.

NOTE: To avoid letting fat spatter on you from a skillet (burns) or on the whole stove and counter (mess), place an inverted metal colander over the skillet while you fry. Steam will escape so that the meat or other food will still be able to brown properly.

Egg (Broken on the Floor): If you don't have an eager dog to lap it up, try these hints.
HINT 1: Hold one piece of pliable cardboard paper in each hand so that you can scoop the broken egg with one piece of cardboard

onto the other one, as if one piece were the broom and the other a dustpan.

HINT 2: Sprinkle the egg heavily with table salt; wait 5 to 10 minutes; sweep into a dustpan.

Garbage Disposal (Classic Shortcut: "Unsticking" with Broomstick): Most disposals have a red Restart button. If you press it, switch on the disposal again, and the disposal still won't start up, try the classic broom handle method.

CAUTION: Make sure the switch is in the off position.

Insert a broom handle or other very sturdy stick into the disposal and turn it counterclockwise to try to unjam the motor. Pull the stick out, run water, flip the switch, and the disposal should start.

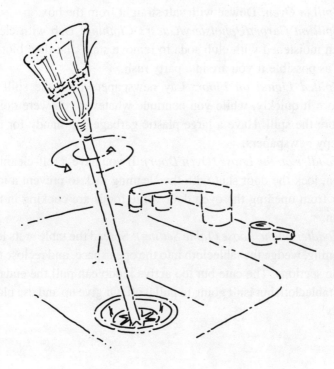

Smoke Removal: If you have a vent over your stove, keep it on while you are cooking, so that in case you burn something on the stove, you'll already have the power going to remove smoke, steam, and odor. Also, if you don't burn anything, your guests will be tantalized by mouth-watering food aromas as they approach the house.

Smoking Odors (Removing Shortcut): Dip a towel in equal parts of vinegar and hot water, wring it out, and wave it gently over your head as you walk about the room. The room will be cleared of smoke odors in a few minutes.

NOTE: This is a great but weird-looking idea. Do it either before guests arrive or after they *all* leave—some people frighten easily! On second thought, it would be a way to end a party that's lasted too long!

Spill in Oven: Dowse with salt straight from the box.

Spill on Carpet/Upholstery/Guest's ·Clothing: Dab with clean cloth moistened with club soda to remove stain and then blot as dry as possible if you are in a party rush.

Spilled Liquid on Floor: Lay newspapers over the spill to absorb it quickly, while you continue whatever you were doing before the spill. Have a large plastic garbage bag handy for the drippy newspapers.

Toddler on the Loose (Oven Door): If you have a self-cleaning oven, lock the door shut with the cleaning lock to prevent a toddler from opening the oven door while foods are cooking in the oven.

Toddler on the Loose (Table Setting): Spread the table at its leaf opening, wedge the tablecloth into the open space, and reclose the table sections. The cute but too active kiddo can pull the ends of the tablecloth but isn't going to pull it off. Or give up and use place mats!

Beverage Service

❃ *Bartender:* If you live alone, arrange for a single friend to help you host your party and to serve the drinks while you put the finishing touches to the food. This is also a good job for a shy person who needs something to do when overwhelmed by a crowd.

❃ *Three Make-Ahead Punches* (From *The Congressional Club Cookbook,* 11th Edition, Washington, D.C.)

Make-Ahead Daiquiri Punch: Combine three 6-ounce cans of frozen limeade, softened, three 6-ounce cans of frozen daiquiri mix, softened, 1 fifth of rum, and 6 cups of water, and freeze in a covered container. Remove from the freezer about 15 minutes before serving and put it into a punch bowl; allow it to thaw to a mush state. Just before serving, stir in 1 quart of club soda. Makes 5 quarts.

Make-Ahead Margarita: Mix five 6-ounce cans of frozen lime-ade, 30 ounces of tequila, 9 ounces of triple sec, 1¾ quarts of water, and chill. Makes 1 gallon of margaritas. Serve chilled drink mix over cracked ice.

NOTE: This mixture can also be frozen, then thawed to a mush before putting it into a glass.

Make-Ahead Sangria: Mix in a large pitcher 26 ounces of red wine, ¼ cup sugar, 1 cup orange juice, 1 cup pineapple juice, ½ cup triple sec, orange and/or lemon slices. Refrigerate for several days to blend flavors. This recipe makes 1½ quarts and will keep as long as 2 weeks in the fridge.

GLUHWEIN

Popular at ski resorts, this drink can warm you anywhere! It is often served in handled glass cups in Germany and Austria.

NOTE: While the recipe calls for heating in a saucepan, you can heat it in a microwave-safe pitcher or bowl in the microwave and then serve from the same container.

1 cup sugar
½ cup water
2 sticks cinnamon
1 dozen whole cloves
Strip of lemon peel (about 2 or so inches)
1 quart hot orange or pineapple juice
1 bottle (about 26 oz.) claret wine or favorite red wine
½ lemon, cut into slices

Combine sugar and water in a saucepan, add spices and peel. Bring to boil and simmer for about 3 minutes. Pour juice and claret wine into a larger saucepan and heat. Strain sugar and spice mixture into the claret-juice mixture. Gently heat to a simmer. Serve in preheated (to prevent breaking) glasses or mugs. Garnish each serving with a lemon slice.

❀ *Serves 12.*

❀ *Less-Mess Jug Wine Service:* If you are serving jug wines to a large group, it's easier, less messy, and more attractive if you serve the wines from a cocktail pitcher or a smaller decanter. Often, during the holidays, certain wines are sold in one-liter decanters, which you can wash and recycle for this purpose.

❀ *Super-Size Ice Bucket:* A large punch bowl or plastic tub filled half-full with ice pieces or cubes will hold liter-size bottles or decanters of wine or champagne. Look in restaurant supply stores for decorative extra-large plastic salad bowls which can double as ice/punch bowls.

❉ *Wine and Champagne:* At a large party, where you are serving drinks from disposable plastic stemmed glasses, you may want to consider clear 4-to-6-ounce plastic cocktail cups for wine instead of plastic stemware, which tends to tip and spill. Of course, champagne should be served in stemware, and you will find tulip-shaped champagne disposables which are better for the bubbly than the traditional flat-based champagne stemware. Or serve wine in handleless punch cups if you have them.

❉ *Opening a Champagne Bottle:* While it looks dramatic to pop the cork and let champagne spout like a geyser, that sort of thing is best left to sports team locker rooms after championship games. When you open a bottle of champagne, put a napkin or clean handkerchief over the cork between your hand and the bottle. Remove the foil and then the wiring, keeping the bottle pointed away from you and not at anyone else. (Once the wiring is off, the cork can pop anytime, especially if the bottle has been jostled before opening.)

Holding the cork in one hand, twist the bottle gently away from the cork. If the cork won't ease out, carefully push it away from the bottle with your thumb. Sometimes running warm water over just the neck of the bottle helps. The trick is to keep the bottle at a 45-degree angle while opening it, to allow more of the champagne's surface to be exposed to the atmosphere and therefore less pressure to build up at the bottle neck, which in turn means that less champagne will be spilled and you'll have more to enjoy.

❉ *Washer Ice Tub:* Line your top-loading washer with a thick towel or two to prevent chipping the drum, add ice and canned beverages, and you have a neatly draining drink cooler.

❉ *Ice Coolers:* Almost anything will hold canned beverages and ice. I've seen people use antique bathtubs, metal washtubs, plastic baby bathtubs or wading pools, plastic bag–lined, wooden-slat garden barrel halves. If it holds ice without leaking, it can be a cooler indoors; outdoors it doesn't matter too much if the container leaks! If the drinks are kept indoors, do place an old plastic shower curtain or plastic tablecloth covered by a rug or thick towel beneath makeshift metal "coolers" to absorb condensed moisture and prevent ruining a floor. Or just put your "cooler" outside the door where it won't drip indoors.

❋ *Coffee Service:* If possible, serve after-dinner coffee from a separate table, such as a card table or a buffet. Then you can set up the cups/mugs, sugar, sweetener, and cream pitcher (pour the cream as the guests are eating the main course) ahead of time.

CAUTION: If you serve from an electric coffeepot, or keep a pot on an electric warming tray, do make sure no wires are dangling to trip anyone.

❋ *Decaf Coffee:* If most of your friends prefer decaffeinated coffee these days, you may want to make your main, larger coffee urn with decaf and just make caffeinated coffee in your everyday coffeemaker. To label, write "decaf" on a card and attach it to the coffee urn handle or lid with a bit of transparent tape so that your guests will know what they are drinking.

NOTE: I've asked servers at large hotel banquets about the decaf to "caf" ratio of drinkers and learned that many banquet managers serve only decaffeinated coffee in the evening unless a guest specially requests "caf," because most people prefer decaf nowadays.

❋ *Coffee "Sweeteners":* For an extra treat, set out Kahlua, Irish cream whiskey, or other liquors so that guests can "sweeten" their coffee. Whipped cream or vanilla ice cream floating on coffee is a tasty touch, too. Or set out artificial flavorings such as chocolate, rum, etc., for those who don't want alcoholic drinks.

❋ *Coffee Mugs:* I've had caterers tell me that it's really better, if you have coffee mugs, to serve coffee in them when you have a large party, even if they don't match. People are comfortable with mugs, and they don't spill as easily as tea-type cups or disposable coffee cups, if people are walking around and visiting while they sip. And you don't need saucers, just small napkins for coasters.

NOTE: Set out coasters on surfaces that need protection from wet drinks and pray that people use them.

NOTE: Many people think marble tops on furniture are like glass, but anyone who owns marble-topped furniture knows that marble is porous and easily stained and/or etched by certain beverages, especially alcoholic and citrus ones. A thick table runner placed strategically can help protect a marble-topped buffet or table. Also, an extra-thick coat of suitable wax can help protect marble and other furniture surfaces.

Special Events, Holidays, and Celebrations

> **Reminder:**
>
> Color the day squares of your calendar with a highlighter marker so you won't forget birthdays, anniversaries, and other special occasions.

General Gift Hints

While it's difficult enough buying a gift for that "someone who has everything," it becomes double trouble to buy gifts when your budget doesn't allow many extras. The good news is that personalized gifts can be kind to your budget, very welcome to a recipient who doesn't need a thing, and fun for you to create "with love," too. Many of the following hints can be put together even by people whose time is as limited as their budgets.

GIFTS FROM AND FOR THE HEART

When you have more talent and time than "treasure," you can still give treasured gifts for all occasions. For specific occasion "gifts from the heart," look under birthday, shower, or other occasions.

Balloons: After they are deflated, save the shiny helium balloons given for birthdays and other celebrations and frame them in wooden embroidery hoops that have been painted colors to coordinate with the balloons. They will brighten up the balloon recipient's room and preserve happy memories of the celebration. For example, birthday balloons for a child's room, congratulations balloons for your home office, special holiday or birthday balloons for a senior's residence, and so on.

Bath Salts: Put 3 cups of Epsom salts into a glass or metal bowl (not plastic because this mixture may stain). Mix 1 tablespoon of glycerin, a few drops of food coloring, and enough perfume to make a fragrant mixture. Slowly add this mixture to the Epsom salts and stir well. Put the bath salts into a pretty jar and add a bow.

Books on Tape: For people who drive for hours to and from work or for elderly people and others with poor eyesight, books on tape help pass the time. If you can't afford to buy commercially recorded books, you can read and record the books yourself; the recipient may get more pleasure from hearing a friendly voice on the tape! Find out which books the recipient likes—mysteries, best-sellers, the Bible?

Calendar of Wishes: Put the month and day on 365 plain 4- by 6-inch index cards and distribute them equally among family members or friends of the recipient. Each person should write a message, quote a verse of poetry or scripture, or write a note. Young children can draw pictures. Then assemble the cards according to the dates and put them in a box. This gift idea came from someone who gave "A Year of Love" index card set to cheer a wheelchair-bound relative. However, it could also be a gift for anyone—we all could use a daily lift with a happy message from a person who cares about us!

"Care Package" for Person Who Has Everything: Instead of guessing at sizes and other needs, put together a "care package" of hair care or other grooming products, favorite canned goodies or boxed foods, and give for holidays or anniversaries. It may be especially helpful for people on a fixed income to receive much needed everyday items.

Cookies: When you make cookies with a grandchild, put some in a container so they can be shared with the child's other grandparents.

Donation Gifts to Shelter: Save plastic baskets from cherry tomatoes or strawberries, weave a ribbon around the top of each, line with a coffee filter or pretty paper, fill with miniature soaps, shampoo, and conditioners collected when you travel, and donate the gifts to your local battered women/adults refuge or to other human services organizations at holiday time or any time.

Floral Gifts: When I receive a floral gift, I take a photo of it to enclose with my thank-you note so that the person who sent it can see what I received and how I've displayed and enjoyed it. Letting the sender know what was received is especially important if the floral gift is sent from out of town. I often get letters from readers who say that they were unpleasantly surprised and even angry when they saw what was delivered in their name to party hosts, hospital patients, funerals, etc.

To get best results when ordering flowers:

1. Order early. Seasonal holiday flowers are always in great demand and may not be available for late orders.
2. Certain seasonal flowers or plants are available only for very short periods, so be sure to ask if they will be available when you want the order delivered.
3. When ordering flowers to be sent to another city or state, do

inside the plastic sheet and beneath the pot to raise it high enough
to let water drain properly.

Floral Gifts to Shut-Ins: When taking cut flowers from your
garden to nursing home residents or hospital patients, do take a
vase. It need not be a "real" vase. A mayo jar, a three-liter bottle
with the top end cut off, or some other recycled container may be
more welcome than a vase, since it's disposable and need not be
stored or returned. Wrap in attractive paper to dress it up.

NOTE: Save the vases from flowers that you receive to "recycle." If you don't give them away, you can wash wide-mouth
vases well and use them to hold cut celery stalks for storing in the
fridge and serving at the table.

Floral Gifts, Transporting: When you have to transport a houseplant, crumple balls of newspaper and place them on top of the
dirt around the base of the plant. Then tape across the pot to keep
the paper from falling out. No more spilled dirt in your car!

Food Gifts for College Students: Send baby food jars of fruits,
puddings, finger foods such as meat sticks, and the usual peanut
butter, jelly, and crackers. Foods which need no refrigeration will
be a blessing for a hungry college student who misses a meal. Use

116

bags of popcorn to cushion mailings so you'll be sending edible everything!

Food Gifts to Elderly People: Bear in mind that tastes change as people age and some elderly people may not enjoy sweets as much as they did previously. Also, some foods, like sweets, certain cheeses, regular coffee, preserves with seeds, and nuts, may be forbidden in an elderly person's diet for health or other reasons. Also remember when you give a food gift to someone with arthritis, try to give it in an easily opened container.

Food Gifts, Safety: When you send or receive food gifts in the mail, such as cheese, meats, and poultry, be aware of safe food guidelines. To make sure, call the USDA's Meat and Poultry Hotline at 1-800-535-4555 from 10 A.M. to 4 P.M. Eastern Standard Time. The hotline staff can answer your questions about the safety of meat and poultry.

NOTE: When you order these foods to be sent, find out how perishable they are, how protective the packaging is (should be insulated containers with cooling agents or dry ice, clearly marked "perishable"), and what the expected delivery date will be.

Do keep in mind that the gift recipient of a large food basket or item may need to save refrigerator or freezer space for it. Also, it's better to send food to someone's home than to the office because of possible mail delays that could cause the package to be delivered on the weekend, when in an office it will sit, unrefrigerated and spoiling, until people come in on a Monday or after a holiday.

Food Gifts, Small Bites: To protect just-a-bit or just-a-bite small food gifts, such as a few cookies, homemade candies, or other goodies, from getting crumbled or mashed, thread ribbon through the lattice sides of plastic strawberry baskets in various colors to suit the season or just use leftover ribbon pieces. Put the food into a "nest" of crumpled colored plastic wrap, and present it.

NOTE: Expand this idea so that you give strawberry-shaped

candies or fresh strawberries dipped in chocolate as a gift in strawberry baskets. Of course, if you give fresh strawberries, they won't keep and must be given the day you dip them.

One reader saves the boxes that mushrooms come in and presents gifts of "mushroom cookies" in them. To make no-bake, easy mushroom cookies, she spreads dollops or blobs of melted chocolate chips on the bottoms of vanilla wafers, and then before the chocolate hardens, she sticks a regular-size marshmallow onto each wafer by pressing one of the marshmallows' flat ends to the chocolate. You need to make just one mushroom at a time to get the chocolate "glue" to stick.

Gift Certificates:

1. Give a person who doesn't drive a car gift certificates for a certain number of free taxi rides. One of my readers gave this gift to an elderly mom who didn't drive anymore.
2. Give a gift of a day's cleaning service to a new mom, any other busy person who just doesn't have time to clean, an elderly person who can't do certain chores anymore, and so forth.
3. Instead of a package with a bow, give a day of shopping, a doctor's visit, or an errand day with a lunch or dinner out to someone who doesn't drive.
4. Gift certificates for dinners out, theater or symphony tickets, or other amusements are terrific gifts for people who have everything.

Gift Records: Keep a notebook and when your friends or relatives say, "Know what I'd like for (Christmas, birthday, anniversary)," write it down. Check off the gifts as you get and give them. The bonus is that you have a handy record so that you won't give duplicates unless that's what the person wants—such as another of those good fruit baskets, etc. You can make note of the sizes of garments and favorite colors, too, for the next time. Toss in your sales receipts, mailing insurance receipts, and other information so that it's all together where you can find it.

Hospital Patient Gifts: If you have one, lend your cellular phone to a hospital patient. Phones on some hospital wards are difficult to get to and often busy. The patient with the phone can shut it off after 8 P.M. so its ringing won't bother others. (Also, see Nursing Home Resident Gifts below.)

Kitchen Gifts: Package seasoning blends or flavored popcorn, fudge, or other goodies (see recipes in the recipe section), your own garden herbs (dried or fresh), or other foods.

Money-Saving for Gifts: One reader records all amounts she saves with coupons at the grocery store and stashes away the amount in cash; then she buys gifts for her family and friends with it.

Newspaper Gift: When you find friends' or family members' pictures or articles about them in newspapers, clip out the article and the header at the top of the page that shows which newspaper and the date, laminate it with clear adhesive plastic, sold at office supply stores and some stationery departments, and then present your "celebrity" with a preserved memento.

Nursing Home Resident Gifts:

1. If the person is unable to go shopping for gifts but likes to give them anyway, make a "pass-it-on" gift box with gifts for people of all ages and either sex. Then the homebound person can just "shop" in the box when it's time to give a present to someone. Do restock the box several times a year.
2. Give all-occasion greeting card assortments and picture cards that are blank inside so that any message can be written, and postcards. Also include appropriate stamps and pens.

Pet Gifts: If your pets breed and provide more offspring than you can live with, and you decide to give a pet to someone, first of all be sure they can care for it properly. It will help if you will write down any pertinent information about the pet, such as when it was born, if it has had any medical attention, its immunizations, and its eating and play habits, add a photo of it when it was a new-born, and then put all the information into an envelope along with the vaccination certificate and license (if any). If you are giving away an older pet, you might want to add cute stories about the animal so that the new owner knows the pet better and feels closer to it.

Photo Collage: Assembling a photo collage of a person's "life story" for a birthday, "life-together story" for a wedding anniversary, or "life-at-work story" for a retirement party is always a welcome gift. One reader found a way to elaborate on this idea: After gluing photos of her son to an 8-by-10 piece of cardboard, she had copies and some enlargements made on a color copy machine to give family members and special friends.

Photo Gifts: Have old and recent family photos duplicated so that you can put them into an album for each child in a family, so each has a personal history. If a family has been the victim of a flood, hurricane, or fire, and has lost precious photos of family members, as so often happens, the best gift you can give is your photos taken of family members through the years.

Plants: Root cuttings from your house and garden plants and give them to friends as "Friendship Plants." Do remember to add a note about plant care and light needs.

NOTE: If you can't buy new pots, spruce up old ones. Wash the pots well with soap and water, rinse well, let dry. Apply craft glue to the pots and wrap them with twine, starting at the bottom and working your way up to the top lip. This technique will also work with some plastic pots. Read directions on your glue to make sure it will glue the twine to the pots. This hint also works well when you want to cover up discolored areas or chips on pots for your own home decorating.

Postage, Money-Saver: One reader saves postage on mailing

gifts to relatives for their birthdays. When she visits her relatives in their hometowns for Christmas or Easter, she takes along birthday gifts, all wrapped and ready to give. Her mother-in-law doles them out on the proper day, and to add to the gift some sentiment of "I'm thinking of you on this day," the reader just sends a birthday card to the birthday person.

Rose Jar Gift from Garden—A Heloise Favorite:

1. To dry rose petals, sprinkle a thin layer of petals on a cookie sheet and put the sheet in a cool, dry place out of direct sunlight for several days. The petals will be ready when they look crisp and brittle and crumble easily.
2. Put the dry petals, 5 drops rose oil, and 5 drops glycerin into a container with a well-fitting lid. Continue to add dry petals as they become available, until the jar is full.

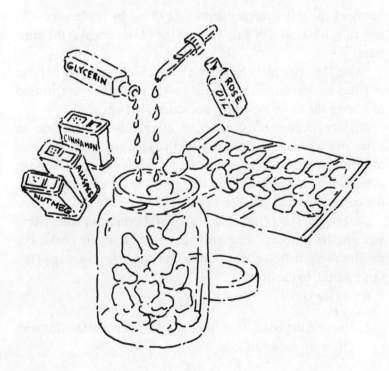

3. Shake the jar every day for two weeks. Add ¼ ounce each of nutmeg, cinnamon, and allspice to the mix.
4. Keep the jar tightly closed in between "sniffings" to help preserve the fragrance.

Stamps as Gifts: Instead of flowers sent to the funeral, one widowed reader received 100 stamps enclosed with a sympathy card, which she said she really appreciated when she sent out her thank-you cards. Stamps could be a good shower gift, too, to the bride or new mom who might not have time to get stamps for her thank-you's.

General Gift Wrapping Hints

Many of the gift wrapping hints sent to me by readers are also recycling hints, so they help you and the environment at the same time.

Bags: Decorate plain handled gift bags with squiggles of paint or glued-on decorations appropriate to the season or event, instead of buying the more expensive decorated gift bags.

Baskets, Decorated: Convert an inexpensive basket into an expensive-looking boutique item. With a glue gun, glue pinecones to cover the outside sides of the basket, place a napkin or fabric as noted below in "Baskets for Food Gifts," or "Easter grass" into the basket, and add your food gift.

Baskets for Food Gifts: Place a colorful printed or solid fabric scrap in the bottom of a basket before you fill it with cookies or muffins as a gift. You can also add a bow, made from a strip of the same fabric, to the handle.

Boxes for Gifts:

1. Recycle the boxes from your checks and cover the lids with gift wrap for small gifts.

2. If they have not come in their own boxes, when you give glasses or ceramic mug sets as gifts, put them in boxes with dividers from liquor stores and you aren't likely to risk breakage.

   NOTE: Do save plastic foam peanuts from packing boxes in large plastic trash bags so that you can pad and protect breakables.

3. Save clean decorated meal boxes from fast-food restaurants, fold them flat for storage, then recycle them as gift boxes for children. If your children have duplicates of the freebie toys, keep the toys and add them to the gifts, too.

Bows (Protection in Mail): Recycle a plastic strawberry basket. Place it over the bow when you mail a gift, to prevent it from getting squashed.

Bows (Storage): To save bows from other packages, if they are in good condition, or store-bought bows, without crushing them, put them in a large plastic bag and add air, then seal.

Decorations Other than Bows:

1. Poke a few colorfully wrapped candies into a fruit basket or silk greenery arrangement by attaching the candies to florists' picks, sold at craft shops. Wrap the wire from the picks around the twisted ends of the candy wrappers to attach the candy to the picks. Use this method to attach wrapped small hard candies to a wreath at Christmas, too.

2. Tape a single flower such as a rose, or several smaller flowers in a bunch, to a gift package.

3. Instead of making bows, crisscross ribbon into a pattern as you wrap it around a box. For example, wrap two strips of ribbon around the length and then around the width of a box about a half-inch apart, either around the center or around the top third of the box's length and width. Tape the ribbon in place on the bottom where it won't show. This type of

decoration works especially well if you have to mail the gift, because there is nothing to crush.

4. Wrap the gift in plain white shelf paper and then dip a sponge into a pie plate of poster paints so you can sponge a design on the paper.
5. If you can print decoratively, wrap the gift with plain white or colored paper and then print the recipient's name in large letters across the box.
6. Cut out an appropriate picture from a magazine, such as an ad for ties, jewelry, or perfume, and glue it to the top of the box, over plain paper. In the case of jewelry or perfume, the box may be small enough to be wrapped in a magazine page without any other paper!

Recycling Wrap: Save large pieces of gift wrap from shower, wedding, and other gifts, and use it to line shelves and dresser drawers. You'll get happy memories every time you open a cupboard, closet, or drawer!

Ribbon (Storage): Hang spools of gift ribbon on wire coat hangers, which then become "dispensers."

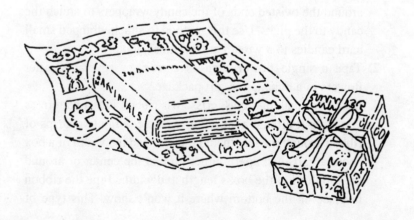

Substitutes:

1. Wrap gifts in the comic section of the Sunday paper or in magazine pages with pictures appropriate to the occasion or which indicate what might be inside. For example, a book can be wrapped in the Sunday book review section.
2. Save the shiny helium balloons you receive for birthdays and other special occasions and then use them for gift wrap after they deflate. Carefully slit the edge of the balloon to make an opening large enough to insert the gift, then realign the open edges and tape them shut with transparent tape. You can also gather the ends and tie them closed with crinkle tie.
3. Disposable paper party tablecloths can wrap many gifts, especially those in boxes which are too large to be wrapped by regular sheets or rolls of paper. You'll save money, too!
4. Wrap a man's gift in a map and tie on a tire gauge or other "manly item" with yarn.
5. Wrap a child's gift in a new T-shirt and tie on a small toy, such as a car, with yarn or crinkle tie.
6. Wrap a young child's gift in a pillowcase, such as one with a

picture of a favorite cartoon character, or one just in the child's favorite color, and tie on a small stuffed animal with yarn or crinkle tie.

7. Cover a coffee can with decorative paper and fill with cookies or other goodies for a neighbor.

8. Wrap gifts in wallpaper remnants; you can decorate a coffee can with wallpaper remnants, too.

9. Put gift soaps and a bath sponge in a basket and wrap with nylon net or tulle trimmed with pinking shears. To do this, place the basket in the center of a square (or squares) of net or tulle cut large enough so that you can bring up the fabric edges, gather a "neck" to tie with yarn or ribbon, and still have a "poof" of the net or tulle on top.

NOTE: If this is a wedding shower gift, wrap with net or tulle in the same color as the bridesmaid dresses.

NOTE: To quick-wrap a small stack of cookies or small cans of paté or other small foods, place two or three squares of colored plastic wrap over one another (more than one color with clear is pretty), place the stack or can in the center, bring up the edges, and twist. You can add a bow or tie with crinkle tie if you wish, but the wrap will stay closed pretty well with just a twist. The "bow" is the "poof" of wrap above the twisted area.

Transparent Tape: Stick a penny or a bread wrapper plastic tab on the end of the tape so it doesn't stick to the roll and become invisible when you want to cut off a piece.

Wrapping Gifts Comfortably: When you are wrapping a number of gifts, do it on your ironing board, adjusted to the best back-saving height.

General Gift and Greeting Card Hints

Address Book:

1. Write the names in ink and the addresses and phone numbers in pencil. The names stand out, and the other information can be neatly erased if it changes.
2. Clip friends' and relatives' address labels from the mail they send to you and stick the labels on index cards with transparent tape or glue.

   NOTE: This is an especially good hint for those of us who can't read our own scribble-notes!
3. Sometimes it's difficult to remember the married names of relatives and friends that you don't see too often. Try leaving the woman's name in the same alphabetical place in your address book or index card file, but write on it "See (married name)."

Card File: Buy greeting cards in quantity when you find those you like or if you buy at a "going out of business sale," and then categorize them by "birthday," "sympathy," "get well," "congratulations," or other categories and store in resealable quart-size plastic freezer bags that you have labeled for easy identification. The bags will keep the cards clean and help prevent moisture from making the envelope flaps stick.

Cards to Children: When you send a birthday or other holiday card or letter to a child who is too young to read, enclose a photo of yourself so that the child will know exactly who the sender is.

Mailing Cards on Time: If you like to get all the cards for each month ready at one time, write the mailing date on the corner where you'll place the stamp; then you won't have to smudge the envelope by trying to erase a date written elsewhere on the envelope.

Stuck Envelopes: Set your iron on medium to hot and then place a damp cloth over the envelope seal and press for a second or two. You should be able to open the flap easily.

NOTE: Next time, store envelopes in recloseable plastic bags to keep them from sticking together.

Stuck Stamp Roll: If a roll of postage stamps gets stuck, try putting the whole roll in a self-sealing bag into the freezer for about an hour. The stamps should pull apart undamaged when you take them out of the freezer.

If this doesn't work, soak the stamps in a cup of cold water for a few minutes, pull them gently apart, and place them facedown on paper towels to dry. You will have to add a drop of glue to the backs of the stamps to secure them to the envelopes.

NOTE: Next time, store stamps in a resealable plastic bag to keep them dry and "unstuck," especially if you live in a damp climate.

SUBSTITUTES

Gift Cards (Make Your Own, Recycling):

1. If you forget to buy a card, cut out one of the design units from the gift wrap and write on the back of it. If you are using crinkle tie, punch a hole in your "card" and tie it to the package with the crinkle-tie curls. If the wrap is not patterned so that you can cut a design "card," cut a rectangle, fold it to a square, and write the "to" and "from" on the inside as you would with a gift card; attach to the package as noted here or put it inside the box with the gift.
2. Save cards you've received from birthdays, anniversaries,

Christmas or other holidays so that you can cut off messages and write on the back of the picture. Backs of silver and gold cards from Christmas can be cut smaller and folded to make cards for weddings and other gifts.

3. Save catalogs and cut out pretty pictures which you think the recipient might like or which are appropriate for the season or that month's holidays (Valentine hearts, St. Patrick shamrocks, or other holiday symbols) and glue them to stationery to make your own birthday, anniversary, and holiday cards, gift enclosures, and stationery. You'll be recycling junk mail, too!

Envelope Is Ruined: Spill your coffee on the envelope? Wrap the gift card in gift wrap to match or to coordinate with the wrap you've used on the present.

Licking Stamps: If licking stamps and envelopes is a big "Yuck" to you, try some of these ideas.

1. Place an ice cube on a napkin in a shallow dish. Rub the stamp or envelope flap over the ice cube, which will provide plenty of "licking" moisture for dozens of stamps and envelopes.
2. Substitute a wet sponge or clean cloth for the ice cube.
3. Spritz stamps with a small atomizer instead of licking.

LETTER OF LAUGHTER: A reader whose large dog liked to watch her with his nose at table level as she prepared the mail discovered that she could moisten stamps on his ever-wet nose. The dog didn't mind and re-moistened his nose with a lick in between stamps.

Sympathy Card: If you enclose a money/check gift in a sympathy card, please include your address so that it's easier for the recipient to acknowledge receiving it.

Writing Computer Notes: If you have a publishing software

program on your computer, use the big, bold print when you write notes to elderly family members or friends to insert in the card. They'll be able to read them more easily.

Friends and Family Feasts
(Life Events, Rites of Passage)

GENERAL PARTY FUN

Borrowed Audio and Video Tapes: Keep a list of all tapes and CDs borrowed for a party and check off the names as you return them. Prompt returns mean that the lenders are more likely to be gracious about sharing their music and videos with you the next time. You can also stick a note on each protective container, as added insurance. If you are the lender, make note of when and to whom you have lent your tapes and CDs so that they don't disappear.

Family Reunion Remembrance: Audio- or videotape older family members as they recall those "good old days" and then make copies for family history collectors.

GENERAL PARTY INVITATION HINTS

❋ If you have a computer with print-shop software and you've learned how to use it, you can make all sorts of party invitations. Only your creativity and time limit what you can do. Make a tri-fold, brochure-style invitation, seal it closed with colored "dots" sold in stationery stores or a small piece of transparent tape, and you won't even need envelopes.

❋ Check all invitations twice to make sure you've given all the information people need. Remember the "who, what, when, where, why, and how." Who is hosting the party, what kind of party is it (brunch, luncheon, dinner, buffet, outdoor barbecue, or other event), when (date, time), where (address, and directions if necessary), why (if it honors a birthday, anniversary, or other occasion, or if it's just for fun), and how (black tie or casual).

NOTE: Be aware that "casual dress" means different things to different age groups and in different communities. If you are new in town, ask your neighbors and coworkers and/or call your newspaper's social columnist to get an idea of what is "casual dress."

LETTER OF LAUGHTER: A parent holding a multigenerational wedding rehearsal dinner at a family-type bar/restaurant planned to put "casual" on the invitations so the guests would know not to wear cocktail party attire or coat and tie. But the bride-to-be said, "Better not, your son's friends will come in shorts, T-shirts, and workout clothes because that's casual to them." Out of the mouths of babes come a word to the wise!

Directions to Party Sites: Copy a section of the map and draw colored lines or highlight streets on the route to the party location if it's off the beaten path.

Child's Party: For a child's party, put the invitation into a balloon, inflate it, and let the guest pop the balloon to get the invitation when you and the "birthday child" deliver it.

RSVP: Be aware that, contrary to how it was years ago, there are now people who don't know the meaning of RSVP ("Respond, if you please," in French). If this is so in your circle, you may want to say, "Please call (number) if you can join us." Or "Please respond regrets only," if you want to know only who won't be there. Still, sadly, many people these days don't respond, and so hosts of catered parties end up paying for uneaten portions of food, or, in the case of cook-it-yourself, the hosts have extra leftovers.

NOTE: If your invitations are to a formal party, and you include a return acceptance card with an envelope, do put a stamp on it to encourage response.

BABY SHOWER

Baby showers used to be for women only, but with so many fathers helping more, the showers are likely to be for couples.

Help for Mom- or Dad-to-Be: Ask each guest or a friend to self-address thank-you card envelopes so that the cards and envelopes can be taken to the hospital and thank-you notes can be written before baby is taken home and parents start living by "baby time" (Definition: No time!).

Baby Shower Games: Have a diapering contest in which the contestants see who can diaper the fastest—but substitute round balloons for the baby.

Provide a basket of nursery aids, such as thermometer, diaper pin, baby wipes, aspirator, medicine dropper, baby bottle, pacifier, or various small toys, and have guests give alternative uses for these items.

Have guests guess the baby's birthdate and time to get a prize later, after the facts are known.

BIRTH OF BABY, CHRISTENING, BRIS GIFTS

Gifts:

1. Save the newspaper(s) of the day that the baby was born and add the news of the baby's arrival from the next day's paper, too.
2. Give or lend the new mom an answering machine. Then have her record a special announcement with the new baby's

name, date of birth, some of the important statistics, and end the message with, "Mom and baby are resting now, and will return your call later." Do set the machine to answer on the first ring to provide even more quiet time.

3. Make sock babies (or snowman dolls). Buy infant tube socks; stuff the socks with cut-up old panty hose; tie the sock shut with yarn about ½ inch from the opening or at the bottom edge of the cuff design. You will be folding the cuff over the tied area to make your sock doll's stocking hat and will slip stitch the edge to the doll's head so that the "hat" edge won't roll up. Sew a piece of ball fringe to the very top of the "hat" to finish it. Next, tie a ribbon or colorful piece of yarn around the midsection of the sock to divide it into the doll's head and its body, and make a bow so the doll has a "bow tie." Either embroider or appliqué fabric scraps onto the doll's head to make facial features, and do the same to put three buttons over the doll's tummy, the way you put coals on a snowman's body to look like buttons. You could sew buttons instead of embroidering or doing appliqué, but they could be dangerous if a small child pulls them off and tries to swallow them.

4. Buy flat colored sponges at the supermarket and cut them into kiddie shapes—fish, ducks, cats, or other easy-to-make shapes—for the bath or for soft toys. (But not as soft toys for children with teeth, who might bite a piece off the sponge!)

5. For a special gift/keepsake, godparents of a girl can give a thin gold necklace as a present at birth and a gold bead each birthday and special occasion thereafter to thread on the necklace; or a bracelet and add an appropriate commemorative charm each year and special occasion.

6. Other traditional gifts are baby cups, dishes, and flatware.

Gift Wrap: Wrap baby things in a baby towel or blanket and pin closed with diaper pins. Instead of a bow, attach a small toy, pacifier, or other baby item to the package.

BIRTHDAYS

Birthday Gifts:

1. *Balloon Money Tree:* Having run out of ideas on what to give Mom, one family got really creative for their mother's eightieth birthday. They made her favorite cake, which had an angel food cake base and therefore a hole in the center. Then they anchored in the cake center a "money tree" of eight balloons with money in them—one balloon for each decade of age. With the help of her grandson and lots of laughter, the birthday grandmom popped the balloons and everyone had a happy birthday party.

2. *Gifts you can't buy:* Give services in the form of a homemade redeemable coupon book to an elderly person who has everything. Clean the house, wash windows, drive the person to the hairdresser, store, or take the person to a movie, dinner, or lunch.

3. *"Read-to-me" gift:* Record as you read the book given to a child for a birthday or other occasion, including, "turn the page now," and then the child will be "read to" even when parents are busy. This is especially good when done by grandparents or other relatives who live in other cities.

Party Favors: When your children get too old to enjoy party favors or "goody bags," you can still give them mementos from the party. Take instant camera pictures of the birthday person with each guest, then put the picture and a "thank you for coming" note from the birthday person into a decorative bag which is presented to the guest as he or she leaves.

Greetings from the President: The president will sign cards for people celebrating their eightieth birthday or older, and for couples celebrating their fiftieth wedding anniversary or more. Requests must be sent at least six weeks in advance to: Attention: Greeting Office, The White House, Office of Communications, Washington, D.C. 20500. Be sure to include the birthdate or anniversary date, complete name (including Mr., Mrs., or Ms.), street address, city, state, and ZIP code of the person(s) to receive the greeting.

Birthstones for the Months (According to the Jewelers of America, Inc.):

January	Garnet	Dark Red
February	Amethyst	Purple
March	Aquamarine, Bloodstone	Pale Blue
April	Diamond	White or Clear
May	Emerald	Bright Green
June	Pearl, Moonstone, Alexandrite	Cream
July	Ruby	Red
August	Peridot, Sardonyx	Pale Green
September	Sapphire	Deep Blue
October	Opal, Tourmaline	Variegated
November	Topaz, Citrine	Yellow
December	Turquoise, Topaz	Sky Blue

Birthday Cakes (General Hints):

1. Stick each birthday candle into a small marshmallow to prevent wax from dripping into the frosting.
2. In a hurry? You don't have time to frost cupcakes for a party or your child told you too late that you are the cupcake person for a class party? Just put a marshmallow on top of each cupcake a few minutes before they are to come out of the oven and you'll have instant frosting.

3. You can make a cake ahead of time, freeze it, and then thaw, frost, and decorate it on party day.

Birthday Cakes for Young Children and Toddlers:

1. Instead of a cake to cut, substitute cupcakes for very young children or toddlers. Put a candle on each cupcake so that each child gets to blow out a candle.
2. Make cupcakes in flat-bottomed, cup-shaped ice cream cones so that small children can eat the cake with less mess. Here's how: Fill the cones ⅔ full with batter; bake according to the timing for cupcakes. Frost and decorate as usual. You can use different flavors of cake batter and colored cone for an even more decorative look.
3. If you feel up to it, bring out the cake iced but not decorated, and let the children draw on it with tubed decorative frosting or add jelly beans and other candies as decorations. You can also provide cupcakes or cookies for children to decorate.

Long-Distance Birthday Party: Mail the party to a college student or other dear one who's far away. Enclose party favors, paper plates, napkins, and nonperishable foods. If you know a responsible friend of the birthday person, send the friend money to buy ice cream and cake, and to invite a few people in for the party. Then arrange to call the birthday person while the party is going on so you, too, can sing "Happy Birthday to You."

RELIGIOUS RITES OF PASSAGE
(Confirmations, First Communions, Bris, Baptism, Bar or Bat Mitzvah)

You can't go wrong by giving a keepsake type of gift such as a symbolic charm for a girl's bracelet or necklace or other appropriate symbolic jewelry (such as a cross for Christian ceremonies or a

Star of David charm or pin for a Bar/Bat Mitzvah), a Bible or other appropriate religious meditation book. Check out religious book and keepsake shops to find appropriate gifts and to get help on selecting what is proper, especially if you are not of the same religion as the celebrant. Also consider gifts that relate to hobbies or special talents such as music, dance, or athletics.

GRADUATIONS

Gifts: Appropriate books or blank journals-to-keep may be good gifts if you don't know the graduate's taste in anything else. Gift certificates and money are useful, too, if you just don't know what to buy. Gifts can relate to hobbies or interests or what is needed in the "new life" ahead.

NOTE: If the gift is small, you can make a mortarboard graduation cap keepsake box for it. Cover with glued-on black, white, or school-color paper or cloth (or spray paint) the bottom and sides of a round box, such as those from some cheeses or one that you buy at a craft store. Do the same to the sides of the box lid. Then cover a proportionately sized square to match and glue the square onto the top of the lid. Glue a school-colored tassel to the center of the square to finish off the job. Fill with candy or a small gift.

High School: Many high school graduates going on to college would be happy with a gift certificate or money to buy things for their dorm rooms. Other dorm gifts can be a small electric water-heating pot or other small appliances that will be allowed in the dorm (check first), bedding, towels, a footlocker or suitcase, or a "care package" of nonperishable goodies to keep on hand when the "munchies" strike.

College: Briefcases, luggage, jewelry, or anything else the graduate will need to enter the awesome world of work can be a good gift.

Party: Find out what the graduate wants! Sometimes graduation schedules are complicated, run overtime, and generally are difficult to time precisely. If you are having a party in your home after the ceremony, you may want to plan something that can be kept warm in the oven or will cook quickly when you get home, because you really won't know when you will be serving. Casseroles and cold buffet foods are a stress-free choice. A cake decorated with school colors can be the dessert.

FAMILY REUNIONS

Memory Lists: At family reunions or holiday gatherings, have each person write down favorite remembrances about family traditions and then read them. The reader who sent in this idea said it was fun to hear the memories of each of the three generations in her family. The lists could be saved and placed in a family history album, too, so that future generations can enjoy them. Gathering and compiling a family cookbook of favorite recipes is another way to celebrate family unity.

Photos: Do take that photo of the aunts or uncles who look so much alike. Future generations will enjoy comparing themselves to their ancestors. It's fun to see that you have Great-Aunt Rosie's curly hair or Uncle Bill's nose!

Where to Hold a Reunion: If your family is large, you may be able to get a group rate at a hotel/motel and a good price on catered meals; then nobody has to work at all. I know of one large family that meets at a cetain resort hotel during the off-season every five or so years and takes over the whole place, getting an extra good rate due to the season.

WEDDING SHOWER

Shower Gift:

1. Give the soon-to-be-weds a pocket datebook in which both sets of parents have entered all birthdays, anniversaries, and other family dates for the year.
2. Share family food "secrets." Put favorite family recipes (include those from grandparents, aunts, uncles, sisters, brothers, friends) on index cards and arrange them in a file box according to appetizers, main dishes, desserts, and special holiday treats. Or type the recipes and put them into a photo album.
3. A reader who's in her seventies says she doesn't want to leave a pile of loose photos behind, so she's sorted them according to family groups, and whenever she goes to a bridal shower, she encloses the photos she has of the bride or groom in with her gift, and she says it's always a hit.

Shower Gift Bows: Collect all bows and ribbons from the shower gifts, affix them to a sturdy paper plate, and fold the plate over a stick or a toilet paper/paper towel roll, to make a bouquet. Then the bride can carry this "bouquet" at the wedding rehearsal.

Shower Gift Wrap:

1. Wrap kitchen items in new dishcloths and hold them closed with chip-bag clips or colored spring clothespins. Add a bow made from two colored scrubbies held together with chenille pipe cleaners. No paper wasted!
2. Wrap gifts in bath or dish towels.

Long-Distance Shower: With family members living so far away from one another, long-distance showers are an idea whose time has come. Here's how you can have a shower for your favorite niece or friend who's moved away. Tell the honoree that you will be calling at a certain time on a certain day. Then have the shower at your home, and when you call, each guest can say "Hi" and give good wishes and, if you like, describe the gift she brought to the shower. Gifts need not be wrapped. Take pictures at the shower and enclose them with the gifts when you mail them to the honoree.

WEDDINGS

Guests' Lodging and Transportation: If you will have many out-of-town guests, call local hotels/motels, guest houses, and bed-and-breakfast facilities to see if you can get a group rate or discount. To transport the guests, rent a van either from a car rental agency or from a limousine company, which will also furnish a driver.

Throwing Rice and Birdseed: Some people like to throw birdseed to wish the "lovebirds" happiness as they leave for their honeymoon. Do get permission to do this; some churches and party locations discourage it because uneaten birdseed sprouts weeds in the lawn and flower beds. Or, prevent the bird seed from germinating by spreading an even layer on a cookie sheet and baking it in a 120-degree oven for about 30 minutes. Be careful not to overcook.

Wedding Gift Giving: I've had this request from many brides and grooms. Please tape the gift card to the gift and write on the card a description of the gift. Too often, the gifts get separated from the cards in the wedding confusion. Then, when the bride and groom try to thank the givers, they can write only "generic" thanks because they don't know who gave what. This request has come from shower honorees, too!

Keepsake Gifts:

1. Make a "wedding cake" keepsake box from a round box bought at a craft store. Cover the box by gluing on white satin fabric and decorate as a cake with white braid and

ribbon bows in various designs. You can glue wedding bells or another appropriate decoration to the center of the lid to finish it off.

2. Cover a photo album as the keepsake box and fill it with the snapshots you took at the wedding shower and wedding. Or just buy a photo album and fill it with family pictures of the bride and groom in their "previous lives" as children and adults.

3. Cover a picture frame and insert your favorite picture of the couple.

WEDDING ANNIVERSARIES

First Anniversary Gift: Gather up baby pictures and special family event photos, put them into an album, and give them to your "child" and spouse on their first wedding anniversary. The reader who sent in this idea had two stepsons among her children and so she included photos of their deceased mother, whom they were too young to remember, so that they would have a complete family history to share with their brides.

NOTE: This could also be a wedding shower or wedding gift.

Silver Wedding Anniversary: Silver dollars are a popular gift for this occasion. Put them into a crystal candy dish or two beautiful crystal wine or champagne glasses, for an elegant presentation.

Collage: Make a framed collage of "happenings" from the couple's life together to hang where they can relive those golden moments everyday.

Wedding Anniversary Gift Traditions: Some of the traditional gifts for specific anniversaries have been revised, but the old favorites are still acceptable. Be aware that many older couples prefer to have a party but without gifts because they truly feel that they do "have everything." If the invitation says, "No gifts, please," and you still want to do something, you can make a donation in their name to the couple's favorite charity, or many libraries will accept donations for books and then put a recognition inside the book to honor the person in whose name the donation was made.

WEDDING ANNIVERSARY GIFT CHART

ANNIVERSARY	TRADITIONAL GIFTS	NEW REVISED GIFTS
First	Paper, plastics	Clocks
Second	Cotton	China
Third	Leather	Crystal, glass
Fourth	Linen, rayon, nylon, silk	Electrical appliances
Fifth	Wood	Silverware
Sixth	Iron	Wood
Seventh	Copper, brass	Desk, pen, pencil sets
Eighth	Electrical appliances, brass	Linen, lace
Ninth	Pottery, china	Leather
Tenth	Aluminum, tin	Diamond jewelry
Eleventh	Steel	Jewelry, accessories
Twelfth	Linen, silk, nylon	Pearls, colored gems
Thirteenth	Lace	Textiles, furs
Fourteenth	Agate, ivory	Gold jewelry
Fifteenth	Crystal, glass	Watches
Twentieth	China	Platinum
Twenty-fifth	Silver	Sterling silver
Thirtieth	Pearls	Diamonds
Thirty-fifth	Coral, jade	Jade
Fortieth	Rubies, garnets	
Forty-fifth	Sapphires	
Fiftieth	Gold	
Fifty-fifth	Emeralds, turquoise	
Sixtieth	Diamonds	
Seventy-fifth	Diamonds	

The revised list was issued by the Jewelry Industry Council in 1948 and is generally used in this country.

WAKES, FUNERALS, SITTING SHIVA

Customs vary according to personal, cultural, and religious beliefs and different parts of the country. If you are new in town and don't want to bother the grieving family, ask the director of the event about what sort of comfort is usual and what sort of activities will be part of the service. Some information will be given in the newspaper obituary.

Taking food to the home (or church or community center) wherever a meal is served after burial services is a common custom in most parts of the country. You can also have sent to the family home food baskets or flowers. Often, the family requests that donations be made to family charities in the name of the deceased person instead of flowers sent to the funeral home. Some services are private with a more public memorial to follow. Please see the section "Portable" Foods on page 64.

HOSPITAL STAYS

Gift to Patient or Nursing Home Resident: Make an audio or video tape of cheery greetings from children or other family members. The type of tape depends on the playback equipment that's available.

NOTE: If you give an audio tape and tape machine to a hospital patient or nursing home resident, a headset may be necessary to prevent the sound from bothering others in the room. If the gift recipient is elderly, check first because some elderly people won't use headsets.

Coin Gift: Often patients have access to vending machines, pay phones, gift shops, and newspaper and magazine stands, so a good supply of change is a most welcome and useful gift.

143

Comfort Gifts: Hand or body lotion, shower/bath gelée, bath powder, nice soaps, warm socks, lap robes, or bed jackets can make a hospital stay more comfortable.

Cures for Boredom: A deck of cards, reading material, TV rental (if necessary), needlework (if it's not too taxing for that person), or photos of loved ones can be given. A special photo of a loved pet is usually a one-of-a-kind gift.

NOTE: If allowed, the newest new-tech gift (to keep or to borrow) for a hospital patient is a cellular phone or phone answering machine so that the patient need not tie up or look for the ward patient phone.

Do's and Don'ts for Visitors:

Do call a relative or the nurses' station before you visit, to find out if visitors are allowed.

Do stay only fifteen or twenty minutes, to avoid tiring the patient, even if the patient says it's OK.

Don't sit on the bed; jiggling a patient, especially one who's had surgery, can cause pain.

Don't bring food unless you know the person is allowed to eat it. Also, don't eat the patient's unwanted food; nurses have to keep track of what the patient is eating and can't do that if visitors snack away!

Don't bring children unless you ask; most hospitals don't allow them because they can both give and catch diseases and can be disruptive. Also, small children can be upset by seeing Grandma hooked up to tubes or looking very ill.

Don't bring a whole bunch of people; most patients can deal only with two or three people at a time.

If you want to bring flowers, make sure the patient doesn't have allergies to them. And *do* bring a vase or other container for cut flowers and put the flowers into it or add water if necessary. The staff may be too busy to get to the flowers before they wilt, and it's depressing to look at wilted flowers if you are a patient who feels "wilted," too.

GOING AWAY AND HOUSEWARMING PARTIES

Gifts: Plants and plant cuttings from your garden are a "warm fuzzy" comfort gift whether a person is going away or arriving in a new neighborhood.

Housewarming: Give a box of long fireplace matches for your gift recipient's fireplace or barbecue.

For a Going Away Party: Hold a potluck party and have everyone write down the recipes for the foods so that the person who's leaving can take food memories along to the new location. Also take instant camera pictures at the party and put them into an album, along with the names, addresses, and phone numbers of all of the guests.

Welcome New Neighbors: Present a list of city service numbers and numbers of your repair service people to help the newcomer when emergencies happen.

When You Move: Take phone books with you for addresses and phone numbers of those you've left behind or in case you have unfinished business and need to call banks, real estate people, or other businesses. Leave behind appliance booklets and a list of names and phone numbers of repair services used on your home; days for garbage pickup; good restaurants and fast-food places in the neighborhood.

Community Events

Often (too often, sometimes) when you are asked to chair a business, church, community, or club social event, you are given a very limited budget to work with. To complicate matters, these events are often fund-raisers, so you really need to be super creative about how you entice people to come for a good time that still makes a profit.

The project gets even more complicated when you are given a committee to work with that's composed of people you hardly know. Remember the old saying that a camel is a horse that was designed by a committee? One of my editors goes beyond that saying. She says a committee functions best if only one person shows up at the meeting!

Invitations: A well-designed postcard will get attention and save postage, too. If you decide to send traditional invitations in envelopes, make sure the size is not too big for first-class postage. Although they are frequently besieged with such requests, some printers will give cut rates to nonprofit organizations, or sometimes you can get your invitations or flyers printed on the remains of someone else's order—the end-run paper; this can save some money, but you won't have a choice of the color or type of paper.

Location: New hotels and new restaurants that want to introduce themselves to the community may donate space for your function. A new office building, museum, showroom, garden center, or community center may let you use a lobby or other space or give you discounted rental to increase community awareness of the facility. The home of a club member is also a possibility.

Food and Beverages on a Budget: Depending on the function, try to get food and beverages donated, perhaps by a wine distributor trying to introduce a new brand, a soft drink distributor with a promotional budget, or a new restaurant which may want to get some public awareness of its specialties and services.

Do consider jug wines, a keg of beer (if it's a very large group), and soft-drink dispensing machines if you are having hundreds of people. Punch is a time-honored budget cutter when planning beverage service.

Consider buffet service for a brunch, luncheon, dinner, or "heavy hors d'oeuvres" (where more substantial foods such as steamship round or fillet of beef, kabobs, and other hot hors d'oeuvres are served instead of just finger sandwiches and small canapés). Buffet service saves money on hiring staff.

Opt for chicken, turkey, pastas, or other entrées that are less costly than beef or veal.

Decorations: Some groups have craft enthusiasts who make table centerpieces for fun. Table centerpieces can be door prizes. If you have many tables to decorate and you want floral arrangements, try asking several florists for donations. Smaller florists may not be able to afford to donate twenty or so centerpieces but may be glad to donate two or four or so. And don't limit your centerpieces to flowers; consider candles in holders, pottery pieces, anything that fits the theme of your event and can be given away as a door prize, too.

NOTE: I once went to a barbecue where Western boots lined with a bandana and filled with silk versions of the state flower were used as table centerpieces! If the shoe fits . . . !

Door Prizes: Do make sure there is a way to give publicity to those who donate door prizes to your event; that's why they do it! Announce the donations and print them in the program if possible. (You can sell "business card" ads to pay for a program, too.)

HINT 1: Table centerpieces can be given away to the one with the stick-on dot beneath the chair, saucer, or anything that remains at the table. But don't mark for door prizes any item that the staff will clear away from the table before you announce who wins those door prizes.

HINT 2: Ask people to put their business cards into a container for door prize drawings and you'll have additional names to put on your mailing list after the event.

NOTE: For people who don't have business cards, do provide paper for them to write their names on for the drawing.

Entertainment: Hiring a disk jockey instead of a band will save money; or if you are *sure* the band is good, a new group may work for less money than established ones. However, do check out a performance before hiring musicians, especially if the new group is recommended by a relative or friend of one of its members. A word to the wise, here! You don't want to be embarrassed!

Guest Speakers: Local celebrities or experts on subjects that relate to your guests can be speakers. Do try to give a gift certificate or some compensation if you are not paying a speaker's fee. A lovely frame or book is always appreciated.

NOTE: Business groups are always glad to hear management consultants, who may speak for reduced or no fees to generate consulting jobs. Writers' groups like to hear from editors and successful writers. Authors are always glad to promote their books, but not all are good speakers; find out who is! Universities may have speakers bureaus on various subjects, too. As well, some chapters of Toastmasters International may have guest speakers available.

Cost-Sharing Parties: When a party is cohosted, for example by a church, school, or office group, food is often potluck and other expenses are shared. To keep things fair, there needs to be a cohosting agreement that equalizes the expenses between those people who will bring expensive foods or beverages and those people who will bring nothing but will contribute cash toward general expenses such as hall rental or entertainment. If you are chairing such an event:

1. Make a chart with columns and head each column so that you can enter information as the donations are received. You'll need to record names, addresses, phone numbers, and descriptions of potluck dishes brought, and gifts or favors, to avoid duplications. Record each guest's cost for the foods or beverages, or cash amounts donated. Then you can easily prorate the costs fairly.
2. Keep all receipts for your expenses as the chairperson of the event and note them as contributions, too. Be aware that nickles and dimes add up when you chair an event and you can end up giving more "treasure" than you thought along with the giving of your talents.

Entertaining Children

CHILDREN'S PARTIES

Contrary to what some people believe, children are not merely small-size adults, and so when you have a children's party, don't expect adult behavior.

❋ Many parents limit the number of guests at a child's birthday party to the age of the child. Two guests for a two-year-old, and so forth. Very young children can get too stimulated when there are too many people, and the result is an exhausting experience for everyone.

❋ Have props, games, food, and everything else ready before child guests arrive, and do plan for every minute of the party so that the children move from one activity to another. The younger the child, the shorter the attention span so have each game or activity last about fifteen minutes or so. Start with a quieter activity such as a craft project, go on to a more active game such as Pin the Tail on the Donkey, and then proceed to the most active game, such as Musical Chairs, after which the children can march to music to the table for refreshments. Plan for a quieter activity after refreshments, to keep children occupied until their parents arrive to take them home.

❋ Games, activities, and organization of the time schedule should be age-appropriate, and it's best if there are not too many lulls in the activities. Also, you need to accept the fact that some children are just not joiners, and after initial coaxing, it may be better to let a shy child enjoy the party in a manner of choice. Some children do prefer to watch, while others have to be in the middle of the action at all times.

❋ One or two hours is enough time for a party, especially for preschoolers (one hour) or elementary school–aged children (two hours).

❋ Give out party favors as the children leave, so that they don't lose them at the party. Provide small bags to hold their party favors, to avoid upsets when parts are lost.

❋ Don't expect children of five, or six, or younger to behave ideally at parties. They may get overexcited by the whole event and forget everything they've learned about appropriate behavior.

WHEN CHILDREN VISIT

Block Boxes: Save any size boxes from things received in the mail, fold the tops so they are closed, and you will have a free, disposable set of giant building blocks which the children can decorate if they want to. If you have a moving box or one from a large appliance, it can be the storage container for the "blocks" as well as something a young child will enjoy crawling into to "play house."

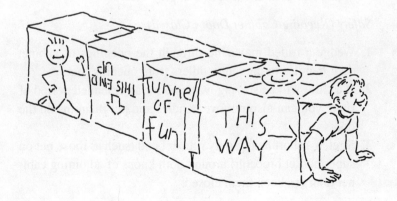

Books for Toddlers: Cut out pictures of people, animals, house hold objects, flowers, and other things familiar to the children and paste them on posterboard pieces cut to 8 by 10. Print one-word descriptions of the pictures at the bottom in large letters. Punch holes in the "pages" so they can be put into a looseleaf binder, and you have an inexpensive book.

Bubbles: If you run out of bubble solution but still have the jar and wand, substitute baby shampoo or mild hand-dishwashing detergent mixed with equal parts water. The bonus with baby shampoo is that it won't sting when younger children get it on their hands and rub their eyes.

Granny Toys (to Keep on Hand When the Grandchildren Visit):

1. Buy toys at garage sales or thrift shops. Plastic blocks, rubber puzzle pieces, and waffle blocks, as well as many other plastic toys, can be washed in the machine. Just put them into cotton pillowcases, stitch the case closed with the largest zigzag machine stitch, and then toss into the washing machine. After air drying, they are clean and sanitary for children to play with.
2. Save "freebie" toys from cereal for children to play with. Save newspaper comics to cut and color and junk-mail letters to draw on the blank side. Save clean, empty food containers so that children can play "store."

Safety (Keeping Cabinet Doors Closed):

1. Wedge a rolled magazine through the openings of cabinet door handles to prevent toddlers from opening them.
2. If a child will be staying with you for an extended period of time, you can also remove handles and put them inside the doors.
3. Stretch a short heavy-duty rubber band (such as those put on supermarket broccoli) around both knobs of adjoining cabinet doors to keep them closed.

Safety (Doors):

1. Throw a heavy terry bath towel over the top of a door and it won't slam shut on toddlers playing nearby.
2. To keep a toddler from opening a door, put a sock or a terry footie on the knob. Older children won't be thwarted by this, but most small toddlers don't have a good enough grip to turn a sock-covered doorknob.

Safety (Table Setting):

1. Use place mats when small children are visiting.
2. Only magicians can pull a tablecloth off the table while leaving the china and crystal still upright and unbroken. To anchor a tablecloth so that small children (yours and other people's) won't pull it off, separate the table as if to insert a table-extending leaf, wedge the tablecloth into the space, and close the table on the cloth. You will have a line where the cloth is inserted, but you will also have unbroken china and glassware.

Special Celebrations Holiday Calendar

In San Antonio, where I live, we celebrate annually the diversity of cultures in our city with a Folklife Festival, held in August at the Institute of Texan Cultures of the University of Texas at San Antonio. The institute published a cookbook called *The Melting Pot: Ethnic Cuisine in Texas* several years ago. To get the most traditional and authentic recipes for the different ethnic groups, the editors sought recipes from first-generation ethnic Texans. I've used some information and recipes from *The Melting Pot* for the Kwanzaa and Jewish Holidays sections so that you could have recipes that are as authentic as possible but with easily available ingredients.

General Holiday Hints

The most important hint I can give you for planning and celebrating holidays is a *Don't*—Don't make your plans so elaborate that you will be too exhausted to enjoy the party or the people with whom you celebrate. If putting a bow on everything that doesn't move is the extent of your decorating time, energy, and creativity level, so be it! The people who matter don't care about *things*—only other *people*! Focus on fellowship and observe my version of the KISS rule—Keep It Simple and Sweet!

Gourmet Party Club: One gourmet group I know ran their monthly dinner parties so that the host(s) chose the theme (Italian, Oriental, Mexican, Cajun) and each guest brought a favorite food in that "flavor," taking care to bring all needed serving implements and dishes. This included heating trays, candle warmers, and other needed items. The hosts coordinated the menu (but casually) so that there would be foods for appetizers, main dishes, and desserts. The guests took home all of the leftovers, serving dishes, and implements after the party (not usually washed, but just put into a large plastic bag) so that the hosts had less to clean up. Guests also brought appropriate wines or their own preferred beverages. Hosts were not even allowed to serve a can of nuts, but provided plates (china or disposable), silverware (disposable or not), ice, coffee, tea, and soft drinks. The parties were fun because nobody had to do all of the work before or after. Such parties could also be adapted for celebrating holidays, whether you celebrate with family or friends.

Traditional and Seasonal Holidays

WINTER HOLIDAYS

Christmas

Hiding Gifts: Curious children and adult "kids-at-heart" probably won't think of looking in suitcases for gifts. But do wrap them first so that if your hiding suitcases get opened by mistake, the gift secret won't be "let out of the bag."

Cards: If you save money by buying your Christmas cards at half price the day after Christmas, the envelope flaps may get stuck while they are stored, especially if you live in a damp climate. Store envelopes in a cool, dry place, even in the freezer. You can also fold the gummed flaps back over the front of each envelope to help keep them from sealing shut. Also, please see Stuck Envelopes in the General Gift and Greeting Card Hints sections on page 128.

Christmas Decorations:

❅ *Christmas Tree:* Buy a potted pine tree to decorate instead of a cut one, and then plant it outside after Christmas. We have been doing this for several years, and each time I go outdoors, I see a living reminder of Merry Christmas Past.

To avoid damage to the tree branches, decorate it with small, lightweight ornaments and bows.

HINT: Since a tree in a pot can be too heavy to move, put it on a skateboard to transport it around the house.

CAUTION: Do put something under the pot to protect floors and carpets from water. Keep the soil moist by placing several ice cubes on the soil each day; watering by the ice cube method prevents spills.

Care of Live Christmas Trees: Here's a list of 12 Christmas trees commonly used as live trees indoors, and the best regions of the country for replanting them outdoors after the holidays are over.

1. Douglas Fir   Northeast, Northwest, Midwest, Rockies
2. Noble Fir   Northeast, Northwest, Midwest, Rockies
3. White Fir   Almost anywhere
4. Norway Spruce   Anywhere except South and deserts
5. Dwarf Alberta Spruce   Anywhere except lower deserts
6. Colorado Blue Spruce   Almost anywhere
7. Scotch Pine   Northeast, Northwest, Midwest Rockies

8. Norfolk Island Pine*	Tropical, subtropical, Southwest, South, Gulf
9. Japanese Black Pine	Almost anywhere
10. Aleppo Pine	South, Southwest, lower deserts
11. Monterey Pine	North, Midwest, East, West in low elevations
12. Mondell Pine	Southwest

Care Instructions: It's best not to keep a live tree in the house for more than two weeks. Keep the tree outdoors and watered well until just before Christmas, then place it indoors where it can get plenty of sunlight (but not in front of an unshaded, south-facing window) and do place it away from heaters, fireplaces or other locations where it may have extreme changes of temperature. Temperature changes can cause the tree to drop needles.

*NOTE: You can keep a Norfolk Island Pine as an indoor tropical plant after the holidays. Place it in a cool room in moderate to bright light, away from drying heat sources such as heater vents, fireplaces and television sets. Keep the soil moist but never allow the tree to stand in water. Fertilize three times a year—spring, mid-summer and early fall. Norfolk Pines grow best in a container that is snug; too large a container retains too much moisture in the excess soil. Well treated, your Norfolk Pine could be your annual Christmas tree; no need to buy one each year!

Christmas Trees (Cut): You need to start with a fresh tree. To test for freshness:

1. Place a needle between your thumb and forefinger and try to bend it. Needles from fresh trees will bend; those from dry trees will break. Fresh tree needles have a strong fragrance and good color, too.
2. Lift the tree a few inches off the ground and then drop it down on the stump end as if you were shaking off snow or dust. If lots of outside green needles fall off, the tree may not be fresh.

After purchase, the tree needs the following care:

1. If it's not yet time to decorate, store the tree outdoors in a cool place, protected from drying sun and wind. Make a fresh *diagonal* cut across the trunk and immediately place the tree in a large container of fresh water. If the water level is allowed to drop, a seal forms on the end and you will have to make a fresh cut to allow the tree to absorb water.
2. Make a fresh cut before placing the tree in your tree stand, cutting *straight* through the trunk, so you have a flat end to insert into the stand.
3. Christmas trees may drink two pints to a gallon of water daily so you need to check the water level every day and add fresh water as needed. Some people like to add a tree preservative with the water to keep the tree fresh.
4. To have a safe and happy holiday, *always* avoid combustible decorations and never use lights with worn or frayed cords, or lighted candles.

❋ *Christmas Wreaths:* You can make your own from greenery or grapevines, which can be purchased at craft or other stores. The benefit of grapevine wreaths is that if you use florists pins (sold at craft and florists' supply stores) to attach bows, artificial flowers or fruit, ornaments or whatever you choose, the Christmas ornaments can be removed after the holidays and then you recycle the wreaths. You can add hearts, lace and bows for Valentine's Day; shamrocks, Irish pipes and elves for March's St. Patrick's Day; bunnies and chicks and greenery for Easter; baby birds, spring flowers and greenery for spring; flags for Memorial or Independence Day; leaves and mini-pumpkins for fall, and so on, according to the season or special holiday of the month. Just take your creativity and imagination to your favorite craft store or florists' supply store. If you don't feel inspired from within, get ideas from craft shows and florist shop displays.

❋ *Evergreen Sap on Hands:* If you rub the sticky areas with baby or cooking oil, the sap will soften and then be easily washed off with soap and warm water.

"FOOD TREE" TABLE CENTERPIECE

We've all seen "Della Robbia" (fruits and greenery) decorations on wreaths and mantel drapes. Here's an idea for an edible Della Robbia Christmas tree or wreath to lay flat on the table. Supplies are available at craft stores and stores that sell florists supplies. You'll need:

12-inch styrofoam cone or 12-inch-diameter wreath
Parsley
Some sticky gum and florists stickpins
Strong toothpicks, multicolored are best
Purple and green grapes
Stuffed olives
Cherry tomatoes
Radish roses
Miniature treetop ornament if using a cone, or a bow
    if using a wreath

Cover the cone or wreath with parsley, sticking it on with florist stickpins. Put some sticky gum on the bottom of the cone or wreath to make it adhere to a round serving plate. Now decorate by sticking toothpicks through the parsley and deep into the cone or wreath, and then impaling grapes, olives, tomatoes, and radishes on individual picks. Top the tree with a miniature star or attach a bow or bows to the wreath with a toothpick or florists pin to finish your centerpiece.

❋ *General Ornament Storage Hints:*

1. Wrap glass balls in newspaper or tissue paper, or store with foam packing peanuts. Egg cartons or sectioned boxes are

the best protection. Gift boxes from apples and other fruits also make good storage boxes.

2. Wrap heirlooms or other treasured items separately and in their own well-marked boxes.

3. Label all boxes so sorting isn't necesary when you take them out the next year.

4. Wrap tree garlands and trims around cardboard gift-wrap tubes and store them on top of breakables to prevent squashing.

5. Store all heavy items on the bottoms of boxes and all lighter and/or fragile items on the top to prevent breakage.

6. Wrap Christmas lights around cardboard tubes to keep them tangle free. Store them in the same box with an artificial tree or box them separately.

7. Artificial trees should be placed into the storage area last because they are the first thing you'll need when you put up your decorations the next year.

8. To prevent a musty smell forming in ornaments that you store in attics, garages, or basements, toss used fabric softener sheets into the boxes before sealing them up.

❋ *Pinecones (Painting):*

1. Shortcut: Place the cones on a newspaper and spray paint the outer edges with festive colors.

2. Environmentally friendly method: This method is more thorough than spray painting. Fill a 3-pound coffee can about ¾ full of water and pour an oil-based paint on the top of the water. Protect your hands with plastic bags or disposable plastic gloves and then slowly dip and swirl the cones in the paint. Place on wax paper or aluminum foil to dry. You may have to repeat the dipping to get the desired color. While the paint is still wet, you can sprinkle the cones with glitter to make them sparkle.

❋ *Pinecones Potpourri:* Put a few pinecones into a plastic bag, add a few drops of cinnamon or other fragrant or Christmas-scented oil (usually sold in ½-ounce containers at craft and other shops). Shake well and leave overnight or longer. These could be gifts, too.

❋ *Christmas Village Scene:* Creativity is the key to recycling some of the most unlikely objects into fixtures of a Christmas village scene for beneath your tree, on a buffet, or elsewhere.

1. Batting can be a base for "snow," and a book or box can be placed beneath the batting to make a hill. Your "snow" will sparkle if you sprinkle glitter over it.
2. A mirror can be a frozen pond. It will blend into the "landscape" if you place a few pebbles and stones around the edges. Also make a walkway to the "lake" with some pebbles or glued-in-place sand or fish-tank gravel.
3. Make a stack of firewood to place beside one of your houses by gluing some twigs together with white household glue that dries clear.

Christmas Mailing: The postal service says it's never too early to do your Christmas mailing and recommends that stateside holiday letters, cards, and packages should be mailed by early December. More time is needed for overseas mail. Your options for mailing are:

1. Space Available Mail (SAM) which is usually least expensive but takes more time to arrive at an overseas destination.
2. Priority Air Lift (PAL) costs more than SAM but takes more time than priority mail.
3. Priority Mail is the most expensive and fastest of the services. You can call your local post office for mail dates or to get a chart with mailing dates listed.

Storing Christmas Gift Wrap: Wrap remnants on leftover rolls. If you have several rolls of wrap of different diameters, stick rolls that fit into one another to save space.

Christmas Photos: What can you do with all those family photos that come in Christmas cards? Buy a photo album and allocate a certain number of pages per family. Insert the newest picture each year and enjoy seeing the changes.

NOTE: The album will help you remember names of new spouses and/or new children in the family!

Santa's Footprints Stencils: To delight a child, make a trail of "Santa's footprints" in the house between the fireplace, the tree, and your child's room. Here's how one reader did it. Cut two foot shapes from paper to make a stencil. Place your stencils on the floor and then sift flour over them. Carefully pick up the foot stencils, shake off excess flour into a bag, and move them to the next step sites. In the morning the child will see where Santa came into the house from the fireplace, and where he tracked "ashes" from the fireplace to the tree, to the room where he kissed the good child, and back again to the fireplace. The flour vacuums up easily. (The Easter Bunny's tracks can be made in the same fashion with paw-print stencils.)

NOTE: If you substitute baking soda for the flour, you will also be deodorizing your carpets at the same time!

Kwanzaa (African-American Culture Celebration)

In Swahili, *Kwanzaa* means "first fruits of the harvest," and the celebration, begun in the USA about twenty-five years ago, combines components of various African harvest festivals with a focus on traditional African-American value systems. It is celebrated by a growing number of African-Americans during the last seven days of December. Each day a family member lights a candle (black, red, or green) and discusses one of the seven principles (*Nguzo Saba*) which, if practiced daily throughout the year, are said to result in making one a changed person. (Source: *Kwanzaa, An African-American Celebration of Culture and Cooking,* by Eric V. Copage, New York: William Morrow & Company, Inc., 1991.) The principles are unity, self-determination, collective work and responsibility, cooperative economics, purpose, creativity, and faith. A feast is held on the next-to-last day of the celebration, December 31, called *Kwanzaa Karamu.* Cities with large black populations hold community celebrations, too. At the end of a celebration, guests select gifts from a *Zawadi* tray to take home. The gifts are traditionally handmade (baked, sewn, knitted, crafted) and wrapped with red, black, and green liberation colors.

Decorations: All reflect Kwanzaa's principles. For example, fruits and vegetables signify the product of unified effort; a straw place mat, the reverence for tradition; an ear of corn represents each child in the family; a communal cup is used for the libation ceremony; and a seven-branched candle holder represents the African continent and the peoples of Africa.

Foods: Traditional African, Caribbean, and regional African-American recipes feature such foods as okra, plantains, sweet potatoes, barbecued meats, candies, and other desserts, such as sweet potato pie. From my Recipe Section, try Caribbean Barbecued Pork, a meat flavored with my Jamaican Barbecue Sauce, Mrs. Geraldine Terrell's Sweet Potato Pone, Chef's Secret Sweet Potatoes, Mrs. Mary Prosser's Pinto Beans, and for a sweet, Buttermilk Pecan Pralines or Lone Star Conefest Pralines.

Beverages: Serve fruit punch, iced teas, or try this recipe for West African Ginger Beer from Eric Copage's *Kwanzaa* book:

1. In a medium saucepan, combine 2 cups water with ½ pound fresh ginger, thinly sliced (no need to peel), and simmer over medium heat for 20 minutes. Stir in ½ cup fresh lemon juice and 1 cup honey, and let cool completely.
2. Strain the ginger mixture into a large pitcher, and add 1½

quarts water. Add ice cubes, and let stand until well chilled before serving. Makes 2½ quarts, about 10 servings.

NOTE: The author says some people like to add a little rum to this "beer," but it's not necessary.

SPRINGTIME HOLIDAYS

Easter

Easter Eggs: If you want colored eggs but don't want to mess with egg dyes, boil eggs with yellow or red onion peels to make them yellow-beige or pinkish, with spinach or turnip tops to make them green, with a fresh beet to make them red, or add a package of unsweetened powdered drink mix to the pot in the color of your choice.

Easter Eggs (Dyeing): Let eggs drip dry on the back side of an egg carton bottom placed over newspapers or paper towels to absorb the drips.

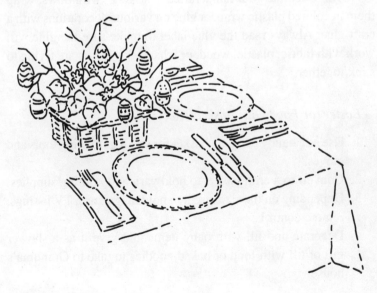

Easter Egg Tree: Fill a clay plant pot with gravel, sand, or a batch of plaster of paris and insert a small tree branch (without leaves). Spray paint all with white or a pastel Easter color. Then you can attach dyed empty eggshells (or plastic foam decorator eggs from craft stores) to the tree with ribbons. (Glue the middle of a length of ribbon to the egg and use the ends to tie the egg onto a branch.) Place a ring of Easter grass around the tree base if you wish.

Easter Basket (Creative Alternatives to Store-Bought):

1. Put "grass" into a recycled plastic strawberry basket and it becomes a free Easter gift basket.
2. Instead of baskets, put goodies into appropriately decorated bowls, mugs, recycled plastic tubs from margarine, whipped topping, or cottage cheese, or plastic drinking cups. For children, you can use a sand pail, hat, football helmet, or other useful item.

NOTE: Decorate your handcrafted "baskets" with bows, wrap them in colored plastic wrap, or glue on various decorations with a craft glue. Always read the glue label to make sure the glue will work with fabric, plastic, wood, or whatever it is you are trying to stick together.

Easter (or Food Gift) Baskets (Recycling):

1. Use as a handy carrying basket for small gardening tools and gloves.
2. Convert to a craft basket to hold yarn and knitting supplies.
3. Depending on the size, use it to hold magazines, TV listings, remote controls.
4. Decorate and fill with baby items and give it as a shower gift or fill with food or baked goodies to take to Grandma's house.

NOTE: If you walk through the woods en route to Grandma's house, don't wear a red hood and don't talk to any strange animals.

5. Fill with rolled hand towels and decorative soaps and place in the guest bath.

NOTE: You can spray paint the basket to coordinate with your bathroom colors.

Easter Grass Substitute: Poke a fluffed-up skein of green rug yarn into a basket instead of paper "grass." You can recycle the yarn at Christmas to wrap presents.

Easter Bunny Tracks: Please see "Santa Footprints" in the Christmas section.

Passover (The Feast of Freedom)

The most dramatic Jewish observance, Passover commemorates deliverance of the Jews from Egypt. It begins with a Seder, a family dinner with certain rituals of prayer, song, and narratives.

Foods: May include gefilte fish, chopped liver, chicken soup, baked chicken, potato cakes, traditional Mandel Brot, tea, sweet red wine, macaroons, and fruit compote. Matzo (flat, white crackers) is placed on the table to symbolize the unleavened bread eaten by the Jews during their flight from Egypt.

Passover Mandel Brot is easily found in supermarkets these days, but if you wish to make some, here's Mrs. E. E. Cooper's Passover Mandel Brot from *The Melting Pot:* Beat 3 eggs and 1 cup minus 1 teaspoon sugar at low speed. Add 1 cup oil, 1 cup chopped nuts, 1 cup Passover cake flour, pinch of salt, and ½ teaspoon cinnamon (optional). Let all stand for 20 minutes. Shape into narrow strips on an oiled cookie sheet. Bake at 350 degrees for 30 to 35 minutes. Slice and return to oven to dry for about 20 minutes, or toast under the broiler, watching carefully.

Mother's Day

Take Mom out to dinner or do dinner home but without Mom doing the work on her special day. Some mothers say they prefer to go out to dinner the night before Mother's Day because the restaurants are quieter. Ask your mom what she prefers!

If you don't choose to go out to a restaurant, you can still give Mom a rest. Bring dinner or fix it for her at her home, setting the table with her "best" china and linens. Most important is: Don't forget to clean up.

Breakfast in Bed: Young children can make Mom some cinnamon toast, or, if the home freezer is stocked with frozen waffles, French toast or bagels, they can toast them and serve them with a sprinkle of cinnamon sugar, syrup or jelly, or cream cheese, whichever is appropriate.

To make cinnamon sugar, mix about 1 part ground cinnamon to 2 parts white granulated sugar (or to taste) together in a bowl or cup; sprinkle on toast or other foods with a teaspoon or store in a shaker container, such as a clean, dry shaker-top spice bottle.

Mother's Day Gifts: Ask any mother and you're sure to learn that the best gifts are those that children make themselves, whether they are kid-art pictures, greeting cards, kid-decorated construction paper place mats, lacy snowflake "dream catchers" cut carefully from newsprint, or traditional paper-plate recipe/letter-holders (punch holes around the perimeter of one whole and a cut half of a plate, decorate with crayons or markers, and then lace the two plates together with colored yarn so that the "eating sides" face each other); the dream catcher will hang in a window and the recipe/letter-holder will hang on a wall until the child leaves for college. And, of course, there are the time-honored homemade "Chores" books in which children make up coupons for various household chores to be redeemed by Mom at *her* time of choice.

SUMMERTIME HOLIDAYS

Memorial Day

Traditionally, Memorial Day signals the beginning of summer, and in our grandmothers' day, you could bring out the white shoes and white clothing which were for "summer only" (which you could wear only until Labor Day in September). While many people don't bother with that tradition, a barbecue is still a good way to celebrate. In the Recipe Section, see Texas Barbecue Brisket, Slow and Easy Barbecue Brisket, Santa Fe Short Ribs, Pinto Beans, Mother's Favorite Potato Salad, and Mother's Coleslaw.

✿ In many parts of the country, Memorial Day is the first day of the swimming season, or for just going to the beach to enjoy the sand, sun and surf. If you can't go to the beach, bring the beach to your house. Have a yard picnic on beach blankets, play volleyball or other beach games, and *enjoy*! Dress is casual and effort is minimal because summer is here!

✿ In many families, Memorial Day is one on which they visit cemeteries to honor and remember beloved relatives who have died. Before you take flowers or plants or flags (to veterans' graves), check with the memorial park's office to find out if there are any special regulations concerning them. Please see the information on transporting plants in the gifts section of this book.

NOTE: It may be possible to plant trees or have them planted in honor of your relatives and friends; again, check with the memorial park office to get the regulations.

Father's Day

Celebrated on the third Sunday of June, this is a good day to let Dad do whatever he wants, even if he wants to sleep all day!

❋ Does Dad want breakfast in bed? Or is he a couch kind of a guy? Try making some of my biscuits from the recipe section to serve with sausages (regular, or, if Dad is watching his cholesterol, low-fat turkey sausages). If you microwave sausages, follow the directions on the package; and, to make them browner, look for the new browning wraps for microwaving found in some supermarkets and housewares departments of other stores.

❋ For "His" day, give Dad a coupon book with coupons for mowing the lawn, washing his vehicle, running his errands, etc.

❋ Does Dad want to play ball or watch a game? Get tickets to your local baseball team's game if the team is in town and go with Dad to bond while eating hot dogs, peanuts and Cracker Jack.

❋ Make this Dad's hobby day, whatever it might be.

Independence Day—Fourth of July

Traditionally, a day at the beach or a barbecue/picnic. Make sandwiches with some of my "Sandwich Fixing" recipes, put them into a cooler with your favorite recyclable-can beverages, and enjoy! Don't forget the sunblock!

If you are going to eat as soon as you get to the picnic site, you can buy carry-out chicken and keep it in a foam cooler so that it stays hot while you drive to the picnic area. Avoid eating picnic foods that have not been kept at their proper temperatures, and see the information on food safety in Section II on page 22.

Decorations: If ever there was a time to wave our country's flag, this day is it.

❀ Identify your house as the one having the party by flying a flag or a flag-type wind sock from your yard light or a flagpole. Or tie a bunch of red, white and blue balloons to your mailbox.

❀ Buy small flags at variety and craft stores to decorate cakes, cupcakes, and table centerpieces.

❀ Stick flags of all sizes into a foam half-round, surround it with bows in red, white and blue and you have an inexpensive centerpiece.

❀ Place red, white and blue runners made from ribbon or crepe paper rolls down the length of your picnic or dinner table. Add a patriotic flower centerpiece.

❀ Don't forget some red, white and blue paper plates, napkins and plasticware. For a picnic table centerpiece, arrange these items in a large straw basket you have spray-painted red, white and blue. Festive, fun and functional!

❀ Bring out your red Christmas tablecloth as a base for your red-white-and-blue-themed decorations. With a red tablecloth, you can save money on fancy disposable plates by buying white ones and using inexpensive blue napkins.

❀ Weigh down a picnic tablecloth by sewing a pocket inside each corner and filling them with rocks.

Picnic Service: Paint a coffee can red, white and blue with craft paints (or paint a flag if you are handy) and poke your picnic paper napkins into it so they won't blow away.

❀ Freeze a marachino cherry in each ice cube of the tray to decorate drinks with a bit of red.

Fireworks: These are banned in most cities due to the many accidents people have had with them. Do check your paper for public displays to attend. Bear in mind that if you live near enough to a public fireworks display, you may be able to see some of them from your yard, so you can have a neighborhood block party to watch the fireworks if your neighbors are so inclined.

Picnic Pests: Buy a citronella candle for your picnic table centerpiece and light it even in the daytime. It will help ward off those uninvited guests that "bug" us at picnics.

Or, dab a bit of full-strength vinegar on your skin with a cotton ball and bugs will stay away from you. (So might people who don't like pickles, but you can't win all of the time!)

Eating garlic is said to repel mosquitoes, but, like vinegar, it may also repel people!

Insect Bites: Avoid them by wearing some sort of insect repellent, and by not wearing perfume, hand lotion, hairspray or aftershave cologne, which attracts biting bugs.

Treat with alcohol, witch hazel or antibiotic preparations. Dabbing on ammonia, vinegar or a baking soda/water solution with a cotton ball can help relieve itchies. Wet ant (and some other insect) bites with water and sprinkle with meat tenderizer.

Protect yourself from ticks by wearing long-sleeved shirts, and long pants tucked into laced boots or with socks and insect repellent over pant legs.

CAUTION: If a bite does not appear to be healing properly, see your doctor.

FALL HOLIDAYS

Labor Day

Traditionally the end of the summer season; barbecues and picnics are popular. Since this is also the harvest time in most parts of the country, add Grilled Vegetables from my Recipe Section to your barbecue meals.

172

Rosh Hashanah (Jewish New Year)

Ten days of repentance and spiritual renewal and a time to take stock of your life.

Foods: May be similar or the same as for Hanukkah. At the Rosh Hashanah dinner, it's traditional for each person to dip a piece of the challah bread in honey to ensure a good life.

Yom Kippur (Day of Atonement)

Held on the tenth and most holy day of the Jewish New Year, this is a day for fasting, repentance, and seeking forgiveness. If your Jewish friends refuse a party invitation, don't feel ignored; this holiest day takes precedence over social events for those who observe it.

Foods: At the end of the twenty-four-hour fast, the ram's horn (*shofar*) signifies the end of the fast and foods eaten can vary according to taste and family customs.

Halloween (October 31; All Saint's Eve)

Food: Try my Heloise's Lighter Pumpkin Bread and make my Harvest Squash Soup recipe with pumpkin (see Recipe Section).

Halloween Party Hints:

Light Decorations: Cut silhouettes of witches, arch-backed cats, or pumpkin faces from black construction paper to tape over your porch light or put in windows to scare the hobgoblins.

Draw spider webs on windows using a black felt-tip (nonpermanent) marker. Add a few plastic spiders by suspending them from the curtain rod. Cleans off easily with window cleaner.

Ghosts: Make tissue ghosts and hang them in rows or put them on a "Halloween wreath"—a straw wreath which you can buy at a craft store. To make ghosts, place a small round cotton ball (or plastic foam ball, candy ball, or candy "kiss") in the center of a piece of white facial tissue and tie a "neck" with a bow of orange-and-black crinkle tie or yarn. Make dot eyes and nose with a black felt-tip laundry marking pen. Then attach the ghosts wherever you please or give them as party favors.

NOTE: The advantage of the straw wreath is that you can change the decorations on it as the seasons change. Attach ghosts for Halloween, fall leaves at Thanksgiving, Christmas ornaments and bows at Christmas.

Jack-o'-Lanterns: A carved jack-o'-lantern is the traditional Halloween table centerpiece, but you can be very creative with the face you carve into it. Pumpkin faces can frown, smile, pout, look like they are saying "ooooh" or any other expression, depending on how handy the carver is with a knife. Make a base of fall leaves for the jack-o'-lantern and you have a centerpiece.

HINT: Remove the pulp from the pumpkin with an ice cream scoop.

NOTE: Sprinkle the inside of the lid and inside bottom of the pumpkin with a bit of nutmeg and cinnamon after carving. Then, as the candle burns, your jack-o'-lantern will smell yummy.

Party Goodies: Bake cupcakes in ice cream cones (as directed in the food section); frost with orange or chocolate frosting, and decorate with candy corn or jack-o'-lantern candies.

Put ice cream in cupcake cups or Halloween drink cups and decorate it with chocolate chip pumpkin faces.

Make popcorn balls and decorate the wrap with Halloween stickers (bought wherever stickers are sold—gift, variety and card stores).

NOTE: Save the homemade goodies for parties. There isn't much point in making homemade goodies to give away to trick-or-treaters because cautious parents are likely to throw away such foods in case they have something harmful in them.

For children old enough to handle a small paring knife, have a Halloween party a day or two before the holiday and let each child carve a pumpkin to take home. Encourage them to carve happy as well as scary faces. Younger children could draw the faces on the pumpkins to take home for a parent to carve.

Games for Young Children: Make a Halloween version of "Pin the Tail on the Donkey" such as "Pin the Tail on the Black Cat" or "Pin the Hat on the Witch."

Games for Older Children: Put some oddly shaped (fake rubber bugs, faucet washers, plastic toys) and yucky things like rubbery-plastic fishing worms (no hooks), cooked rice or oatmeal, or gelatin into several non-see-through containers and have the children put their hands inside to guess the contents, which you can say can be witches' eyeballs, tarantulas and spell-casting scary things.

Trick or Treat Hints:

❋ *Give-Away Jack-o'-Lantern Treat Bags:* On brown lunch bags, draw pumpkin faces with a felt-tip marker or paste on features cut from black construction paper. Put candy inside and tie the "neck" shut with black-and-orange crinkle tie or yarn.

❋ If you don't want to give away sweets, give small toys, such as plastic dinosaurs or cars, or gift certificates for a cold drink at a fast-food or convenience store if your city's businesses offer them.

Trick or Treat Costumes:

❋ *For Small Children:* Pajamas can be the start of just about any costume.

❋ *Clown:* Sew or pin large yarn poofs on the front of pajama tops. Add face paints, a wig or silly hat, and you have a clown costume.

❋ *Mouse:* If you have a mouse-ear hat, add a tail to sleeper pajamas and you have a mouse costume.

❋ *Bunny:* Make a hat with long, floppy ears, add a cotton fluff for a tail, and you have a bunny sleeper.

❋ *Devil:* Red sleepers with a red tail made from a stuffed tube of red cloth, and a red hood or cape make a scary devil costume.

❋ XX-large T-shirts can be the base for all sorts of costumes, too. The quickest one is to write on the front of a plain T-shirt: "MY PARENTS FORGOT TO BUY ME A COSTUME SO THIS IS IT." Sympathy will yield lots of treats for such a trickster.

❋ *Pumpkin:* Take an orange XX-large T-shirt and insert elastic in the hem casing. Put the T-shirt on the child and stuff crumpled tissue paper up inside to form a round body. Draw up elastic and secure. Top the "pumpkin's" head with a green or brown beret. (Use a red XX-large T-shirt and follow the above "stuffing" directions to make a tomato costume. Or, a purple XX-large T-shirt to make a purple grape costume.)

❋ Make a Robin Hood/elf costume from a large green T-shirt over black tights; add a tri-cornered hat.

❋ *Paper Bag Costume:* Cut holes in the bottoms of big paper (paper, not plastic!) grocery bags for the head and cut holes on either side for arms. Let the child decorate the "costume" with crayons or large markers. An XX-large T-shirt can substitute for a paper bag in this hint if your grocer no longer offers paper.

❋ *Goggles for Costumes:* Make silly goggles to wear with a costume by cutting a pair of "holes" from plastic beverage six-pack rings. You can hold the goggles on with the elastic from a discarded pair of panty hose or a large rubber band looped on the "frame." Cover up the elastic/band with a hat.

❋ *Thrifty Costume Basics:* Search through the racks at thrift shops for old evening gowns, bedspreads, curtains, draperies and fabric remnants to use for making costumes. With a bit of luck you may even find some costumes already made in a thrift shop. Also search in your own or another person's attic for old formal clothing, ballet tights and tutus, hats and other accessories that can be converted into costumes for children or adults. Get out your stapler and glue to add decorations; no need to sew unless you want to.

❋ Glue or staple large fall leaves to an oversized shirt or a vest to make a "leaf monster."

❋ A sequined vest or jacket over tights and a turtleneck top can be a fairy costume if you make a wand by gluing sequins or glitter to a fly swatter.

❋ Need a ballerina skirt? Try running a string or elastic through the tops of sheer cafe curtains of an appropriate length.

❋ An oversized turtleneck over tights can be a clown or elf costume depending on the hat or makeup added.

❋ An Indian costume can be made from a striped bathrobe worn over a T-shirt and tights topped with a turban made from a scarf (neck or dresser scarf, depending on what you found at the thrift shop).

Costume Finishing Touches: Look for face paint, wigs, and fake moustaches and beards at variety and costume shops, or draw on witches' warts, Frankenstein scars, moustaches, and beards with eyebrow pencil and color features with regular cosmetics.

NOTE: If you put a thin layer of cold cream on the child's skin before drawing on exotic makeup, it will be easier to get off.

Halloween Safety Hints:

1. Children should not play with candlelit jack-o'-lanterns. Use a flashlight instead of a candle. If you just don't like the idea of a flashlight inside the jack-o'-lantern, light it with a votive light glass. If you use a real candle, you must keep the pumpkin "lid" off to prevent it from catching fire. Also keep such jack-o'-lanterns away from curtains or draperies that can catch fire if they are blown over a windowsill pumpkin decoration. Do be sure the jack-o'-lantern is in a safe place where it can't be tipped over by children or pets.

2. Stick reflector tape on strategic places on costumes, shoes, and even trick-or-treat bags, to make children and adults more easily seen in the dark.

3. Children should carry flashlights when trick-or-treating so they are noticed when walking in the dark, even when accompanied by adults or older children. You can cut a witch, arched-back cat, or jack-o'-lantern silhouette from black construction paper and tape it to a flashlight so that scary shadows can be cast when the flashlight is lighted.

4. When planning costumes, be aware that face paint or makeup is safer than a mask because it allows clear vision when crossing streets and walking on unfamiliar paths. If you choose a mask, make sure vision is not obstructed; if

necessary, make the eyeholes larger. Also, make sure costumes are not so long and flowing that children trip on the hems.

5. Go only to homes of people you know, or hold a neighborhood party to keep the children in one safe place. Do watch newspapers for community-sponsored Halloween parties.

6. Keep pets in a safe place where the tricking and treating won't frighten them into panic. Scared pets can bite strange, costumed children. Also remember that chocolate (especially dark) can kill small dogs, or at the least make them very sick if they eat enough. Keep those treats away from pets!

Thanksgiving Day

Thanksgiving Decorations:

❋ If your family can all get together at Thanksgiving but not Christmas, have Christmas in November, complete with a "Thanksgiving Tree." Plant a medium-size tree branch in a coffee can that is weighted with rocks and sand. Put the can into a nice basket or other decorative container. Decorate the tree with fall leaves, bows in fall colors, and other Thanksgiving motif "ornaments." Put gifts beneath the tree as you would at Christmas.

❋ For a fall family table, place fall leaves on the table in various designs or randomly, and then place a clear plastic tablecloth over all.

❋ Supermarkets feature dried corncobs and gourds at this time of the year. If you don't feel like wiring them together to hang as a door decoration, just heap some of these fall harvest symbols in a wooden salad bowl, and you have a minimum-effort centerpiece.

❋ Keep children busy by making brown-paper-bag turkeys. Draw a turkey head (with neck) in profile on a piece of brown paper bag or cut one from a magazine or coloring book. Draw and color the face on both sides. Stuff a brown paper lunch-size bag with a ball of crumpled newspaper to fill the bag about half full and make the round-ball turkey "body." Tie the bag shut with a piece of string or fall-colored yarn so that the open end of the bag flares and becomes a turkey tail. With glue or clear tape, stick the head/neck to the bottom of the bag, and you have a squatty, sitting turkey.

Foods: My Recipe Section has a traditional Roast Turkey and a dressing recipe, but if your family wants to break with tradition, try some of the Turkey Variations. Add Mrs. Terrell's or Chef's Secret Sweet Potatoes to the meal, too.

If you don't bake pumpkin pie, ask a guest to bring dessert or look in the freezer or bakery section of the supermarket for pumpkin desserts. If you bake your own pumpkin pies, try my Healthy Pie Crust recipe with your favorite pumpkin filling. Do follow my KISS (Keep It Simple and Sweet) rule for such major holidays, to avoid exhaustion!

Hanukkah, also spelled Chanukah (Festival of the Lights)

Usually in late November or December, Hanukkah is determined by the Jewish calendar and signifies the triumph of Jewish religious freedom over the Syrians in 165 B.C. On each of the eight days of joyful celebration, one of the nine candles of the menorah (candelabra) is lit. A traditional game played with a spinning top (dreidel) is played and presents are opened each night. The presents are usually personal and not too elaborate.

If you are not Jewish but are invited to a Hanukkah celebration, you can bring a simple present (such as a flowering plant); however, if the present is food, it must be kosher (deemed so after inspection by a rabbi).

Foods: Can include *latkes* (pancakes), the special Jewish challah bread, sweet wine, honey pastries, and other foods featured in kosher sections of supermarkets and food stores. A Sabbath meal might include gefilte fish as an appetizer, chicken broth with dumplings, noodles, rice, and barley, and boiled or roasted chicken as the entrée. Please see the recipes for Mrs. A. H. Gans's Latkes and Chicken Soup, and Mrs. Solomon J. Jacobson's Matzo Balls in the Recipe Section.

Alternative Celebrations Calendar

Don't wait for traditional holidays. Celebrate the minor ones, too, either with a party for friends or family. Eating a marshmallow sandwich on the anniversary of man's first steps on the moon, July 20, 1969, may be just the silly "fun thing" you need to cope with one of those weeks when every day is a bad day.

There are many significant celebrations and heroes' birthdays in each month of the year, so in addition to some of the more commonly celebrated holidays I'm listing some of the lesser known and some frivolous ones found in the *Chase's Annual Events* directory (Contemporary Books, Inc., Chicago, IL). I hope you have as much fun observing these events as I did writing about them. I also hope the silly celebrations will inspire you to develop your own offbeat ideas and menus for parties. You can use your newspaper's television schedule to select themes for parties from popular shows. For example, ask your guests to wear plaid shirts to a party themed to *Home Improvement* and give a prize (a child's tool kit) to the person with the best (or worst) "Tim, the Toolman" home improvement story. Or, have a *Beverly Hills, 90210* party for your favorite local zip-coded friends. Consider a movie that's currently popular in your town or any other local happening or political event that inspires you. The idea is to have fun planning your party. If the host has fun planning the party, the guests are sure to enjoy it, too. *Enjoy!*

JANUARY

January is National Hot Tea, Soup, Prune Breakfast, Oatmeal, and Family Folklore/Family History Month. Football bowl games are great excuses for parties, and celebrating the Rose Bowl Parade, the Hall of Fame Bowl Game, and others on January 1 can be fun, casual parties even the hosts enjoy.

Football Bowl Games

Football Snacks: Try Heloise Recipes for Tri-Colored Popcorn (make the colors of your favorite team) or Gourmet Popcorn, Hot Open-Faced Tomato and Cheese Sandwiches, Sausage Biscuits, Easiest Ever Delicious Donuts, Sonia's Seven-Layer Dip, or any of the Heloise candies.

National Soup Month

Souper Soup Bowl Party for Bowl Games: Serve my hearty Beef Minestrone in between games so the cook can watch and have fun, too.

National Hot Tea Month

Have a tea for your card-playing group. High tea, English-style is held at many hotels throughout the country. Also, there has been an upsurge in openings of tea and coffeehouses. Entertaining with a tea or coffee is an easy way to have a party and can be less expensive than a dinner, if you are on a strict budget.

Tea Concentrate for a Crowd: You can prepare the concentrate ahead of time whether you serve the tea hot or iced. This recipe makes 40 to 50 cups of tea.

1. Bring 1½ quarts of fresh, cold water to a rapid boil.
2. Remove water from heat and immediately add ¼ pound loose tea. Stir to immerse leaves and then cover. (Double this recipe for 80 to 90 cups.)
3. Let stand 5 minutes. Strain into a teapot for serving.
4. To serve this concentrate as hot tea, bring out a second pot of boiling fresh water, pour about 2 tablespoons of tea concentrate into each cup, and fill up with the hot water. The strength of the tea depends on the water-to-tea ratio.

If you are using this concentrate for iced tea, add 50 percent more tea to allow for melting ice—it's 6 tea bags or 6 teaspoons of tea for 4 glasses of iced tea.

NOTE: When you buy tea in tea bags, the number of tea bags per pound will tell you how strong the tea is. Most teas come 200 bags to the pound; if you get 1 to 2 cups per bag from such a tea, then you may get 4 cups per bag from a tea that has 150 bags per pound and may need 2 bags for one cup if the tea has more than 200 bags per pound.

Serve the tea with my English Tea Biscuits and My Favorite LoCal Grape Jelly, or any of the cookies and candies from my Recipe Section. (Please see National Oatmeal Month below.)

Sun Tea: To save energy (yours and electricity), make Sun Tea in the summer.

1. Put the appropriate number of tea bags (about the same number of bags for the amount of water as for hot tea) into a glass container (quart or gallon).
2. Fill with fresh cool water and put the container on a sunny patio or doorstep where it will be safe from curious children and

pets. Depending on the weather, you'll have tea by noon or at least by 4 P.M. teatime.

3. Pour over ice and add flavorings of choice.

"Sun Tea" in Microwave: If there's no sun or if you are in a rush, boil water in a glass jar or pitcher in the microwave, toss in the appropriate number of tea bags, and let the tea steep on the kitchen counter until it's the proper strength (5 minutes or so).

NOTE: I once tried to speed this process along by simmering the tea bags in the pitcher in the microwave oven. What a mess! The bags broke and I had to strain the tea to use it. So let the tea steep out of the microwave. To get stronger tea faster, add extra tea bags.

TEA HINT 1: If a pitcher of iced tea becomes cloudy, add a small amount of boiling water and stir; the tea will usually clear up. Teas sold especially for iced tea are less likely to get cloudy.

TEA HINT 2: When you make a pot of tea with tea bags, loop the strings to the teapot handle so that the tags don't fall into the tea and add a "papery" taste to it.

TEA HINT 3: If only one person in the group wants tea, boil the water in the microwave in the cup and add a tea bag.

National Oatmeal Month

Oatmeal Goodies: Have some friends over for coffee or tea and make a batch of an oatmeal candy from my Recipe Section— Lorraine's No-Bake Fudge Cookies. (The recipe requires 3 cups of oatmeal, so is this nutrition combined with decadence?)

Oatmeal Beauty: Take an oatmeal beauty bath as a "party of one" to relax after or even before a party. Some people dangle a cloth bag containing about 2 cups of oatmeal from the faucet as the tub fills, then rub their skin with the bag after it's moistened by the water, and then soak in the tub. Others just add the oatmeal to the water and soak.

NOTE: If you use tea bags for tea, put the used ones in the fridge and save them to put on your eyes when you take your oatmeal beauty bath.

Microwave Oatmeal: For the past few years, as I've traveled around the country on my book tours, I've noticed that more and more people order cooked oatmeal for breakfast in hotels and restaurants. If you have only one houseguest asking for oatmeal, check out the microwave directions on the oatmeal box. You can make and serve your guest's oatmeal in the same bowl and save mess!

Oatmeal Garnishes: Raisins, nuts, dried cherries or prunes (It's also national prune month!), fresh fruit, a dollop of fruit or plain yogurt.

National Family Folklore/History Month

Compiling Family History: As relatives remember those "good old days" at family gatherings, make an audio or video tape to duplicate for others and to save as a family history record.

Family Photo History: Collect duplicate photos and put them into an album which you can take to a family gathering. The pictures can trigger even more memories to record for your family history project. (Please see the Family Reunion Section.)

January Birthdays to Celebrate

Tom Sawyer's Cat's Birthday (January 3): This celebration focuses on Tom Sawyer's penchant for doing things the hard way and satirizes government bureaucracy. It is sponsored by The Puns Corps, c/o Bob Birch, Box 2364, Falls Church, VA 22042-0364, Phone 703-533-3668. Give your cat a treat and have a casual luncheon for cat lovers. The menu could include "goldfish" crackers and sushi for snacks, a canned tuna casserole, and a taffy pull with my Vinegar Taffy recipe.

Millard Fillmore's Birthday (January 7): Fillmore didn't get his party's nomination for the presidency in 1856, so he ran as a candidate of the Know Nothing Party. Traditionally, his birthday functions as a reason for a party when there is no other one. Whatever you choose to serve, finish off your dinner with a cheese board decorated with "sour grapes."

Elvis Presley's Birthday (January 8): Since his death on August 16, 1977, his fans have remembered Elvis annually. Elvis look-alike costumed guests could sing on a rented Karaoke machine and eat cheeseburgers! For dessert, serve ice cream with some of the toppings suggested in my Recipe Section.

FEBRUARY

February is the month to celebrate National Creative Romance, Great American Pies, Cherry (not a surprise!), Embroidery, Snack Foods, and Robinson Crusoe. It's also Afro-American History Month.

Robinson Crusoe Day (February 1)

A shipwreck party is a natural for this event. Cut out mock "Friday's footprints" and place them outside your door to indicate where the party is. You can also place "footprints" inside the house to direct people to the bathrooms, where to place coats, etc. Serve rum punch as the seafaring beverage, if you wish. Your menu can include "island" foods such as fruit salad with coconut and/or a paella made from various seafoods.

Heloise Recipes: Caribbean Barbecued Pork, or any meat with Jamaican Barbecue Sauce; Chef's Secret Sweet Potatoes; No-Mix Cherry-Pineapple Nut Cake for dessert.

National Creative Romance Month

What else but a Valentine's Day party? Try a party of two! A menu of "love foods" from the Recipe Section could include Hearts of Palm and Artichoke Salad; lamb chops which have been lovingly tenderized by my Marinade for Beef, Veal, or Lamb; Chef's Secret Sweet Potatoes or Peking Double-Baked Stuffed Potatoes; and for dessert, serve anything chocolate or a cake decorated with "message heart" candies. (Buy a plain cake at the store and put the "message heart" candies on it yourself—now you've made the cake!)

Valentine's Day Roses: Traditionally, the colors of roses have certain symbolic meanings. Pink roses symbolize perfect happiness and "sweetheart." Red roses symbolize love. Yellow roses symbolize friendship. White roses symbolize innocence and purity.

Valentine's "Mixer": Cut cheap valentines in half and give halves to guests as they enter. Their dinner companions are their valentines' "other halves." If you need to group guests at small tables, please see Valentine's Bridge/Card Party below.

Valentine's Bridge/Card Party: Buy a pack of cheap children's valentines that has a number of valentines of each design and

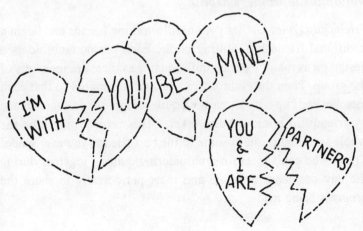

187

have each guest draw a valentine from a basket that contains four of each design. Then assign four people with matching designs per card table.

Great American Pies Month, National Cherry Month

Take a Pie to Lunch: Wash and save plastic food containers, such as those from store cookies, carry-out burger boxes, or other recyclables, that will hold a piece of pie safely and unmashed in the bottom of your lunch bag.

NOTE: If you bake your own pies, do try my Healthy Pie Crust recipe.

Make It Cherry: Try the No-Mix Cherry-Pineapple Nut Cake from the Recipe Section.

Easy Cherry Cobbler: Into a buttered baking dish, pour a can of cherry pie filling, top with canned biscuits from the dairy section, dot with butter or margarine, sprinkle cinnamon and sugar on top, and bake at 325–350°F until the biscuits are lightly browned.

National Embroidery Month

Friendship Quilt: Gather your needleworking friends and begin a traditional friendship quilting circle. Each person embroiders a design on as many separate quilt squares as there are members of the group. Then the embroidered designs are shared so that each member ends up with a treasured quilt composed of squares made by friendship circle needleworkers. This project may take the whole year and result in some of the best friends you ever made! Those who can't meet for embroidering/quilting together during the day can work at home and meet periodically to share the progress being made.

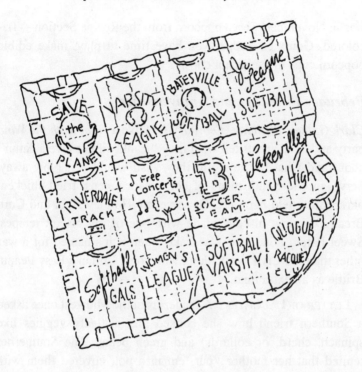

Serve Heloise flavored coffees or teas from January's Tea section and Friendship Cake to the quilting group. Please see the Recipe Section.

National Snack Food Month

Popcorn: Since February 22 is the anniversary of the day popcorn was first introduced to the colonists by a Native American named Quadequina, do serve popcorn at your February parties. Impress your friends by telling them that Quadequina, who by the way was the brother of the Massasoit chief, brought a deerskin bag filled with popped corn to the first Thanksgiving, which was celebrated February 22, 1630. And everyone thought the first Thanksgiving was in November! Serve popcorn from the Recipe Section—Tricolored, Gourmet, and, if you have time to play, make edible popcorn cups to use as nut cups.

February Birthdays and Anniversaries

Clark Gable's Birthday (February 1): Give a *Gone with the Wind* party and have guests tell what they "frankly don't give a damn" about and what in the world they wish would just blow away. Serve an Old South menu of cornbread, greens, fried chicken, okra, Smithfield ham, etc. Or serve my Holiday Ham and Corn Bread Dressing, biscuits made with one of my biscuit recipes, Sweet Potato Pone, and War Cake (even if it's named for a war other than the Civil War), along with some Lillian's Easy Peanut Brittle as an extra treat.

LETTER OF LAUGHTER: A reader from the Midwest once asked a Southern friend how she cooked greens (leafy veggies like spinach, chard, or collards) and green beans. The Southerner replied that her mother "put 'em in a pot, covered them with water, added bacon grease, and then cooked the ever-livin' hell out of them," but as a citizen of the "new South," she preferred to cook them for a shorter period of time!

NOTE: You can buy powdered ham bouillon in some stores and add it to vegetables and other dishes to get that traditional Southern ham bone/pork flavor without adding fat or real meat.

Vanna White's Birthday (February 18): Have your party start at the time your city shows Vanna turning letters on that famous TV wheel game and have guests play the game after the show. You can buy it wherever board games are sold and/or ask guests who may own the game to bring it to the party. Plan an alphabet menu, such as one with my recipes: A = Angel Biscuits, B = Baked Barbecue Chicken, C = Chinese Beets, and so on.

Erma Bombeck's Birthday (February 21): Have a family fun party with just your family or with friends and relatives. Make it a point to share funny family stories. (But please not those that mortify or embarrass, because hurt feelings are not fun or funny!) Tape the stories so that they become a family history.

On the menu, serve unpretentious family fare and "kid food." Appetizer: Carrot sticks, "ants on a log" (celery sticks spread with peanut butter and sprinkled with raisins). Main Dish: Spaghetti or lasagna made with my Spaghetti Sauce from the Recipe Section; "mac and cheese," chicken drumsticks, etc. Please see the Recipe Section. Salad: Current family favorite gelatin or other salad. Dessert: Ice cream cones or frozen pops.

M*A*S*H: The Final Episode Anniversary (February 28): Rent or borrow tapes of this episode or the original movie for entertainment. Dream up your own menu based on the characters, such as Hawkeye Pierce's Maine clam chowder or his favorite Chicago-style barbecued ribs; Colonel Potter's Beaver Biscuits; Winchester's stuffy stuffing; Radar O'Reilly's farm fresh corn; Klinger's Toledo hot dogs. Dessert can be B. J. Hunnicut's wife's cookies from home served from a cookie tin; Frank Burns and Margaret Houlihan's stolen sweets, etc. Identify the foods with signs made to look like the road signs in the TV show. If your friends like to wear costumes, you could offer a prize to the best Klinger or other character look-alike. The prize could be a *M*A*S*H* video tape or some object from the show, such as Hawkeye's cocktail glass, Klinger's necklace, Colonel Potter's horse blanket, a bottle of Margaret's hair bleach, Radar's hat, Frank Burns's socks, anyone's army boots, and so on. Army surplus stores have many items that you could buy, and you might also find old military items at flea markets and thrift stores.

NOTE: Any favorite movie or TV show theme can be worked up in this manner at any time. Let your imagination soar!

191

MARCH

National Craft Month

Get together with your "crafty" friends and have a sale (so that you can learn what others are doing while you earn enough money to do more crafts of your own.) Make it a crafty party, too.

Heloise recipes for potlucks: Heloise's Lighter Pumpkin Bread; any of the salads or sandwich fixings from the Recipe Section; side dishes, such as either sweet potato recipe, Southwestern Veggie Rice, and any of the sweets and desserts.

National Noodle Month (National Frozen Food Month)

Noodle dishes are terrific party fare. Many can be frozen so that they can be made ahead and just thawed and cooked on the day of the party. Lasagna is a party favorite. Make your lasagna with my Spaghetti Sauce. Please see the Recipe Section. For directions on making lasagna without boiling the noodles first, please see the food shortcuts in Section II of this book.

National Peanut Month and Peanut Lover's Month

Make a batch of Lillian's Easy Peanut Brittle and serve it at the end of your meal or as a snack when friends visit.

National Women's History Month

Have your best women friends over for coffee or lunch. Check out the tea hints in the January celebrations section, and also the Recipe Section for Chocolate Extract Coffee and Heloise Classic finger sandwich spreads and desserts.

March Birthdays and Anniversaries

Glenn Miller's Birthday (March 1): Bring out the "moldy oldies" and dance, whether or not you can roll up your rugs.

Theodor Geisel's Birthday (March 2): Celebrate the birthday of the *Dr. Seuss* author with a brunch. But try not to serve green eggs with your ham. Eggs get green when they are cooked with too-hot temperatures.

Casmir Pulaski's Birthday (March 4): Birthday of the American Revolutionary War hero and Polish patriot who died in the siege of Savannah. Toast his memory with The Brunnemann's Krupnik (from *The Melting Pot: Ethnic Cuisine in Texas*): Bring to a boil 1 cup honey, 1 cup water, a 2-inch piece of vanilla bean or 1 teaspoon vanilla extract, several cloves, a dash of cinnamon or a cinnamon stick, ¼ teaspoon of fresh ground nutmeg, and a piece of lemon rind. Add 2 cups vodka and allow to boil again. Remove from heat, cover, and set aside for at least 20 minutes to steep. Heat and serve piping hot.

Funky Winkerbeen's Anniversary (March 27): Fans of the nationally syndicated comic strip created by Tom Batiuk can gather for a high school party. The menu can include roast "Band Turkey" (such as those sold by Funky's high school band as a fundraiser), and any other cafeteria-type foods that you recall as being edible. Or serve one of the side dishes from my Recipe Section. Serve the infamous "Band Candy" chocolate bars for dessert.

Eiffel Tower Anniversary (March 31): Bring out your own French cookbook and cook a meal that awes your guests, or take guests to a French restaurant. You can also cook up the easy recipes listed below and found in the Recipe Section.

For an appetizer, serve Easy Escargot with French bread. Add a green salad with vinegar-and-oil dressing and more crusty French bread to Mrs. M's Beef Burgundy Stew and a dessert of French cheeses served on a cheese board garnished with grapes—an easily served buffet feast.

International Working Women's Day (March 8)

If you are a woman, you are probably working whether it's in the home or out of it, so do nothing to entertain anyone on this day. Pamper yourself, take a nap, and eat out!

St. Patrick's Day (March 17)

Think Green! It's said that everyone becomes Irish on St. Patrick's Day. Green beer is a popular beverage on this day; a few drops of food coloring will do the trick. Serve green gelatin salads. Also, see the Recipe Section for Hearts of Palm and Artichoke Salad, Olive Nut Sandwich Spread, or Mother's Coleslaw. If you have time to "play" in the kitchen, mix up a batch of Soda Scones, which are popular teatime snacks or dessert treats in Ireland.

Soda Scones: Sift together the dry ingredients (1 pound flour, 1 teaspoon baking soda, ½ teaspoon salt, 1 teaspoon cream of tartar) and cut in 1 tablespoon of margarine. Add just enough buttermilk to make a stiff dough. Roll on a floured surface to ½-inch thick and cut with round cookie cutter. Bake at 350 degrees. When brown on one side, turn and brown the other. Scones are eaten warm. (Recipe by Joan Moody in *The Melting Pot: Ethnic Cuisine in Texas.*)

American Chocolate Week (March 20–26)

I love this one! Have a chocolate lovers dessert party. Dessert parties are popular with parents of young children since the party can begin after children have gone to bed. They are also popular with working singles and couples who like to socialize after dinner. The advantage is that you can entertain without cooking and cleaning up after a full meal.

Serve my Chocolate Extract Coffee and any of the chocolate

194

sweets from the Recipe Section, such as Heloise No-Fail Fudge, Heloise Dusty Ricotta, No-Bake Fudge Cookies, and No-Bake Sandwich Cookies.

National Goof-Off Day (March 22)

Do the same as on International Working Women's Day, but you don't have to be a woman to celebrate this one!

APRIL

Perhaps because it begins with April Fool's Day (April 1), April is National Humor Month. Easter is often in April, and you will find Easter ideas in the "Springtime Holidays" section.

National Humor Month

Have an April Fool's party, and during dessert (or perhaps *for* dessert?), have guests tell their all-time, lifetime, favorite jokes.

This April Fool menu from a 1979 *San Antonio Light* newspaper food section features unlikely ingredients that you can ask your guests to guess. Begin with a Sauerkraut Hors d'oeuvre Loaf (usually mistaken for a crab dip), Coca Cola Chicken (more unlikely ingredients), Mystery Mashed Potatoes, a salad named "Watergate," which could have its name updated to "Irangate," or "Whitewatergate," and Beef Brownies (that don't taste beefy). Please look in the Miscellaneous part of my Recipe Section for the recipes.

International Guitar Month

String your guests along (sorry to pun so shamelessly, but sometimes the urge is uncontrollable) with the April Fool's Day menu.

And for music, get out your records and tapes of Eric Clapton (plugged and unplugged) or another guitar-picking favorite musician.

National Fresh Celery Month

Heloise Recipes for Celery Appetizers:

✻ *"Kid Food" for Children's Party:* Traditional "Ants on a Log" celery sticks with peanut butter in the groove sprinkled with raisin "ants."

✻ *Crisp and Serve:* Put celery sticks into a wide-mouth vase containing water to crisp them in the fridge, then at serving time, spill out the water, dry the outside of the vase, and put the celery on the table.

✻ *Colored Celery:* Remember your elementary school science lessons about osmosis (water absorption through membranes)? Put the celery into a container as noted above, but add a few drops of food coloring to the water. It takes several hours for the celery to absorb the coloring.

✻ *Celery Leaves:* Don't toss out the leaves. Cut them up and toss them into stews and soups for flavoring.

Egg Salad Week (Annually, the Week After Easter)

Celebrated to use up uneaten Easter eggs if you've kept them safely in the fridge. You can stuff celery with egg salad for appetizers at any party. Or make Heloise's Humdinger of a Salad. Other egg recipes include Heloise's Lower-Calorie Eggnog and Egg Drop Chicken Soup.

April Birthdays and Anniversaries

Hans Christian Andersen's Birthday (April 2): This author's more than 150 children's fairy tales are considered classics of children's literature. Have a theme party for children or people who are "kids at heart" that features foods named for Andersen's tales. Do serve Hansel and Gretel's Gingerbread for dessert. You can easily make gingerbread cookies or cake from a mix.

Discovery of the North Pole Anniversary (April 6): Serve frosty drinks with your dinner party. See the "Make-Ahead" freezer drinks elsewhere in the book.

NOTE: Here in San Antonio, where I live, you can have frozen-drink dispensing machines delivered to your door along with the mix and cups in which to serve. When you have a party and you don't have the time or inclination to "do it all," always check out catering and other party services that can at least provide some of the menu/beverage items. You may be surprised at what's available when you look under "Caterers" in the yellow pages.

Samuel Beckett's Brithday (April 13): Celebrate the birthday of the famed Irish author, critic, and playwright by attending a local play with friends and having an after-theater party or dessert.

NOTE: This is a good way to entertain if you have small children, because the sitter will have put them to bed while you are at the theater. You may want the sitter to remain in case the children wake up.

Heloise recipes that can be prepared during the day and served after the theater include: any of the salads and sandwich spreads, any of the sweets and desserts. Or if you wish, as an entrée, to save your time and energy, buy a sliced, ready-to-serve ham. Add such side dishes as Mother's Potato Salad and Mother's Coleslaw. Dishes such as Mrs. M's Beef Burgundy Stew can be prepared ahead and reheated, too.

NOTE: If you want to make this theme into a family-style party on a weekend, have the children play "costumes" in one area of the house, supervised by a sitter, while adults visit in another.

Income Tax Payday (April 15, also my birthday, please see below)

Not exactly a day to celebrate joyously unless you focus on it as a good occasion for friends to get together as a support group—that is, "supporting the government"! The colors are green for money and black for mourning! Play money-oriented real estate board games and hope you don't "Go Directly to Jail!" Serve a pauper's meal—broke from tax payments—or a feast—last meal before going directly to jail?

Heloise's Birthday (April 15)

Have a party, serve some of my recipes, have guests write down their favorite hints, and then send them to me! Mail to: HINTS FROM HELOISE, P.O. Box 795000, San Antonio, TX 78279, or FAX to: 1-210-HELOISE.

NOTE: Never think any hint is too simple to share. So often, people read my hints and say, "Now, why didn't I think of that . . . it's so simple!" One good example of a "so simple" hint is this one for changing light bulbs. To avoid burning fingers when removing a hot, burned-out light bulb, remove the new bulb from its corrugated box, slip the box over the hot bulb, and unscrew it. You won't burn your fingers, and the old bulb can be safely discarded.

National Kiss Your Mate Day (April 28)

Make a special dinner for a "party of two." Please see February's Valentine's Day dinner for two.

Duke Ellington's Birthday (April 29): Bring out those jazz records and tapes. The color theme is indigo-blue for "Mood Indigo." Ellington became famous while playing at the Kentucky Club in New York. Serve a "Big Apple" dessert in his honor such as apple pie made with my Healthy Pie Crust.

Willie Nelson's Birthday (April 30): I'm a Texan, what can I say! This is one to celebrate! Get out your country and western music and serve a Texas barbecue to commemorate Willie's "Austin Sound" music. See recipes for Texas Barbecued Brisket, Slow and Easy Barbecued Brisket, and Pinto Beans. Serve Lone Star Canefest Pralines as a sweet.

MAY

You can still have parties even though May is Better Sleep Month!

May Day Party (May 1)

May Day is celebrated in various ways, including as a worker's day, throughout the world. In Hawaii, where I lived as a child, May 1 is Lei Day. The floral necklaces are made, worn, and given, and lei-making contests are held. You can substitute paper leis for fresh flower ones, if you wish, and have a Hawaiian Luau.

Mother Goose Day (May 1)

Have a young children's party themed to Mother Goose rhymes.

National Salad Month

Have a salad luncheon for your card or other club. See my salad recipes.

National Barbecue Month

Have a backyard barbecue party. See my barbecue recipes.

May Birthdays and Anniversaries

Celebrate May as Older American's Month by Celebrating Kate Smith's Birthday (May 1): Famous for singing "God Bless America," Smith's signature song was "When the Moon Comes Over the Mountain." The colors are red, white, and blue. Serve an entrée of your choice with my Chinese Beets (red), Mother's Potato Salad (white), and blueberry-topped ice cream for dessert.

Discovery of Jamaica by Columbus Anniversary (May 4): A good excuse to serve rum drinks, rum cake, and island food! Include my Carribean Barbecued Pork or a meat flavored with my Jamaican Barbecue Sauce and your choice of side dishes.

NOTE: I heard of a couple in the landlocked Midwest who actually brought in sand to cover the floor of their garage, where they held a most memorable beach party!

Cinco de Mayo (National Mexican Holiday, May 5): One of our favorites in San Antonio! A good excuse to serve Mexican food, which is economical and popular! Try taco chips with Pico de Gallo, Sonia's Seven-Layer Dip, Mexican Meatballs, Chicken Fajitas, and one of the praline recipes for dessert from my Recipe Section.

Decorations can include a sombrero centerpiece with the hat brim filled with chips, a serape (blanket) for a tablecloth, crepe paper flowers arranged in a bean pot. ¡Olé!

Rudolph Valentino's Birthday (May 6): Since his death in August 1926, at least one "weeping woman in black" has brought flowers to this actor's tomb in Hollywood every year on this date.

Have a 1920s party. Toast the silent screen star with drinks served in coffee cups to recall Prohibition days.

David Attenborough's Birthday (May 8): Celebrate the famed naturalist's birthday with an outdoor picnic. Think "green" and focus on "healthy planet" ideas. Serve drinks in recyclable cans. Follow the "green" suggestions for disposable party ware: In areas where landfill is scarce, avoid "throw-away" anything; where drought is common and water must be conserved, serve on disposable ware.

NOTE: It is possible to wash the better-grade plastic forks, knives, and spoons and save them for your next party.

Menu: Serve a vegetarian meal. Include any of the meatless soups in my Recipe Section, and/or some of the meatless sandwich fixings, Southwestern Veggie Rice, Heloise's Humdinger of a Salad, or other meatless side dishes.

Bono's Birthday (May 10): Recycle your St. Patrick's Day ideas to celebrate this Irish musician's birthday.

Bea Arthur's Birthday (May 13): Have a TV's *Golden Girls* party for your senior friends to celebrate Dorothy's day and to say "Thank You for Being a Friend" (the TV show's theme song). Serve a Friendship Cake for dessert, from the Recipe Section.

Arthur Conan Doyle's Birthday (May 22): Celebrate the Sherlock Holmes detective story writer's birthday by finding the clues when you play a mystery board game. Serve the "mystery" foods suggested for April Fool's Day and have guests guess the ingredients.

Vincent Price's Birthday (May 27): Celebrate the horror movie actor's birthday by bringing out your Halloween ideas.

Clint Eastwood's Birthday (May 31): Send out invitations to a "Make My Day" party. Life-size, cardboard photo cutouts of Clint in his best Western movie pose are available in catalogs and some specialty stores for about $25; guests can have their photo taken with "Clint" at your party. Serve Western fare or make up a *Dirty Harry* menu as for the *M*A*S*H* party (see February).

JUNE

If you aren't busy with attending graduations, weddings, and anniversary parties, you can have a party of your own.

National Turkey Lovers' Month

Invite your favorite "turkeys" to a party and serve—what else? Turkey made with the variations from my Recipe Section.

National Accordion Awareness Month

Like the bagpipe, the accordion proves that beauty is in the ear of the beholder (or something like that). Play accordion music from Lawrence Welk or Weird Al Yankovich—but not too much of it, please. You'll know it's "too much" if some of your guests start to leave! Dance the polka and serve a bubbly drink in honor of Welk's famous "bubble machine." To find out how much champagne to buy, please look in the Party Planning Section.

June Birthdays and Anniversaries

Mighty Casey Has Struck Out Anniversary (June 3): Watch your favorite baseball team and you can serve the same type of menu as for January football bowl games. Do include traditional baseball fare from the "Take Me Out to the Ball Game" song—peanuts and Cracker Jacks as snacks. Also, no ball game is complete without cold beer and "red hot" hot dogs. Look for nonalcoholic beers to serve, too, for the designated drivers and nondrinkers.

Judy Garland's Birthday (June 10): Make rainbows the party colors to commemorate her singing "Over the Rainbow" and have a bunch of munchkins (children) over for a Wizard of Oz party. You can show the video for part of the entertainment, too. Restless children can "follow the yellow brick road" (bricks or pieces of scrap wood painted yellow, or just yellow construction paper cut to brick shape) as they skip around the house and yard to where you'll serve refreshments. For a children's party, try serving simple fare like sandwiches from the Sandwich Fixings and any of the cookie recipes for dessert.

Flying Saucer Sighting Anniversary (First Contemporary Recorded Sighting, June 24, 1947): Have fun with this "Beam me up, Scotty" theme, especially if you have some "Trekkies" among your friends. Play *Star Trek* trivia. Serve snacks on saucers or flying plastic disks. If your friends like costume parties, they can dress up as their favorite *Star Trek* characters. The menu can be any recipe renamed to suit *Star Trek* themes.

JULY

Anti-Boredom Month

If ever there was an excuse to have a party, this is it. Have an outdoor picnic potluck because it's too hot to cook seriously for a crowd. Please see "Gourmet Party Club."

Dog Days (July 3–August 15)

Celebrate the hottest days of the year in the Northern Hemisphere, caused, according to tradition, by the rising of Sirius, the Dog Star. If you have a pool, this is the time to have a pool party. Provide old towels, a pathway to the bathroom marked with runner rugs layed end-to-end to collect bathing suit drips, and make sure guests know it's a casual event. Easy foods include some of the cold soups from the Recipe Section, such as Gazpacho, Avocado, or Double Berry, and Grilled Swordfish with Mustard Sauce accompanied by Grilled Vegetables and/or Mother's Fried Rice or Southwestern Veggie Rice. For dessert, try the Cold Oven Cake or the Ice Cream Cake from the "Make-Ahead, Take-Along" recipes.

July Birthdays and Anniversaries

Pete Fountain's Birthday (July 3); Louis Armstrong's Birthday (July 4): Celebrate the birthdays of these two New Orleans jazz musicians with an outdoor crawfish or shrimp boil. Many super-markets now sell boiled crawfish and shrimp so you don't have to do the work unless you want to. If you boil them yourself, include small ears of corn on the cob and small new potatoes so the whole meal is prepared at once in one pot. To avoid mess when serving these boiled critters in their shells, serve them Louisiana-casual style. Spread several thicknesses of newspaper over the table and pile the drained shrimp or crawfish (or crabs) in the center. If you wish, you can serve the corn and potatoes in a large bowl to pass. Furnish each person with a small bowl to hold "dipping sauce." Also provide lots of napkins for this ultimate finger-food meal, and lots of cold beverages to wash it all down. When the meal is finished, just roll up the newspapers and throw the mess away.

Clement Clarke Moore's Birthday (July 15): Celebrate the birth-day of the author who wrote "A Visit from Saint Nicholas" (" 'Twas the Night Before Christmas") with a Christmas-in-July party to make everyone feel "cool." Use some of the Christmas ideas from the Christmas section.

Moon Day (Anniversary of Man's First Landing on the Moon, July 20, 1969): Think "heavenly." Serve my Angel Wing Biscuits with Meteors (any of the meatballs), and other suitable dishes.

AUGUST

National Smile Week (First Week of August)

Put on a happy face and have a beach party/picnic. Please see Frankie Avalon's birthday in September.

National Night Out (First Tuesday)

Annually on the first Tuesday of August, this event promotes police and community awareness and participation in crime prevention. Organize your neighbors to bring snacks and beverages to a central point on your block (and chairs, too) so that you can have a block party Neighborhood Watch event. Try some Pico de Gallo and Sonia's Seven-Layer Dip with taco chips for an easy but somewhat substantial snack.

August Birthdays and Anniversaries

Burkina Faso: National Day (August 4): If you say you are having a party for this day, you will stump just about any guest, but talking about Burkina Faso is sure to be an ice-breaker. Actually, it's the anniversary of the name change of the Republic of Upper Volta to Burkina Faso, or Bourkina Fasso (another spelling), in case you actually know somebody familiar with this holiday. Serve anything you like!

Lucille Ball's Birthday (August 6): Have an *I Love Lucy* party. Say on the invitation that you will give a prize to anyone who has red hair, and make sure you have lots of prizes if you have friends who are always "dyeing" to do something silly. This is an opportunity to try new party recipes. If they fail, you can say that you are just "doing a Lucy!" You could also serve some of the April Fool's Day recipes.

Garrison Keillor's Birthday (August 7): Celebrate with the National Public Radio star of *Prairie Home Companion* fame and pretend you and your friends are in Lake Wobegon, Minnesota, "where all the women are strong, all the men are good-looking, and all the children are above average." You don't have to try to serve Lutefisk, unless you know a lot of Norwegians who will eat it—just Midwest foods like roast beef, potatoes, corn, and apple pie for dessert. For an appetizer, try my Norwegian Meatballs!

Danielle Steel's Birthday (August 14): If you read her best-sellers, get together with other fans and swap her books over coffee. Make some of my spice-flavored coffees while you talk about those spicy novels. Whip up a Better Than Sex Cake (alias, No-Mix Cherry-Pineapple Nut Cake) or bake a Cold Oven Cake, depending on your whims.

Mother Teresa's Birthday (August 27): Remember the kindnesses of the famous missionary nun by performing a kind act such as taking someone who can't drive to a luncheon or dinner party. Or gather items to take to a local charity.

SEPTEMBER

Great American Breakfast Club Month

This is a month designed to encourage people to eat pork for breakfast, but you can celebrate it with any food that you like to serve for brunch. Try making pancakes with my Favorite Biscuit or Pancake Mix. For an extra zip, sprinkle pancakes with coconut, chocolate bits, or nuts after you pour the batter on the griddle and before you flip them. You can also make latkes (Jewish pancakes) and add fresh fruit. Other brunch recipes include Sausage Biscuits, Heloise's Lighter Pumpkin Bread, Heloise's Lower-Calorie Eggnog, or Double Berry Soup.

National Chicken Month (Chicken Boy's Birthday, September 1)

Chicken Boy—in case you didn't know, and I'm sure few people do!—is a twenty-two-foot statue of a boy with a chicken's head, holding a bucket of chicken, which was formerly the sign for the Chicken Boy restaurant in Los Angeles. It has become a pop culture icon. No surprise on the menu here—serve deviled eggs for an appetizer, chicken soup, chicken as a main dish, eggplant as a vegetable, and a dessert to cluck about like my Heloise Fudge or Shortcut Maple Nut Candy.

September Birthdays and Anniversaries

Emma M. Nutt Day (September 1): So you never heard of Emma M. Nutt, eh? This day honors the first woman telephone operator, Emma M. Nutt of Boston, Massachusetts, who began working on September 1, 1878, and continued as a phone operator for thirty-three years. Call up your friends and have a party. Serve Harvest Squash Soup as a first course to take advantage of the seasonal specials on squash during this time of the year.

Queen Elizabeth I's Birthday (September 7): Get Brit at your party for the daughter of Henry VIII and Anne Boleyn, who was born in 1533 and died in 1603. Serve cider if you can't get Medieval mead (and you probably can't!). Or serve British ales and stouts for beverages. On the menu: Say good-bye to British involvement with Hong Kong by serving Egg Drop Chicken Soup, Mrs. Yu's Beef and Pea Pods, Mother's Fried Rice, Chinese Beets, and for dessert, English "Tea" Biscuits. Or plan a less political menu with your own recipes.

Frankie Avalon's Birthday (September 18): The beach party movie and singing star was born in 1940. Serve picnic foods and play fifties records to get in a nostalgic mood.

Larry Hagman's Birthday (September 21): Do *Dallas* to

remember the TV series star as the big, bad J. R. Ewing! Serve Texas barbecue, Mrs. Prosser's Pinto Beans, or Southwestern Veggie Rice from the Recipe Section. Top off the meal with "J.R.'s Just Desserts" of your choice.

Jim Henson's Birthday (September 24): Remember the late great Muppets puppeteer with a party for Kermit the Frog, Big Bird, Rowlf, Bert, Ernie, Miss Piggy, and Oscar the Grouch for children *or* adults. With or without costumes, your guests of any age will enjoy party ware with the Muppets theme and Muppet food. Don't forget cookies for the Cookie Monster!

OCTOBER

If you want to celebrate something other than Halloween, read on.

International Association of Culinary Professionals' Cookbook Month

Have a potluck dinner such as the one recommended in "General Party Hints Gourmet Club" and ask all of the guests to write down the recipe of the dish they bring, even if all they write is the name of the store where they bought the ready-made food. Then copy all of the recipes and send a mini-cookbook/pamphlet to the guests. They'll surely remember your party!

National Dessert Month

Have a dessert party instead of a dinner. See the "Sweets" section in the Recipe Section.

Octoberfest

Munich, Germany, isn't the only place where October means a month-long *Gemuchlicheit* (good fun, friendship, harmony) party.

Many U.S. cities have Octoberfests. The menu is one of the easiest to prepare for a casual party. It can include bratwurst or other sausage, sauerkraut, and German (or other) potato salad. Don't forget the mustard and beer—alcoholic or nonalcoholic! At these events in Germany, sausages are held with a napkin wrapped around the end, dipped into mustard, and eaten without benefit of utensils or sandwich rolls. So if you feel like being authentic, you simplify serving, too! Gingerbread cookies are the dessert. Theme colors are from the German flag—red, black, and yellow-gold.

Extra-Effort Pretzels: If you feel in the mood to do something extra, make pretzel or gingerbread hearts into necklaces by threading ribbon (or crinkle tie) through them. Guests hang the goodies around their necks and munch away, just as the tourists and locals do at German Octoberfests. Buy or bake soft pretzels that are at least 4 to 6 inches across; thread about 36 inches of thick, colored yarn or crinkle tie through the top pretzel loops, and tie the ends in a tight bow.

Extra-Effort Gingerbread: Gingerbread cookies should be made crisp and in a heart shape. You can use a gingerbread mix. To make holes for threading the yarn or crinkle tie, punch them (about ¾ to 1 inch from the edge), with the end of a plastic drinking straw, at strategic places in the top heart lobes before you bake them. The hearts should be about 6 inches across at the widest part. To thread the ribbon or yarn, enter the first hole from the back of the cookie. In Germany, the cookies are decorated and you can write *Ich Liebe Dich* (I love you) or just *Liebe* (Love) on them with cake decorator frosting. You may want to wrap the cookies with clear plastic wrap to keep from damaging the frosting before you hand them out at the party.

October Birthdays and Anniversaries

Charlie Brown's and Snoopy's Birthday (October 2): Charles M. Schulz's "Peanuts" comic strip was "born" in 1944, so many ages of guests can celebrate this one. Peanuts and popcorn are the appetizers and The Great Pumpkin is your centerpiece. For dessert, serve some Elephant Ears from the Recipe Section in honor of Snoopy and add some Peppermint Patties.

Phileas Fogg's Wager Day (October 2): The anniversary of the famous wager in Jules Verne's *Around the World in Eighty Days.* (You can also celebrate this one on Phileas Fogg Wins a Wager Day on December 21.) Fogg bet £20,000 that he could tour the world in eighty days or less and return to London on Saturday, December 23, at "a quarter before 9 P.M." Have your party start at "a quarter before 9 P.M." and have your menu go around the world; decorate with small international flags from craft stores. Please see the Recipe Section.

Paul Simon's Birthday (October 13): Celebrate the musician's birthday with a Scarborough Fair entrée—chicken or other meat flavored with parsley, sage, rosemary, and thyme. Your beverage, of course, is "troubled water" from the Simon and Garfunkel classic "Bridge Over Troubled Water," and the entertainment is—you guessed it—*bridge!* You'll have a bridge party-dinner that will be remembered!

Marie Antoinette Execution Anniversary (October 16): What else but a dessert party at which you "let them eat cake." Try my Heloise Funnel Cakes, Cold Oven Cake, War Cake, Friendship Cake, and/or No-Mix Cherry-Pineapple Nut Cake.

Annette Funicello's Birthday (October 22): Remember the Mickey Mouse Club by celebrating the birthday of one of its favorite stars. The decorating is easy: Mickey anything. Do serve at least one course of cheese, as an appetizer or after dinner, to remember the mouse! If you have a mouse-ear hat, it can be part of the decor!

John Cleese's Birthday (October 27): If you're a fan of the British TV series *Fawlty Towers,* this is your day to celebrate. Any menu that resembles the Fawlty Towers dining room specialties probably ought to be avoided. Instead try some Heloise recipes such as Fresh Tomato and Basil Soup, Salmonettes, Lamb (marinated in the Marinade for Beef, Veal, or Lamb), Quick Potatoes à la Heloise, and serve English "Tea" Biscuits or one of my cakes for dessert.

NOVEMBER

Thanksgiving Day is the biggie this month, but you could try some others.

Sadie Hawkins Day (First Saturday in November)

Daisy Mae's endless attempts to "catch" Li'l Abner are still celebrated throughout the United States although Al Capp's Dog-patch comic is no longer in the newspapers. The tradition was established in the 1930s as an occasion for women and girls to ask the men or boys of their choice out on a date. This could be a good opportunity for a group of women or girls to invite interesting men and boys for a party. The beverage could be the comic strip's "Kickapoo Joy Juice" punch, but with less "kick" than the comic strip advised, for safety's sake!

Great American Smokeout (Third Thursday)

Sponsored by the American Cancer Society, this event is designed to help smokers quit one day at a time. If you still smoke and want to quit, form a support group by holding your first smoke-free party. Serve "comfort foods" such as puddings, chocolate chip cookies, Heloise flavored coffees, and soup (please see my soup recipes). Soup takes a long time to eat and makes you feel satis-fied. Finger foods like barbecued ribs and chicken are good foods to keep empty fingers occupied (see my barbecue recipes). Pro-vide peanuts in the shell to keep those fingers occupied, too, and also carrot and celery sticks to help ease the need to crunch and munch when there are no cigarettes to put into the mouth. Provide lots of chewing gum. Good luck!

November Birthdays and Anniversaries

Roy Rogers's Birthday (November 5): Celebrate the "Happy Trails" cowboy's birthday with Western foods from my Recipe Section. For fun, find out how many guests know Roy's real name. It's Leonard Slye, and he was born in 1912.

Buffalo Bob (Bob Smith)'s Birthday (November 27): It's "Howdy Doody Time" on this day if you are old enough to remember the freckle-faced puppet who starred with Buffalo Bob on one of TV's first children's shows. If you are having a children's party, puppets, even if not Howdy Doody, can be the theme for prizes or guest gifts.

Dick Clark's Birthday (November 30): And you thought Dick Clark of *American Bandstand* fame never had birthdays! For the record, he was born in 1929. Have guests guess the year of the youthful-looking emcee's birth. If you don't have the space to dance to whatever music was popular when you were a teen, you can still listen to the music. Since you are probably busy preparing for the traditional holidays, make this a simple party with no real work: Serve teen food such as pizza (order it delivered) and cookies such as my Snowball or Candy Cane cookies.

DECEMBER

It's difficult to consider holidays other than the traditional December celebrations of Christmas and Hanukkah, and recently, in many African-American communities, Kwanzaa.

I'm sure you have the idea from the parties above—it's celebrate anything any way you wish with food, decorations, or entertainment. Use any menu that you think suits the occasion and use any occasion to have a party. You work hard. You deserve some fun!

Just in case you want some birthdays other than the Main One (December 25) to celebrate in December, here are a few lesser-known ones:

- Jazz Great Dave Brubeck, December 6.
- Marie Tussaud, Creator of Madame Tussaud's waxwork museum in London, December 7.
- Mexican mural artist Diego Rivera, December 8.
- Poet Emily Dickinson, December 10.
- Talk-show host Phil Donahue, December 21.
- Singer-songwriter Frank Zappa, December 21.
- Composer-musician Bo Diddley, December 30.

Recipes for All Occasions

Throughout the years, we have published recipes in the Heloise columns, and I often get requests to repeat the favorites. Many Heloise Classic recipes are real shortcuts and time-savers because, for many of us, time is the "all-out-of" ingredient when we cook. Other recipes take more effort and are fun when you have time to "play" in the kitchen. I hope these Heloise recipes become your favorites as much as they are mine. Enjoy!

❀ **Beverages** ❀

HELOISE'S LOWER-CALORIE EGGNOG

3 eggs, separated
3 tablespoons sugar or artificial sweetener equivalent
1 pinch of salt, if desired
1 to 2 tablespoons powdered milk or coffee creamer to
   make richer
3 cups skim or low-fat milk
3 tablespoons bourbon or bourbon extract to taste
3 teaspoons vanilla
Dash nutmeg or cinnamon

Beat the egg yolks and mix in the sugar or sweetener and salt. Dissolve the powdered milk or creamer into the milk and stir into the mix. Add bourbon or bourbon extract and vanilla and blend in a blender to make extra smooth. Whip egg whites until frothy and fold into the mixture. Chill and serve with a dash of nutmeg or cinnamon. Serve with a cinnamon stick "stirrer" for a special treat!

❋ *Yields 4 servings*

HOT COCOA MIX

Made in a jiffy, this cocoa will warm you and your guests on a cold winter's day. It's also a terrific mix for campers.

Basic Recipe:
2 cups powdere milk
¼ cup cocoa
1 cup powdered sugar (or equivalent in sugar substitute)
Dash of salt

For a richer mix add:
⅓ cup powdered nondairy creamer
And/or 1 to 2 tablespoons of malted milk powder

To use, stir about four tablespoons of the mix (to your taste) into a cup of boiling water. Add a dash of whipped topping or vanilla ice cream, if you wish. Store in a tightly covered container.

CHOCOLATE EXTRACT COFFEE

We flavor food, why not coffee? This is my morning treat, but you could serve it when you and a friend take an afternoon coffee break.

For 4 cups: Add a couple of drops chocolate extract to taste to coffee. For 8 cups: Add ½ teaspoon chocolate extract to pot. For 24 cups: Add about 1½ teaspoons of chocolate extract to pot. You can substitute cocoa for chocolate extract.

❁ **Breads** ❁

MY FAVORITE BISCUIT OR PANCAKE MIX

I like this mix 'cause it's less expensive than the store-bought kind and the "dry" ingredient mix keeps well in the cupboard. It stays fresh longer if stored in the refrigerator. Make a batch and then impress your houseguests with your delicious breakfast biscuits or pancakes!

8 cups all-purpose flour
⅓ cup baking powder
2 teaspoons salt
8 teaspoons sugar (optional)
1 cup shortening
⅓ cup milk for each cup of mix used for biscuits
  (Use more milk for pancakes.)

Mix all dry ingredients together. Using a pastry blender, cut in the shortening until the mixture resembles coarse meal. Store in well-sealed container in pantry or fridge. When making biscuits, use ⅓ cup milk for each cup of mix. When making pancakes, add enough liquid for the batter consistency desired. Bake biscuits as you would biscuit mix, at 450°F for 12 to 15 minutes.

EVERYONE'S FAVORITE BEER BISCUITS

These melt-in-your-mouth biscuits are favorites with my readers, and I get many requests for this recipe.

2 cups biscuit mix
1½ tablespoons sugar
6 ounces warm beer (Can use nonalcoholic beer
  if desired.)

Dissolve sugar in the beer and add it to the biscuit mix. Mix the dough as you would with any other biscuits and bake them as you normally would any biscuit mix. If you make your biscuits from scratch, just add beer instead of the liquid called for in the recipe and be sure to add the amount of sugar as listed above. However, you can't substitute beer for liquid in recipes in which milk is the liquid, such as the homemade mix above.

ANGEL WING BISCUITS

This recipe makes biscuits that really are as light as angel wings.

1 package dry yeast
¼ cup warm water
2½ cups flour
1 teaspoon baking powder
1 teaspoon salt
⅛ cup sugar
½ cup shortening
1 cup buttermilk

Let yeast dissolve in the warm water and set aside. Mix all dry ingredients together as listed. Cut shortening into the dry mixture as you do for pie dough. Stir in the buttermilk and the yeast mixture. Thoroughly blend the mixture. The dough can be refrigerated or can be kneaded lightly. (After you have removed the dough from the refrigerator, it should be allowed to rest at room temperature, to allow it to rise.)

Roll dough out on a floured board. Cut out the biscuits with a biscuit cutter. Place biscuits in a greased pan and allow the dough to rise a little before baking. Bake them at 400°F for about 12 to 15 minutes.

HELOISE'S LIGHTER PUMPKIN BREAD

1⅔ cups whole wheat flour
10 to 12 packets (about 2 tablespoons) artificial sweetener
    (the kind you can cook with)
1 teaspoon salt
1 to 2 teaspoons each of allspice, cinnamon, nutmeg
1 to 2 teaspoons baking soda
½ cup chopped nuts (optional; may substitute bran, wheat
    germ, sesame seeds)
2 eggs, slightly beaten
½ cup salad oil
1 cup (half of a 12-ounce can) pumpkin (a half cup more
    will give a stronger pumpkin taste)

Sift dry ingredients and add nuts or seeds. Mix eggs, oil, and
pumpkin; add to dry ingredients. Pour into greased and floured
loaf pans. Bake at 350°F for 50 to 60 minutes. I bake this bread
in 2 small loaf pans because it cooks about 20 minutes faster.

❀ *Yields 20 slices*

❀ **Main Dishes, Fish** ❀ **and Meats**

HOLIDAY HAM

1 fully cooked ham (12 to 14 pounds)
Heloise's Corn Bread Dressing (see below)
¼ cup brown sugar
1 can pineapple juice (6-ounce)
1 fresh pineapple
1 tablespoon Dijon mustard

While preheating the oven to 325°F, remove the bone from the ham. Spoon corn bread dressing into the ham bone cavity and reshape the ham around the dressing, tying a string around it to hold the shape. Set aside remaining dressing.

Put ham on rack in roasting pan, fat side up. Make diagonal diamond slashes half an inch deep in the fat side of ham. Place meat thermometer in the middle of the lean meat and cook for about 18 to 20 minutes per pound, or until the thermometer reads 140°F.

One hour before it has finished cooking, prepare a glaze. In a small saucepan, combine ¼ cup brown sugar, the can of pineapple juice, and the tablespoon of mustard. Stir at medium heat until brown sugar dissolves. This makes enough glaze to baste the ham two or three times while it is still cooking.

Cook remaining corn bread dressing in the oven at 325°F for about 30 to 45 minutes.

Allow the ham to sit for 20 minutes after cooking, then carve. Cut ½-inch pineapple slices and broil until light brown. Place around ham on a platter.

❈ *Makes about 20 servings*

221

HELOISE'S CORN BREAD DRESSING

2 to 3 cups cooked corn bread, crumbled
1½ cups chopped onion
1 loaf bread, toasted
2 cups chopped celery
1 cup chopped celery tops
1 tablespoon sage
1 tablespoon poultry seasoning
2 cups water
1 cup chicken bouillon or turkey drippings
2 eggs

Crumble the bread into a large pot. Put the remaining ingredients (except the eggs) in a saucepan and let it cook for about 10 minutes or until the celery and onions are tender. Mix this with the bread crumbs; if the dressing isn't as moist as you would like, add more liquid.

Add the eggs and mix thoroughly. Place it in a greased baking dish and bake at 300°F for 30 minutes.

If you would like a moist dressing, use a smaller baking dish and pile the dressing higher. For a drier, crustier dressing, spread it in a dish no more than 2 inches deep. The baking times will vary with this method, so watch the dressing carefully so that it doesn't burn.

GARLIC SHRIMP

¾ cup (1½ sticks) butter or margarine
10 large garlic cloves, minced
2 tablespoons fresh lemon juice
1 teaspoon cayenne pepper
36 uncooked large shrimp, peeled and deveined, tails left
  intact
Fresh rosemary sprigs

Melt butter in a small saucepan and simmer for 1 minute; add garlic, lemon juice, and cayenne pepper and mix. Thread shrimp on wooden skewers and brush with seasoned butter. Grill shrimp on hot barbecue for about 3 minutes until pink. Turn and grill for about 1 minute until opaque, basting with butter mixture. Serve on a bed of fresh rosemary sprigs.

✻ *Serves 6*

GRILLED SWORDFISH WITH MUSTARD SAUCE

8 half-pound swordfish steaks, about 1-inch thick
¼ cup fresh lemon juice
5 tablespoons Dijon mustard
¼ cup (½ stick) butter or margarine

Rinse fish and pat dry. Brush with lemon juice and spread mustard on one side. Dot with butter. Grill fish—mustard side up—on hot barbecue for about 20 minutes, until just opaque; do not turn. Arrange fish on plates, mustard side down. Spoon on mustard sauce (see below) and serve.

✻ *Serves 8*

223

MUSTARD SAUCE

6 tablespoons butter or margarine, melted
3 tablespoons fresh lemon juice
2 tablespoons Dijon mustard

Heat butter, lemon juice, and mustard in a small saucepan and mix thoroughly.

MEATBALLS

Heloise Meatball Shortcuts

Swedish, Italian, or other ethnic flavored meatballs make delicious hot hor d'oeuvres. If you've avoided making them because frying mass quantities of meatballs is a chore, try the oven method.

Shortcut, Less-Mess, Meatball-Making Method: Instead of frying, shape meatballs and place on a shallow baking dish; bake at 350–375°F for 10 to 20 minutes, depending on size. No need to turn them! If you need to drain grease off as they cook, place the balls on an oven rack inside another solid oven pan (to catch the drained grease).

Quick-Thawing Ground Meat Hunk: Unwrap the meat; slice it with a sharp knife; place slivers in a bowl or other dish, and they will thaw in about 1 hour.

Speed-Shaping Meatballs: Mold meatballs with a release ice cream scoop. If you want little burgers instead of balls, flatten the scoops with a pancake turner. If the scoop gets too sticky while you work, rinse it periodically in hot water.

Keeping Meatballs in Shape When Frying: If you refrigerate meatballs for about 20 minutes before frying, they aren't as likely to fall apart while you fry them.

Freezing Ground Beef for Shortcut or Unplanned Guest Foods: When ground meat is on special, buy large packages of it and then divide the meat into meal-size portions before freezing it. You can make hamburger patties or mix up recipes of meat loaves and meatballs before freezing. Store meatballs in a plastic bag so that you can remove only the number you need for one meal or for hot hors d'oeuvres; save the remainder for another time.

"Beefing Up" Ground Turkey: If you substitute ground turkey for beef in a recipe, you'll get a "beefier" flavor if you mix beef bouillon powder into ground turkey.

NORWEGIAN MEATBALLS

Make small meatballs, seasoned with ginger and nutmeg to taste. Brown well in butter or margarine; make a flour gravy from drippings; return meatballs to gravy and simmer until done. Serve with mashed or boiled potatoes. To make the gravy even more delicious, add a bit of sour cream to it at the very last minute before serving.

MRS. M'S BEEF BURGUNDY STEW

An easy party dish, served with or without snails as an appetizer, and accompanied by a simple green salad with vinegar-and-oil dressing, crusty French bread for dipping in the wine sauce, and a robust Burgundy red wine. Dessert can be cheeses and fruit—French/European style.

½ pound salt pork, sliced about ¼-inch thick and cut into inch squares

24 small white onions (If fresh ones aren't available, you can use well-drained canned ones.)

4 pounds lean chuck beef, cut into 2-inch cubes

1 tablespoon flour (optional)

Peppercorns (about 6 or 8)

Garlic (1 or 2 cloves to taste)

Orange peel (from ½ small orange)

Bouquet Garni:
    2 small bay leaves
    Sprig of thyme
    Small sliver of nutmeg or mace
    4 sprigs of parsley
    ½ teaspoon marjoram or oregano

½ bottle dry red table wine, heated (a robust-flavored one)

1 cup tiny button mushrooms, browned in butter (May substitute canned, browned-in-butter mushrooms— whole, sliced, pieces—if fresh are not available. If you use the canned, add the juices to the stew.)

Put salt pork bits into a heavy pan or Dutch oven, preferably made from cast iron. Brown until crisp and remove pork bits to drain on paper towels. Leave the melted fat in the pan. Sauté the white onions in the fat until golden brown. Remove onions when browned and reserve. In the same fat, brown the meat pieces.

Stir frequently with a wooden spoon so that the meat browns well on all sides. (Do be sure to have a pan big enough to prevent crowding and proper browning of the meat.)

Return the salt pork bits to the pan, sprinkle them with 1 tablespoon flour, if you wish (flour is optional). Sprinkle the meat liberally with freshly ground peppercorns. Add 1 or 2 crushed cloves of garlic, a piece of orange peel (fresh or the kind that comes in a jar), and the Bouquet Garni tied up in a cheesecloth or in a tea ball.

Heat the wine and pour it over the meat. It should just barely cover the meat pieces. Cover tightly and cook over very low heat on the top of the stove, or in a slow oven (150–300°F) for about 3 hours. If too much liquid evaporates, you can add a bit more hot wine or stock, but do not add too much or the result will be too soupy.

About 15 or 20 minutes before serving, add the browned onions to the stew and place the mushrooms in the center.

At serving time, sprinkle the top generously with fresh finely chopped parsley. Add pieces of bread that have been browned lightly in butter (or substitute crispy plain, unseasoned, commercially made croutons).

NOTE: If you choose the oven method and cook this Beef Burgundy Stew in a heavy casserole, you can bring the dish to the table for easier serving.

✿ *Serves 8–10*

MRS. YU'S BEEF AND PEA PODS

This scrumptious recipe came from a friend of my mother's, Mrs. Byung P. Yu, and it's a favorite of Oriental food fans.

2 tablespoons dry cooking sherry
2 teaspoons sugar
4 to 6 tablespoons soy sauce
2 tablespoons cornstarch
¼ to ½ teaspoon powdered ginger
2 pounds round beef roast, sliced thin
5 tablespoons salad oil
2 ten-ounce packages frozen pea pods or Italian green beans
Water
Cooked rice

Combine cooking sherry, sugar, soy sauce, cornstarch, and ginger in a bowl. Add meat and toss to coat with the sauce. Let stand for at least 30 minutes. Heat 2 tablespoons salad oil in an electric skillet, blazer, or chafing dish. Add pods (or beans) and cook just until hot and still crisp, about 2 minutes. Spread in a single layer on a platter.

Add the remaining oil to the skillet and sauté beef slices. Turn to cook evenly, about 5 minutes. Add the pods or beans and heat with the beef. Place in serving dish.

Add a small amount of water to the skillet with the drippings. Heat and pour over beef and pea pods. Serve with hot rice.

❉ *Serves 4–6*

PEKING ROAST

This roast uses any cut of beef, even the least expensive, and the result is fork-tender meat with delicious gravy.

To marinate:
3- to 5-pound roast beef
Garlic (optional) and onion slivers to taste
1 cup vinegar
Water

To cook:
2 cups of strong black coffee
2 cups of water

Add 20 minutes before serving:
Salt and pepper to taste

With a sharp knife, cut slits into a roast and insert slivers of onion and garlic. Put meat into a bowl and slowly pour vinegar over it. Add enough water to cover the meat. Cover with plastic wrap and refrigerate 24 to 48 hours, basting the meat occasionally with the vinegar and water.

When the meat has marinated long enough and you're ready to cook it, pour the vinegar off. Place the meat in a heavy pot (iron Dutch ovens are best) and brown in oil until very dark on all sides. Pour coffee over the meat and add the 2 cups of water. Cover.

Cook slowly for approximately 6 hours on top of the stove. You may need to add more water at some point, so check it once in a while. Add only a small amount of water at a time. Do not add salt and pepper until about 20 minutes before serving.

❀ *Serves 6–10*

TEXAS BARBECUED BRISKET

Brisket is a favorite party-barbecue meat in Texas, and traditionally it's mesquite-smoked.

1½ to 2 pounds mesquite wood chunks
¾ cup water
¼ cup Worcestershire sauce
2 tablespoons cider vinegar
2 tablespoons cooking oil
2 cloves garlic, minced
½ teaspoon instant beef bouillon granules
½ teaspoon dry mustard
½ teaspoon chili powder
¼ teaspoon ground red pepper
1 five- to six-pound beef brisket
½ cup ketchup
2 tablespoons butter or margarine
Additional ketchup

Soak wood chunks in enough water to cover for at least 1 hour before cooking.

In a small bowl, mix water, Worcestershire sauce, cider vinegar, cooking oil, minced garlic, instant beef bouillon granules, dry mustard, chili powder, and ground red pepper to make cooking sauce. Set aside ½ cup of this sauce.

Drain wood chunks. In a covered grill, arrange coals around a drip pan; test for slow heat. Place about ¼ of the drained wood chunks on top of the preheated coals. Place brisket fat-side up over drip pan and brush with sauce; cover grill. Cook for 2½ to 3 hours or until tender, brushing with cooking sauce every 30 minutes and adding more dampened wood chunks as necessary.

Meanwhile, make the table sauce. In a small saucepan, combine the ½ cup reserved cooking sauce with ½ cup ketchup, brown sugar, and butter or margarine. Heat the mixture through and add more ketchup as needed to achieve desired consistency. To serve, slice brisket across the grain and pour on table sauce.

❀ *Serves 15–18*

SALMONETTES

This is a Heloise Classic. Be sure to watch the salmonettes closely when you deep fry them; they brown fast! They also disappear fast!

14 ounces (approximately) canned salmon or tuna
¼ cup liquid from salmon or tuna
½ cup flour
1 egg, slightly beaten
Pepper (optional, to taste)
1 heaping teaspoon baking powder
Oil for deep frying

Drain the salmon or tuna and reserve ¼ cup of the liquid. Put salmon or tuna into a mixing bowl, breaking it apart well with a fork. Add flour, slightly beaten egg, then pepper (no salt), if desired, and mix well.

Add the baking powder to the reserved liquid and beat well with a fork until foamy. Pour this back into the fish and stir until blended.

Using 2 teaspoons, scoop out the mixture with one of them and use the other to push the mixture off the teaspoon into a deep fryer which is half full of hot oil. After they are browned (watch 'em, it doesn't take long), drain on a paper towel and serve.

❀ *Serves 4–6*

SLOW AND EASY BARBECUED BRISKET

This recipe has a long cooking time but a very short preparation time, so it's nice for parties because the "chef" gets more time to visit with the guests as it cooks.

2 pieces of beef brisket, about 9 pounds each
1 teaspoon salt
1 teaspoon pepper
1 teaspoon paprika
2 cups ketchup
1 tablespoon sweet relish
1 tablespoon margarine
½ teaspoon liquid smoke
1 tablespoon Worcestershire sauce

232

Mix salt, pepper, and paprika together and sprinkle on brisket. Cook slowly over coals for 6 hours, adding a few briquettes every hour or so to maintain temperature. To make sauce, bring ketchup, relish, margarine, liquid smoke, and Worcestershire sauce to a boil. Add salt, pepper, and paprika to taste. Serve as a sauce on the brisket after it is cooked.

NOTE: While meat cooks on the grill, you can grill vegetables, too. Please look in the vegetable section.

❊ *Serves 30 or more*

SANTA FE SHORT RIBS

Unseasoned meat tenderizer
6 pounds lean beef short ribs, cracked
1½ cups dry red wine
3 tablespoons olive oil or salad oil
1 small onion, chopped
2 cloves garlic, minced or pressed
1 teaspoon salt
½ teaspoon pepper
1 bay leaf
½ cup red chile salsa

Apply tenderizer to ribs according to package directions, then place ribs in a large heavy-duty plastic bag. In a bowl, stir together wine, oil, onion, garlic, salt, pepper, bay leaf, and salsa. Pour over meat in bag; seal bag securely and shake. Put the bag in a shallow baking pan and refrigerate for at least 4 hours, or until the next day, turning occasionally.

To cook, drain ribs (save marinade for basting) and place on a lightly greased grill 4 to 6 inches above a solid bed of medium coals. Cover grill and cook, turning and basting occasionally with

233

marinade, until meat near bone is done to your liking; cut to test (30 to 40 minutes for medium-rare).

❀ *Serves 6*

ROASTED TURKEY

1 turkey, approximately 12 pounds
5 tablespoons dry mustard
2 tablespoons Worcestershire sauce
2 tablespoons olive oil
Salt and pepper to taste
1 tablespoon vinegar
2 sticks celery
Parsley
1 onion, halved
2 slices bacon
1 stick butter, cut into small pieces
1 cheesecloth soaked in olive oil
2 cups rich chicken stock

The day before cooking, rub the turkey inside and out with a paste made from the dry mustard, Worcestershire sauce, oil, salt, pepper, and vinegar (for a larger turkey, increase the amounts given proportionately). Just before roasting, place the celery, parsley, and onion inside the bird. Lay bacon across the breast. Insert small pieces of butter between the drumstick and the body. Soak a cheesecloth in olive oil and place over the turkey, then put it in a roaster, add stock, and roast at 300°F for 20 minutes per pound for a 10- to 12-pound turkey, 18 minutes per pound for a 15- to 18-pounder, and 15 minutes per pound for an 18- to 20-pound bird. Baste several times while roasting. Remove the cheesecloth during the last 30 minutes to brown.

❀ *Yields 24 servings*

VARIATIONS

Mayonnaise Method: Rub the turkey thoroughly all over with mayonnaise before cooking. Make an aluminum-foil tent over it and cook at 325°F for the calculated time. Remove the aluminum during the last 20 to 30 minutes and the turkey will roast to a gorgeous golden brown. It will not only be delicious-looking but also especially moist and tender.

Peanut and Paprika Method: Baste the turkey with peanut oil and then rub all over with paprika. Place it in a roasting pan and make an aluminum-foil tent as above. Cook at 300–325°F, removing the foil to brown. Turkey will be exceptionally succulent.

TURKEY LOCO

This method cooks the turkey on the barbecue and leaves the rest of the stove free for other dishes.

10- to 12-pound turkey
About 4 limes, cut into halves
About 4 teaspoons oregano leaves
Salt and pepper

Remove turkey neck and giblets and discard any large lumps of fat. With poultry shears or a knife, split turkey lengthwise along one side of backbone. Pull turkey open; place, skin-side up, on a flat surface and press firmly, cracking breastbone slightly until bird lies reasonably flat. Rinse and pat dry.

Before cooking, squeeze 1 or 2 lime halves and rub over turkey; sprinkle with oregano and add salt and pepper.

Barbecue turkey by indirect heat, placing turkey, skin-side up, on grill above drip pan, not coals. Cover and cook for 1½ to 2 hours, until a meat thermometer inserted in the thickest part of the thigh (not touching bone), registers 185°F, or until meat near thighbone is no longer pink (cut to test). Every 30 minutes, squeeze 1 or 2 lime halves and rub over the turkey.

When cooked, place turkey on a platter, cut off legs and wings, and slice meat from breast and thighs.

✻ *Serves 12–16*

HELOISE ORIGINAL ITALIAN SPAGHETTI SAUCE

This makes a large pot of sauce. You can freeze the leftovers, if there are any left from this favorite!

¼ cup olive oil
½ cup butter
1 cup finely chopped onions
1 pound ground beef
4 strips finely chopped bacon
4 cloves garlic, finely chopped
3 tablespoons finely chopped fresh parsley
1 bay leaf, finely chopped
1 tablespoon salt
Fresh ground black pepper to taste
1 teaspoon crushed dry red pepper
2 ounces red wine
2 (15-ounce) cans of whole tomatoes or tomato sauce
1 (small) can of tomato paste
1 cup water
1 finely chopped carrot

Heat olive oil over low heat in a pot large enough to hold all ingredients. Add butter and simmer until melted. Add onions and sauté until lightly browned. Add ground beef and bacon; sauté until browned, stirring occasionally.

Add garlic, parsley, bay leaf, salt, black and red peppers. Cook over low heat for 10 minutes. Add wine, cover, and steam for a few minutes more.

Add tomatoes or sauce, paste, and water. Bring the mixture to the boiling point and add carrot. Cover and cook over very low heat for 1 hour, stirring occasionally. Serve over your favorite cooked pasta.

BAKED PINEAPPLE CHICKEN

1 cut-up chicken or equivalent in chicken parts (about 2½ pounds)
Paprika, garlic, and onion powder to taste
2 to 3 tablespoons low-sodium soy sauce
1 (20-ounce) can of juice-packed chunk pineapple

Spray casserole dish with nonstick spray. Place chicken in a dish. Sprinkle with paprika, garlic, and onion powder. Add soy sauce to juice from pineapple and mix, then baste chicken with the mixture. Pour pineapple over the top. Bake at 350°F for about 1 hour. Serve over rice and add a salad.

BAKED ITALIAN CHICKEN

1 cut-up chicken or equivalent in parts (about 2½ pounds)
Nonfat Italian salad dressing
1 onion, sliced
Sliced potatoes (one, medium, per person)

Spray casserole dish with nonstick spray. Place chicken in dish and cover with Italian dressing. Top with sliced onions and sliced potatoes. Bake at 350°F for about 1 hour, until done. Serve with a salad.

CHICKEN FAJITAS

This recipe cooks on the grill.

2 pounds boneless chicken breasts
Fajita seasoning to taste, such as McCormick's (buy in
    packets at most supermarkets)
1 (8-ounce) bottle Italian dressing
½ cup white wine
12 flour tortillas, warmed
1 onion, thinly sliced and sautéed

Sprinkle chicken breasts thoroughly with fajita seasoning. In a large bowl, combine Italian dressing, white wine, and chicken. Marinate overnight.

Remove chicken and grill over hot coals for 5 to 8 minutes per side, depending on thickness of the chicken breasts. Baste with marinade. Do not overcook. Slice into lengthwise strips. Place chicken on hot platter and scatter sautéed onion slices on top. Serve tortillas on the side to make fajitas at the table.

❋ *Serves 4–6*

CHICKEN FAJITAS

This quick recipe cooks in the microwave. Serve with South-western Veggie Rice (see page 247).

1 pound skinned and boned chicken breast
1 fresh lime
1 clove garlic, minced
¼ teaspoon oregano leaves
¼ teaspoon chili powder
¼ teaspoon cumin
1 small green pepper, sliced
1 small onion, sliced
6 tortillas (8-inch size)
Sliced lettuce
1 medium tomato, chopped

Cut chicken into thin strips. Place in a 3-quart microwave-safe casserole. Combine juice from lime with garlic, oregano, chili powder, and cumin; then pour the mixture over the chicken. Allow to stand 20 minutes at room temperature or cover and allow to marinate overnight in the refrigerator. Add green pepper and onion to chicken. Microwave on High, uncovered, for 6 to 10 minutes or until chicken is tender, stirring once.

Heat tortillas by layering them between paper towels; micro-wave on High 45 to 60 seconds or until heated. Wrap chicken mixture in tortillas by placing it in the center, topping with lettuce and tomato and folding up the sides.

❀ *Serves 6*

MARINADE FOR BEEF, VEAL, OR LAMB

Here's a marinade to tenderize cheaper cuts of meat prior to grilling, roasting, or broiling.

1 cup dry white or red wine
¼ cup cider vinegar
1 cup salad oil
2 teaspoons salt
½ teaspoon black pepper
⅛ teaspoon dry tarragon
1 bay leaf, crushed in small pieces
½ teaspoon thyme or marjoram
1 large clove garlic, finely chopped

Combine all ingredients in medium bowl. Soak meat in marinade for about 4 hours, turning it from time to time. Keep in refrigerator but let stand (either in or out of the marinade) at room temperature for 1 hour before cooking. (Optional additions: sliced onion, a large sliced carrot, and some celery ribs.)

❀ *Yields about 2¼ cups*

CARIBBEAN BARBECUED PORK

1½ pounds boneless pork steaks
1 large red onion
¾ cup fresh lime juice
1 teaspoon salt
¼ to ½ teaspoon cayenne pepper

Trim excess fat from pork. Thinly slice red onion. Place pork and onions in a nonmetal baking dish. Combine lime juice, salt, and cayenne; pour over pork; cover and refrigerate for several hours. Remove pork steaks from marinade, brushing off onions. Cook over hot coals, 3 inches from heat, for 8 to 10 minutes, or until thoroughly cooked, turning once. Heat onions and lime juice to boiling and serve with cooked pork.

❊ *Serves 6*

❀ **Salads and Side Dishes** ❀

CHINESE BEETS

A Heloise Classic, this is one of my most requested recipes.

6 cups cooked, sliced beets, or 3 (16-ounce) cans sliced
   beets
1 cup sugar
1 cup vinegar
2 tablespoons cornstarch
24 whole cloves
3 tablespoons ketchup
3 tablespoons cooking oil (optional)
1 teaspoon vanilla
Dash of salt

Drain the beets, reserving 1½ cups of the beet liquid. Place the beets in a medium saucepan with the reserved liquid and the remainder of the ingredients.

Mix well, then cook for 3 minutes over medium heat, or until the mixture thickens. Let it cool, then store in the refrigerator.

GRILLED VEGETABLES

If you cook the side dishes that go with the meats being grilled at the same time, your vegetables get extra flavor and you save energy—mostly yours, because you have no extra pots to clean after dinner and you were going to clean the grill anyhow!

Bell Peppers: Cut into quarters, remove seeds, grill skin-side down for 12 to 15 minutes until tender.

Corn: Soak corn and husks in cold water for 30 minutes. Peel back husks but do not remove. Do remove corn silk. Pull husks back over corn and twist closed. Cook on grill for about 15 minutes, until husks start to brown or corn is tender.

Eggplant: Cut off ends and slice into ¼- to ⅓-inch slices. Oil and cook until brown, 5 minutes per side.

Mushrooms: Cut stems level with caps. Brush on olive oil and cook until tender and brown, about 2 minutes per side.

Potatoes: Baking or new potatoes are best for this recipe. Slice to ¼- to ½-inch thick. Place slices on foil squares with dots of butter or drops of olive oil on top. Sprinkle with herbs such as minced garlic, chives, parsley, and rosemary. Seal foil into packets and cook on the grill until tender.

Potato Skins: Prebake potatoes in microwave or conventional oven until tender. Cut in half lengthwise and scoop out centers, leaving about ¼-inch shell. Cut each shell in half lengthwise again. Brush with butter and sprinkle on salt and pepper. Cook on grill until crisp, about 4 minutes per side.

Red Onions: Peel, cut onions in half, brush with oil, and cook until brown, about 10 minutes per side. Do brush with more oil while the onions cook.

Zucchini: Trim ends and slice lengthwise into ½-inch-thick strips. Brush on oil and cook until brown and tender, 4 minutes per side.

HELOISE'S HUMDINGER OF A SALAD

*I cook as my mother did—without exact measurements—so
please tolerate my "to taste" ingredient amounts. This is a
great recipe to stretch a can of tuna or chicken.*

1 can tuna, chicken, or turkey
3 celery stalks
1 egg, hard-cooked and diced
1 (4-ounce) can sliced mushrooms
10 to 12 black olives
1 to 2 tablespoons hot mustard to taste
Salt and pepper to taste
Dashes of celery salt to taste
Mayonnaise or salad dressing to bind mixture
Leaf or iceberg lettuce
Paprika for garnish

Slice the celery stalks very thin and on the diagonal instead of
chopping them. Dice the egg. The cheapest brand of sliced mushrooms is fine for this recipe. Slice the black olives, using any
amount you like. Mix all the ingredients with enough mayonnaise
or salad dressing to bind the ingredients.

Serve on a bed of lettuce and sprinkle with a dash of paprika
for an extra garnish. This salad tastes better if it can stay in the
fridge for a few hours, but it can be eaten immediately if
you're in a hurry.

MRS. MARY PROSSER'S PINTO BEANS

From The Melting Pot: Ethnic Cuisine in Texas

1 pound pinto beans
⅛ pound salt pork
3 quarts water
1 onion, chopped
1 teaspoon oil
2 teaspoons salt
1 teaspoon baking soda
2 teaspoons chili powder

Wash beans to remove rocks and grit. Add beans and pork to water and cook on high heat until tender. Lower heat and add onion, oil, salt, baking soda, and chili powder. Simmer gently for 1½ hours.

❋ *Serves 8–10*

PEA SALAD

This simple add-on or main-dish salad keeps in the fridge so you can make it the day before the party or in the morning of party day if you wish.

1 can baby peas, drained
2 eggs, hard-boiled, peeled, and chopped
¼ cup grated sharp cheese
2 tablespoons onion, finely chopped
Mayonnaise
Salt and pepper to taste

Mix all ingredients together and add enough mayonnaise to moisten. This will keep in the fridge for a couple of days in an airtight container.

❋ *Serves 4–6*

MOTHER'S POTATO SALAD

My mother's potato salad is still a reader favorite, and again, this is a "to taste" recipe; my mother didn't measure ingredients; she just added them "to taste." I like to eat it as a meal served on a lettuce leaf, but it can also be a veggie accompanying a meal.

Potatoes (boiled in jackets)
Enough mayonnaise to moisten
Bit of vinegar
Celery salt to taste
Savory salt to taste
A nice amount of chopped pimiento
Dash of pepper
Some chopped eggs
Several stuffed olives (optional)
Bit of chopped onion (optional)
Dab of prepared mustard
Sprinkles of paprika

Boil potatoes in their jackets until done, then peel and dice them. Mix mayonnaise, vinegar, celery salt, savory salt, pimiento, and pepper together and pour over warm potatoes. Add eggs, olives, onion, and prepared mustard, and mix all ingredients well. Sprinkle with a bit of paprika for color before serving.

MOTHER'S COLESLAW

This slaw is better if made a bit ahead of time so that all flavors have time to blend together, so it's a good party food.

2 ounces vegetable oil
1 ounce vinegar, lime or lemon juice (not all three)
½ teaspoon prepared mustard
¼ teaspoon celery salt
1 ounce mayonnaise

Salt and pepper to taste
Dash of paprika
1 cabbage, shredded

Mix together vegetable oil and vinegar, lime or lemon juice. Add prepared mustard, celery salt, mayonnaise, salt, pepper, and paprika. Pour mixture over shredded cabbage and refrigerate until ready to use.

MOTHER'S FRIED RICE

My mother got this recipe while she lived in China, and it's one of my favorites, too.

1 cup uncooked rice
4 to 5 slices bacon (diced) and drippings
3 or 4 eggs
3 or 4 cut green onions (or scallions), tops and all
Leftover bits of pork, beef, or ham, chopped into small
    pieces (optional)
Soy sauce to taste

Cook and cool rice a day ahead or earlier in the day. It's better if it's had a chance to dry out a bit. Brown bacon in a heavy skillet until crisp. Remove bacon and turn down heat. Slightly beat eggs and pour them into the hot bacon drippings. Add rice and onions; mix together. Add bacon and leftover meat. Mix. Add soy sauce until the rice is as brown as you like it. Stir well and cook on low heat 15 to 20 minutes.

❋ *Serves 4–6*

❋ ✿ ❋

SOUTHWESTERN VEGGIE RICE

This is a microwave oven recipe that goes well with Chicken Fajitas or barbecued dishes.

3 tablespoons salad oil
1 large onion, chopped
2 cloves garlic, minced or pressed
1½ cups rice
⅛ teaspoon cayenne pepper
2 chicken bouillon cubes
2 cups boiling water
10 ounces frozen peas and carrots, thawed
1½ cups peeled, seeded, chopped tomatoes

Cook oil uncovered for 2 minutes on high in a 3-quart microwave-safe casserole. Add onion, garlic, and rice. Cook uncovered on High for 3 minutes until onion is limp and rice is opaque. Stir once. Stir in cayenne and bouillon cubes dissolved in boiling water. Cover tightly and cook on High for 4 to 7 minutes or until liquid begins to boil. Reduce power to Medium, and cook for 10 to 12 minutes, or until most of the liquid is absorbed and rice is tender. Let stand covered for 5 minutes. Stir peas, carrots, and tomatoes in at the end of the standing time.

❋ *Serves 8–10*

CHEF'S SECRET SWEET POTATOES

Mother got this recipe from a hotel chef who wanted to stay anonymous so nobody'd know he used canned sweet potatoes.

Liquid from potatoes
1 cup water
12 cloves
1 whole fresh lemon, thinly sliced
½ cup brown sugar
Canned sweet potatoes (one 1-pound, 13-ounce can or two
   1-pound cans)

Pour juice from the can into a saucepan and add water, whole cloves, very thinly sliced lemon (with seeds removed), and brown sugar. Boil mixture until a thin syrup is formed.

Add canned potatoes which have been cut in half. Allow to boil for just a few minutes. You'll have tangy, delicious spuds with no peeling and precooking sweet potatoes.

MRS. GERALDINE TERRELL'S SWEET POTATO PONE

From The Melting Pot: Ethnic Cuisine in Texas

6 medium sweet potatoes
2 cups brown sugar
1 stick butter or margarine
½ teaspoon cinnamon
½ teaspoon nutmeg
½ teaspoon allspice
1 cup molasses

6 eggs
2 tablespoons flour
1 cup milk
½ teaspoon cloves

Grate potatoes. Mix all ingredients well and cook in a greased baking dish at 350°F until set and slightly brown on top.

❋ *Serves 6–8*

LEFTOVER MASHED POTATO PATTIES

Good for that last "Feed 'Em Well Before They Go" hearty brunch you'll serve your guests before they leave after a fun weekend!

1 cup mashed potatoes
½ cup flour
2 tablespoons baking powder
2 beaten eggs
½ teaspoon salt
Pepper to taste

Combine all of the ingredients above. Form into pancake-size patties. Fry on both sides until golden brown. Serve for breakfast, lunch, or dinner.

❋ *Serves 2*

QUICK POTATOES À LA HELOISE

My mother concocted this one day to use up some juice from a canned ham. Since it requires cooked meat and canned potatoes, you can have all the ingredients ready the day before, and you can put them all together long before any guests arrive.

Juice from a canned ham (or beef or chicken bouillon
    cubes dissolved in water)
Salt and pepper to taste
About 1 tablespoon cornstarch or flour to thicken juice
1 can (2 to 3 servings) small whole potatoes, sliced
1 small onion, very thinly sliced
1 stalk thinly sliced celery (optional)
Leftover bits of meat (optional)
Grated cheese (any kind you like, including Parmesan)

To the ham juice or bouillon, add salt, pepper, and cornstarch (or flour) and stir. Slice canned potatoes with an egg slicer and layer them into an oven-proof casserole, alternating with onions (and celery and meat bits if you are using them) until the casserole is full. Pour juice over all; top with cheese and bake in 325°F oven until bubbly and hot.

Bonus Hint: If you'd rather have melty, soft, chewy cheese inside a casserole instead of browned cheese on top of it: Layer potatoes and onions (celery and meat bits if you use them) until the casserole is only half full. Then add a layer of grated cheese and continue to layer potatoes, etc., until the casserole is full. Bake until bubbly hot.

Leftover Potatoes and Onions Hint: If you have too many potatoes and onions for your casserole, save them, mash 'em or toss 'em into a blender or food processor for a few seconds, and make patties to fry with your next breakfast/brunch bacon or sausage.

PEKING DOUBLE-BAKED STUFFED POTATOES

Mother called these Peking potatoes and some folks call them stuffed potatoes. Whatever the name, they're terrific because you can make them ahead of time and refrigerate them until you're ready to reheat them!

Baking potatoes
Milk to moisten
Drop or two yellow food coloring
Bit of margarine
Salt and ground black pepper to taste
Grated cheese (your choice)
Grated raw onion

Optional ingredients for variety:
Parmesan cheese
Garlic juice or salt to taste
Chopped chives
Sliced tops of green onions
Pimientos

In conventional or microwave oven, bake potatoes until done. Cut each one in half, scoop out the center with a spoon, and place pulp in a mixing bowl. Mash while *dry*. (I use my beater for this, but a potato masher will do.) Add a little milk to moisten, yellow food coloring, margarine, salt and pepper.

Grate cheese and raw onion using coarsest holes of the grater or food processor. Add cheese and onion to mashed potatoes and stir well with a fork. Do *not* beat or use mixer or masher for this. Then fill each baked potato half shell with this mixture, place in a baking dish, cover with clear plastic wrap so that you can see what's inside, and freeze.

To serve, thaw and heat until thoroughly warm. After rebaking the potatoes and just before removing them from the oven, I like to sprinkle Parmesan cheese (or other cheese) on top and let it melt slightly, to a brown tinge.

If you like garlic, add the optional garlic juice or salt before filling the shell, or sprinkle the garlic on top before reheating the potatoes. Chopped chives, green onion tops, and pimientos are colorful garnishes for these delicious potatoes.

If you bake extra potatoes when you are oven-cooking a meal, you can use them for this recipe without heating up an oven just for one cooking project. And baking potatoes in the microwave will just take a few minutes, saving you time and energy.

 **Sauces**

JAMAICAN BARBECUE SAUCE

Mother got this recipe from a hotel chef in Jamaica, and it's so good it can be used on anything, not just meats.

1½ cups cider vinegar
4 teaspoons lemon juice
3 tablespoons Worcestershire sauce
2 teaspoons brown sugar
1 tablespoon prepared mustard
¾ teaspoon salt
½ teaspoon flavor enhancer
1 cup ketchup
1 tablespoon liquid smoke
1 teaspoon garlic powder
1 teaspoon cayenne pepper
½ cup tomato puree

Mix all ingredients together well. Pour into a quart jar, cover, and refrigerate until you're ready to use it. It keeps well several weeks in the refrigerator. Just heat and use when needed.

❊ *Yields 1¾ pints of sauce*

❊ ❀ ❊

STEAK SAUCE

This recipe from a budget-conscious reader tastes surprisingly good for being so simple to make.

1 cup Worcestershire sauce
1 cup tomato ketchup

Mix. Store in fridge. Use on any meats.

❀ **Sandwich Fixings** ❀

OLIVE NUT SANDWICH SPREAD

One of my favorites, this makes a great lunch when spread on a lettuce leaf (to save bread calories), and it can be a delicious make-ahead spread for party finger sandwiches.

6 ounces softened cream cheese (or low-cal)
½ cup mayonnaise (or diet mayo)
½ cup chopped pecans
1 cup sliced salad olives
2 tablespoons olive liquid from the jar
Dash pepper (But no salt!)

Mix all ingredients well. This spread will keep in the fridge for weeks.

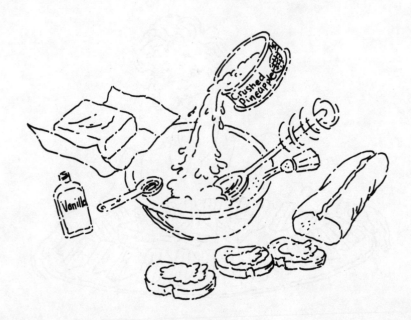

MOTHER'S PIMIENTO CHEESE SPREAD

Another of Mother's favorites, this recipe uses the cheapest kind of 2-pound boxed soft cheese. Use the other pound later.

1 pound boxed soft cheese
1 cup mayonnaise
4 ounces of the cheapest pimientos on your shelf
½ cup super-finely chopped sweet or sour pickles

For variations:
Juice from 1 jar of pimientos
4 ounces chopped salad olives
Chopped onions to taste

Grate the cheese coarsely. (Use the large openings of a grater or food processor.) Now the fun part—layer ingredients as if you are making lasagna. Place a large piece of wax paper or plastic wrap on the counter first, then start the process: Put down a layer of grated cheese, a layer of mayonnaise, a layer of pimientos, and a handful of pickles. Use a spatula to fold it over and over, starting from the bottom.

Repeat the process, folding again and again until you have used all of your ingredients. I divide this up into two batches. Put it in jars, seal well, and pop into the fridge.

If you want a thinner spread, add the juice from 1 jar of pimientos and mix well. Vary the spread by adding chopped, cheap salad olives and onions.

PINEAPPLE CREAM CHEESE SPREAD

The reader who sent me this recipe says it's better than an ice cream cone "if you want to lose yourself." Delicious!

8 ounces softened cream cheese
⅓ cup undrained crushed pineapple
1 teaspoon vanilla
Dash of salt
Sugar to taste (optional)

Mix all ingredients thoroughly and spread on fresh sourdough or French bread. I've never put it into an ice cream cone, but I suppose you could if you wanted to!

MEDITERRANEAN SANDWICHES/RAISIN TAPENADE

Source: California Raisin Advisory Board

½ cup pitted ripe olives
¼ cup golden raisins
1 clove garlic
2 tablespoons fresh chopped basil leaves or
    2 teaspoons dried basil
1 tablespoon drained capers
2 tablespoons olive oil
1 teaspoon red wine vinegar
¼ teaspoon pepper

Blend the olives, raisins, garlic, basil, and capers in a food processor bowl. Add olive oil, vinegar, and pepper; pulse to combine.

To make sandwiches:
4 large crusty sandwich rolls
4 lettuce leaves

½ pound sliced Jarlsberg or Swiss cheese
2 small tomatoes, sliced
½ cup drained, prepared, roasted red peppers

To make each sandwich, halve one roll horizontally; spread each cut side with 1 tablespoon Raisin Tapenade. Layer bottom half with 1 lettuce leaf, 2 ounces cheese, ½ sliced tomato, and 2 tablespoons red pepper. Cover with top of roll, cut-side down.

✽ *Makes 4 sandwiches*

HOT OPEN-FACED TOMATO AND CHEESE SANDWICH

This recipe came from a disabled reader who, because she lost the use of her left side, had to learn new and easier ways of one-handed cooking. It's a nice spur-of-the-moment lunch when your neighbor drops by.

Mixture of:
Sliced tomatoes, zucchini, onions, and ground beef
English muffins or bread slices
Mozzarella or cheddar cheese slices

Mix tomatoes, zucchini, onions, and ground beef, then cook mixture in microwave. (If you can't slice the veggies, you can easily "chop" them with a pizza cutter or some types of potato mashers after they are cooked.)

Divide mixture into single portions. Reserve one portion for the day's meal and pour the remainder into zipper-type freezer bags to freeze for other meals.

To serve, toast English muffin or bread slice; pour thawed tomato mixture on bread or muffin, top with cheese slice, and microwave until the cheese melts.

SAUSAGE BISCUITS

This is an easy recipe for breakfast biscuits or for serving at a brunch or cocktail party.

Refrigerated biscuits
1 pound ground pork (75–80 percent lean)
½ cup of your favorite barbecue sauce
Cheddar cheese, shredded

Press one biscuit into each cup of a muffin tin, forming a cup with the biscuit. Brown and drain pork, stir in barbecue sauce, spoon mixture into biscuit cups. (You could substitute lean pork sausage for the ground pork.) Top with some shredded cheddar cheese and bake at 375°F for about 20 minutes.

❀ Soups ❀

A soup course, even if you serve only about a cup of soup to each guest, gives you time to put those last-minute touches on the main course while the guests are busy sipping their soup. Don't be afraid to substitute ingredients in soups; most soups taste good because they are made so creatively!

NOTE: Traditionally, stock or broth for soup base is made by slow cooking beef, chicken, or fish bones with vegetables such as carrots, onions, and celery. The bones and solids are removed, the fat is skimmed off, and you have stock. However, so many people are so busy today that they don't have time to make homemade stock. Canned stocks and bouillon cubes are alternatives even if they make professional chefs and serious foodies "boil." If you are concerned about the salt content of bouillon or canned stocks, look for low-sodium ones at the market.

HOT SOUPS

EGG DROP CHICKEN SOUP

A very filling Chinese favorite

4½ cups water
4 chicken bouillon cubes
4 ounces cooked chicken, shredded
½ cup carrot, finely shredded
½ teaspoon dried parsley
1 teaspoon soy sauce
2 eggs, lightly beaten
4 teaspoons scallions, sliced

Dissolve chicken bouillon cubes in 4½ cups water in a large saucepan over medium heat. Add shredded chicken, carrot, parsley, and soy sauce and bring to a boil, stirring occasionally. Cook for 5 to 6 minutes, then slowly dribble lightly beaten eggs into the boiling soup, stirring constantly until the egg has cooked. Serve sprinkled with sliced scallions as a garnish.

CREAM SOUP (BASE)

You can cut calories and fat by cooking with nonfat, dried milk powder instead of whole milk.

1 cup nonfat dried milk powder
1 tablespoon dried onion flakes
2 tablespoons cornstarch
2 tablespoons chicken bouillon powder
½ teaspoon dried basil
½ teaspoon dried thyme
¼ teaspoon black pepper

Mix all ingredients and store in an airtight container. To make soup base, add 2 cups cold water to the mix in a large saucepan and stir constantly over medium heat until thick. You can use the base to make any flavor cream soup. Just add your main ingredient to the mix—mushrooms, for example—and cook for a few minutes longer.

If the soup is too thick, add more water and stir thoroughly, still over medium heat. You can add other seasonings if you like, too.

❀ *Makes 4–6 cups*

CREAMY CAULIFLOWER-CARROT SOUP

1 tablespoon cooking oil
1 cup chopped onions
1 pound carrots, peeled and diced
12 ounces cauliflower, broken into small pieces
4 chicken bouillon cubes
4 cups water
6 tablespoons nonfat dried milk

1 teaspoon cumin
Salt and pepper to taste
Dash ground nutmeg
1 scallion, finely chopped

In a large saucepan, heat the oil and add the chopped onion, carrots, and cauliflower pieces. Cover the pan and cook for 5 to 10 minutes, stirring at intervals. In a bowl or pan, dissolve the chicken bouillon cubes in 3 cups of water, then stir in 4 table-spoons nonfat dried milk. Pour this mixture over the vegetables and add 1 teaspoon of cumin and salt, a dash of nutmeg, and salt and pepper to taste. Cover and bring to a boil, then lower heat and simmer for 20 minutes or until vegetables are cooked.

Strain the vegetables and leave the liquid in the saucepan. Puree the cooked vegetables with ½ cup of the liquid and 2 tablespoons of nonfat dried milk until the consistency is smooth and even. Pour the pureed vegetable mixture back into the saucepan and stir in the finely minced scallion. Add a little water if the consistency is too thick, stir, reheat, and serve.

❋ *Serves 6*

HARVEST SQUASH SOUP

Any of the hard-shelled winter squashes, such as butternut, pumpkin, or acorn, or a mixture of different varieties, can go into this delicious soup. For extra flair, serve pumpkin soup in the pumpkin shell.

2 tablespoons cooking oil
1 large onion, chopped
¼ teaspoon thyme
¼ teaspoon mace
3 pounds winter squash, peeled and cut into chunks
1 pound new potatoes, peeled and cut into chunks
1 pound parsnips, peeled and cut into chunks
4 chicken bouillon cubes
4 cups water
1 teaspoon hot-pepper sauce
Salt and pepper to taste
Mace for garnish

Heat the oil in a large saucepan and add the onion, thyme, and mace. Cook, stirring frequently, for about 5 minutes, then add the squash, potatoes, and parsnips. Cook over medium heat for about 30 minutes, stirring occasionally, until the vegetables start to soften.

Mix 4 chicken bouillon cubes in 4 cups of water in a bowl or pan to make chicken broth. Pour broth over the vegetable mixture and add hot-pepper sauce and salt and pepper to taste. Bring to a boil, then cover, lower heat, and allow to simmer for another 30 minutes. The vegetable chunks should now be completely cooked.

Tip the mixture into a blender container a portion at a time, and puree until smooth. Use the bowl or pan used for mixing the broth to hold the soup until you have pureed all the vegetable mixture, then return the mixture to the saucepan and reheat. You can sprinkle each portion with a pinch of mace before serving.

✳ *Serves 8*

RED PEPPER SOUP

It's tasty and pretty, too!

4 cups water
4 chicken bouillon cubes
1 tablespoon cooking oil
4 cups onion, chopped
8 large sweet red peppers, seeded and chopped
1 tablespoon wine vinegar
Salt and pepper to taste
8 parsley sprigs

Dissolve the chicken bouillon cubes in 4 cups of water in a bowl or pan to make chicken stock. Heat the oil in a large saucepan, add the onion, and sauté for about 5 minutes, until translucent. Add the chicken broth and the red pepper and bring to a boil, stirring occasionally. Reduce heat, cover, and simmer for 15 to 20 minutes.

Pour the pepper mixture into a blender container a portion at a time and puree until smooth. Use the bowl or pan used to mix the broth to hold the soup until you have pureed all the mixture, then return the mixture to the saucepan and reheat over medium heat. Add 1 tablespoon wine vinegar and salt and pepper to taste. Stir thoroughly and make sure the soup is piping hot before serving. You can top each portion with a sprig of parsley before serving.

 Serves 8

SOUTHWESTERN VEGETABLE LENTIL SOUP

This soup's flavor is complete when served with corn bread.

1 tablespoon cooking oil
2 cups onions, chopped
½ cup celery, chopped
¾ cup parsnips, peeled and chopped
¾ cup carrots, peeled and chopped
6 cups water
½ pound dried lentils
4 vegetable bouillon cubes
1 teaspoon chili powder
1 teaspoon cumin
1 (14½-ounce) can whole tomatoes
1 teaspoon hot-pepper sauce
1 jalapeno pepper, seeded and sliced

Heat 1 tablespoon cooking oil in a large saucepan, add the onion, and sauté for about 5 minutes, until translucent. Add the celery, parsnips, and carrots, 6 cups of water, and ½ pound dried lentils, and crumble 4 vegetable bouillon cubes into the mix. Stir in the chili powder and cumin and bring to a boil, stirring frequently. Reduce heat, cover, and simmer for 30 minutes. Add the can of whole tomatoes, including the liquid, the hot-pepper sauce, and the sliced jalapeno pepper. Stir well and simmer for another 45 minutes or until the lentils are tender.

❀ *Serves 8*

MEXICAN MEATBALL SOUP

This south-of-the-border soup is tasty but low in fat!

½ pound lean ground beef
4 teaspoons parsley, chopped
½ teaspoon black pepper
1 clove garlic, minced
1 teaspoon oregano
5 tablespoons fresh cilantro, chopped
2 tablespoons long-grain rice
1 egg white
6 cups water
6 beef bouillon cubes
2 teaspoons light cooking oil
1 medium onion, finely chopped
1 cup tomatoes, peeled and diced
2 cups celery, diced
4 cups carrots, peeled and sliced
1 cup fresh or frozen corn

Mix the beef, parsley, pepper, garlic, oregano, 1 teaspoon of cilantro, rice, and egg white, and form into small meatballs, no larger than 1 inch in diameter.

Dissolve the beef bouillon cubes in 6 cups of water in a bowl or pan to make beef broth and set aside. Heat the oil in a large saucepan and add the onion. When cooked, add the tomatoes, celery, carrots, and stock. Bring to a boil and drop in meatballs. Reduce heat and add the fresh or frozen corn, then simmer gently for 25 to 30 minutes. Stir in 4 tablespoons chopped cilantro just before serving.

❀ *Serves 8*

BEEF MINESTRONE

Served with crusty bread, this soup will feed a houseful of hungry people at a weekend lunch or supper, and it won't take hours to prepare.

1 teaspoon cooking oil
½ cup onions, minced
¾ pound lean ground beef
2 cloves garlic, minced
½ pound fresh green beans, sliced
2 (14½-ounce) cans whole tomatoes
4 cups water
4 beef bouillon cubes

2 cups cabbage, shredded
1 cup zucchini, diced
½ cup carrots, peeled and diced
2 (8-ounce) cans cannellini beans
4 ounces vermicelli, uncooked
Salt and pepper to taste
Parmesan cheese

Heat the teaspoon of cooking oil in a large saucepan and add the onions, ground beef, and garlic. Cook until the meat is browned, stirring frequently. Remove from heat and drain, then blot up any remaining fat in the pan with paper towels.

Add the fresh green beans, which should be sliced into 1-inch pieces, and the tomatoes, including liquid. Dissolve the bouillon cubes in 4 cups of water and pour into the mixture. Stir thoroughly and bring to a boil. Reduce heat, cover, and simmer for 15 minutes.

Now add the cabbage, zucchini, and carrots. Drain the cannellini beans (these are white kidney beans) and add to the mixture together with the vermicelli, broken into 1- to 2-inch pieces. Season with salt and ground black pepper to taste.

Bring back to boil, reduce heat, and simmer until the vermicelli is cooked (test with a fork), about 15 to 20 minutes. Sprinkle Parmesan cheese on top of each serving.

❋ *Serves 8–12*

MATZO BALLS

These dumplings for chicken soup are traditionally served at Passover but can be served at any other time, too. From Mrs. Solomon J. Jacobson, San Antonio, TX.

2 eggs
1 cup boiling water
2 tablespoons shortening (chicken fat is preferred for its flavor)
Salt and pepper to taste
1 cup matzo meal

Beat eggs lightly. Add water, shortening, salt, and pepper. Mix in matzo meal. Refrigerate several hours or overnight. Shape into balls and drop into a large pot of boiling water. Keep you hands moist while forming the balls to prevent the dough from sticking. Cover pot and boil for about 20 minutes. Do not uncover pot during this time. The balls will have puffed up while boiling. Remove them from the water and put them into the Chicken Soup, recipe above.

CHICKEN SOUP

This Jewish "comfort food" may not actually cure your cold, but it will certainly make you feel better. From The Melting Pot: Ethnic Cuisine in Texas

1 slice breast of beef flanken (flank)
1 beef knee bone, split
Small bunch of fresh curly parsley, tied with a thread
1 chicken (about 4½ pounds) and giblets, quartered, with
    wings and legs disjointed
4 stalks celery, leaves and all, cut into halves and scraped
1 knob celery, pared and quartered
1 large petrushka (root parsley) with leaves, pared and
    washed well
4 large carrots, scraped and cut in half lengthwise
2 large onions, quartered
Chopped fresh dill
Salt
White pepper

Place flanken and bone in a 2-quart saucepan and cover with salted water. Boil uncovered for 10 minutes and remove from range. Strain in a colander and rinse with cold running water. Set remains aside on paper towel. Put parsley in a container covered with cold water and refrigerate. Place chicken, giblets, flanken, bone, and all vegetables except curly parsley into a 6-quart sauce-pan. Fill with water and bring meat and vegetables to a boil, lower heat, and simmer covered for 1 hour, then add salt and white pepper. Drain parsley and add it to the soup. Cook, covered, until done.

NOTE: Can be served with Matzo Balls recipe on page 267, also from *The Melting Pot: Ethnic Cuisine in Texas.*

COLD SOUPS

Super starters for summer meals, and easy to prepare!

GAZPACHO

3 cups tomatoes, peeled, seeded, and chopped
1½ cups tomato juice
1 cup cucumber, peeled, seeded, and chopped
½ cup green bell pepper, seeded and chopped
½ cup onions, chopped
1 (4-ounce) can diced green chilies, drained
1 clove garlic, minced
2 tablespoons balsamic vinegar
¼ teaspoon hot-pepper sauce
Salt and pepper to taste
6 small sprigs mint

Mix tomatoes, tomato juice, cucumber, bell pepper, onions, green chilies, and garlic in a large bowl. Transfer portion by portion to a blender container and blend until smooth, pouring the pureed portions into another bowl until all the mixture has been processed. Stir in 2 tablespoons balsamic vinegar, ½ teaspoon hot-pepper sauce, and season with salt and pepper to taste.

Cover and chill well, for at least 2 to 3 hours. Serve in individual bowls with a sprig of mint on top of each to garnish.

✳ *Serves 6*

FRESH TOMATO AND BASIL SOUP

I've collected hundreds of recipes for tomato soup, and I'm working my way through trying them all. This one is delish!

3 cups water
3 vegetable bouillon cubes
2 pounds tomatoes, peeled and sliced
3 cloves garlic, sliced in half
3 fresh basil leaves
4 tablespoons parsley, finely chopped
1 tablespoon virgin or extra virgin olive oil
Salt and pepper to taste
4 to 6 parsley sprigs

Dissolve vegetable bouillon cubes in 3 cups water in a bowl or pan to make vegetable stock. Pour a little stock into a large saucepan and add tomatoes, garlic, basil, and parsley. Cook over medium heat, stirring frequently, until garlic is cooked through, then remove and discard all but 2 half cloves. Pour the tomato mixture into the blender container and puree on medium speed until the consistency is smooth.

Return the puree to the saucepan and add the remaining vegetable stock and 1 tablespoon of virgin or extra virgin olive oil. Stir throughly and simmer gently until the soup has reduced a little in volume and thickened. Season with salt and pepper to taste, cover, and chill for 2 to 3 hours. Before serving, garnish each bowl with a sprig of parsley.

NOTE: You can also serve this soup hot. It's extra delicious served with a few "fingers" of whole-wheat toast floating on top of each portion.

❀ *Serves 4–6*

AVOCADO SOUP

If you like guacamole, you'll love this soup!

2 medium avocados	2 cups water
2 cups light sour cream	2 chicken bouillon cubes
2 teaspoons lemon juice	6 small mint sprigs
½ teaspoon hot-pepper	
sauce	

Peel the avocados, remove the pits, and slice. Put the slices in a blender container with the sour cream, lemon juice, hot-pepper sauce and water; crumble the bouillon cubes on top. Blend on medium speed until smooth and evenly colored. Pour into bowls and chill in the refrigerator for 2 hours. Garnish with mint springs before serving.

❀ *Serves 6*

DOUBLE BERRY SOUP

Cool fruit soups can be a first course or dessert. Some versions of this recipe add blueberries to the mix; a West Coast variation includes kiwi fruit. Choose your fruits for this soup by what is in season for best taste and economy.

1 cup orange juice, unsweetened
2 cups cranberry-raspberry drink
1½ cups water
½ orange rind, cut into quarters
2 tablespoons cornstarch
3 tablespoons water
2 cups fresh raspberries
2 cups fresh strawberries, sliced
¼ cup strawberry or raspberry schnapps (optional)
6 small mint sprigs

Mix the orange juice, cranberry-raspberry drink, and water in a large saucepan (not aluminum) and add the orange rind (first remove as much of the white pith as possible). Bring the mixture to a boil and simmer for 2 to 3 minutes.

Thoroughly mix the 2 tablespoons of cornstarch with 3 tablespoons of water in a cup and slowly stir this into the juice mixture. Keep the saucepan over the heat and stir constantly until the mixture is clear and thickened. Remove from the heat; take out and discard the orange rind.

Add the sliced strawberries and raspberries, and the schnapps if you are including it, and stir thoroughly. Pour into a bowl, cover, and chill for at least 2 to 3 hours before serving. Garnish with mint sprigs.

❀ *Serves 6*

❀ **Sweets** ❀

CANDIES

BUTTERMILK PECAN PRALINES

I use a 6- to 8-quart pot for this because the mixture foams to great heights while cooking.

1 cup buttermilk
2 cups sugar
1 teaspoon baking soda
1 tablespoon butter or margarine
1 teaspoon of vanilla
2 cups pecan halves

Pour buttermilk into the pot and stir in sugar and baking soda until dissolved. Cook mixture over medium heat, letting it bubble until it turns brownish in color and reaches soft ball stage (235°F) on a candy thermometer. If you don't have a candy thermometer, test the candy by dropping a small amount into cool water and working with it to see if it forms a soft ball. While cooking the mixture, you will need to stir it constantly so it won't stick.

At the soft ball stage, remove the pot from the heat and add butter or margarine, vanilla, and pecan halves. Return to stove and heat the mixture until it becomes glossy and starts to crystallize. On wax paper or a greased baking sheet, quickly spoon out the candy into little patties about 2 inches in circumference. (You can decorate each patty by placing a pecan half on it while it's still warm.)

Let them cool and store in an airtight container. If the candy starts to turn sugary and hardens too fast, return the pot to the heat for a few minutes, then spoon it out again.

NOTE: The cooking stages are crucial to the outcome of this candy. Overcooked, it's very sugary; undercooked, it won't be firm. That's why a candy thermometer is so important. It takes the guesswork out of candy making.

LONE STAR CANEFEST PRALINES

I got this recipe from my friends at Imperial Sugar, in Texas, during the Lone Star State's 1986 sesquicentennial. It's slightly different from my other praline recipe.

2 cups granulated sugar
1 teaspoon baking soda
1 cup buttermilk
⅛ teaspoon salt
2 tablespoons butter or margarine
2½ cups pecan halves

273

In a large (3½-quart), heavy saucepan, combine sugar, baking soda, buttermilk, and salt. Cook over high heat about 5 minutes or to 210°F on a candy thermometer. Stir often and scrape the bottom of the pot. The mixture will foam up; then add butter or margarine and pecans.

Over medium heat, continue cooking, stirring constantly and scraping bottom and sides of the pot until the candy reaches soft ball stage (234°F) on a candy thermometer. Remove from heat and cool slightly, about 2 minutes. Beat with a spoon until thick and creamy. Drop from a tablespoon onto a sheet of aluminum foil or wax paper. Let cool. Enjoy!

❀ *Makes 20 (2-inch) pralines*

SHORTCUT MAPLE NUT CANDY

While nothing replaces sugary smooth buttermilk pralines, this recipe is a tasty substitute and is a good way to use up leftover ready-made frosting.

1 tub ready-made vanilla frosting
¾ teaspoon maple flavoring
½ cup toasted chopped pecans

Heat vanilla frosting and maple flavoring in a 2-quart saucepan until thin. Stir in pecans. Drop mixture by level teaspoonfuls onto a wax paper–covered baking sheet. Refrigerate until set, about 4 hours. Store candy in the refrigerator.

❀ *Makes about 6 dozen candies*

HELOISE FUDGE

You can't control calories with this treat, but one piece is worth squandering a few extra ones. Be sure to read the entire recipe and directions *before starting on this sinful fudge.*

4½ cups granulated sugar
1 (12-ounce) can evaporated milk
3 (6-ounce) packages semi-sweet chocolate chips
1 (10-ounce) package miniature marshmallows
½ cup butter or margarine
1 teaspoon vanilla
2 cups chopped nuts

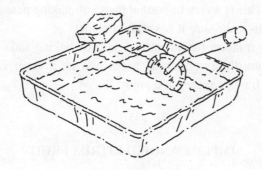

Mix sugar and evaporated milk in a large, heavy saucepan and *slowly* bring the mixture to a rolling boil (takes about 10 to 15 minutes) and then let it boil for exactly 8 minutes while constantly stirring. This is a slow but *important* process.

Remove the saucepan from the heat and immediately add the chocolate chips, marshmallows and butter (all at one time, not in stages). Mix only until the chips and marshmallows are completely melted. Add the vanilla and nuts, then blend.

Spread the mixture in a large (13 × 9 × 2) ungreased pan; allow to cool and then cut into bite-sized pieces. This fudge is best stored in the fridge—that way it doesn't disappear as soon as it's cool enough to eat!

LILLIAN'S EASY PEANUT BRITTLE

This recipe in response to a reader's request came from my secretary's grandmother, Lillian R. Graves.

1 cup sugar
1 cup light corn syrup
2 cups raw shelled peanuts
1 teaspoon baking soda
Pinch of salt

Bring sugar and corn syrup to a boil and add raw shelled peanuts. Stir constantly and cook until mixture turns light brown in color.

NOTE: This is a very important phase of making peanut brittle. You want to make sure it has a good color!

Remove mixture from heat and add the baking soda and salt. Pour mixture thinly onto wax paper and let it cool. Then, just break into bit-size pieces and enjoy.

SIMPLE CANDIED CITRUS FRUIT

This delicious Christmas treat can be enjoyed the year round, too. It keeps indefinitely in the fridge.

Peels of 4 lemons, 4 oranges, 4 grapefruits
1 cup water
¼ cup corn syrup
2 cups sugar

Wash and dice the peels of lemons, oranges, and grapefruits as you collect them; freeze them in freezer-safe containers. When you have peels of 4 of each of the fruits, you can start.

Slowly bring to boil water, corn syrup, and sugar and then simmer for 30 minutes over low heat. Then add peels and cook for 55 minutes to 1 hour until all the syrup has been absorbed.

Lay out a large piece of wax paper and sprinkle it liberally with sugar. Put the candied peel on the wax paper and toss so the peels will be covered. Let it sit for a day or two to dry. Store in refrigerator.

LORRAINE'S NO-BAKE FUDGE COOKIES

2 cups sugar
½ cup butter
Pinch of salt
½ cup milk
4 tablespoons cocoa

Mix all ingredients in saucepan; bring to boil and then boil together for 1 minute. Remove from burner and add:

½ cup peanut butter
2 cups oatmeal (uncooked)
1 teaspoon vanilla
½ cup nutmeats

Stir well and drop by teaspoons onto wax paper–covered cookie sheets. Let cool. Store in tins.

LORRAINE'S NO-BAKE CHOCOLATE "SANDWICHES"

1. Spread Ritz crackers with peanut butter; place a second cracker on top for a "sandwich."

2. Melt either white (almond bark) chocolate or chocolate chips in the top of a double boiler.

3. Dip "sandwiches" in the melted chocolate, holding them with tongs.

NOTE: You can also place them on a metal-grate potato masher for dipping.

4. Place "sandwiches" on wax paper–lined cookie sheets to allow chocolate to harden. You can place the sheets in the fridge to harden them faster if you wish. Store in a tin—if there are any left after they are sampled.

HOLIDAY COOKIES

Many families have a tradition in which they make cookies together on holidays, and it's a source of many fond memories. You'll find cookie cutters of all shapes and motifs wherever cookware is sold and also in some craft shops. You'll also find many frosting or candy decorating ideas for Hanukkah, Valentine's Day, Easter, Thanksgiving, and other festive occasions. If you think cutting with cookie cutters is too messy, consider getting a cookie press or cookie gun, or bake cookie recipes you can form into a log and just slice before decorating or baking as is.

SNOWBALL COOKIES

Now you can have snowballs any time of the year!

1 cup butter or margarine, softened
1 cup powdered sugar, sifted
2 cups flour, sifted
2 teaspoons vanilla
¼ teaspoon salt
2 cups chopped pecans

Combine butter or margarine and ½ cup sugar in a large bowl, blending on medium speed until fluffy. Mix in flour and remaining ingredients. Chill dough in refrigerator until firm enough to work with. Roll spoon-size portions of the mixture into balls and place on a greased cookie sheet approximately 2 inches apart.

Bake at 350°F for 15 to 18 minutes or until golden brown. Remove from oven and roll baked cookies in remaining powdered sugar. Allow to cool, then roll once again in sugar.

❋ *Makes 30 or more cookies*

BONUS COOKIE HINT: When you roll cookie dough, substitute powdered sugar for flour on your board. It will make your cookies a wee bit sweeter, but they will not get tough as they sometimes do when they are rolled out on a floured board.

NOTE: This may be an extra helpful hint when children are rolling cookie dough, because they tend to process the dough over and over, which makes it tougher.

CANDY CANE COOKIES

1 cup butter
1 cup powdered sugar

1 egg
1 teaspoon vanilla
2½ cups flour
Red food coloring
1 package candy canes, crushed into small pieces

In a large bowl, mix together butter, powdered sugar, egg, and vanilla. Then stir in the flour to make dough. Divide the dough in half and add a few drops of red food coloring to one half and mix well. Take 1 teaspoon of each dough and roll into strips about 4 inches long and ¼-inch thick. Twist the strips around each other and form into candy-cane shapes on an ungreased cookie sheet.

Bake in a 350°F oven for 15 to 20 minutes. Remove from oven. While cookies are still warm, sprinkle crushed candy-cane topping on each cookie.

✽ *Makes 24 cookies*

HELOISE DUSTY RICOTTA

Substitute cocoa or carob powder for the espresso and make it wonderfully triple-chocolate.

1 pound ricotta cheese
½ cup powdered sugar (or sugar substitute to equal ½ cup)
2 tablespoons rum or substitute brandy (or ¼ tablespoon
    rum or brandy extract)
1 or 2 tablespoons instant espresso (and/or 1 tablespoon
    cocoa or carob powder)

Mix ricotta, sugar, rum (or brandy), and espresso and/or cocoa (or carob powder) in a bowl. Whisk until thoroughly blended. Put into small serving bowls or pretty sherbet glasses. Chill well. Dust with dash of instant espresso and cocoa just before serving.

ENGLISH TEA "BISCUITS"

In England, a small cake is called a biscuit. I found this tea cake recipe to help a reader who was hungry for them.

1 cup sugar
2 eggs
1½ cups milk
1 heaping teaspoon baking powder
¼ cup butter
Flour to make a stiff batter
1 pint of fresh fruit or berries (optional)

Combine ingredients and, if you wish, stir in a pint of fresh fruit or berries (drained). Bake at 400°F until golden brown and serve while warm with afternoon tea.

ELEPHANT EARS

You don't need the memory of an elephant for this tasty treat that's easy to make for a brunch. Enjoy, and don't even think about calories!

½ cup cinnamon
1 cup white sugar
1 can cinnamon buns (found in the dairy case)

Preheat oven to 375°F. Mix cinnamon and sugar together and spread mixture evenly on a sheet of foil or wax paper. Remove cinnamon buns from the can one at a time and lay them on the sugar and cinnamon mixture. Using a rolling pin, roll each of the cinnamon buns out thin, turning it often so it absorbs as much sugar and cinnamon as possible. The diameter should be 6 to 8 inches when you finish. Place on foil-lined cookie sheets (only 3 "ears" may fit on a cookie sheet) and bake in a hot oven on the center rack or as close to the center as possible. Check often so they don't scorch or overbake—they are very thin.

EASIEST-EVER DELICIOUS DOUGHNUTS

The store brand is just as good and more economical than name brands for this quick and very easy treat for a coffee break party, a brunch, or a late-night snack.

Oil for deep frying
Canned refrigerator biscuits
Powdered sugar or sugar-cinnamon mixture

Heat cooking oil—enough to cover. Shape or cut the biscuits into doughnut shapes or just break them in half and shape them into balls so they'll be "doughnut holes." Drop them into hot oil and cook until golden brown. Don't cook them too fast or you'll have a doughy, gooey center.

Drain on a paper towel and roll in powdered sugar or cinnamon and sugar. If you use granulated sugar, you can save mess by dropping the doughnuts into a brown paper bag containing the sugar. Shake and let cool slightly on paper towels. These taste best when still warm.

FUNNEL CAKES

They'll melt in your mouth and are best if eaten while still warm.

Oil for deep frying
2 eggs
1½ cups milk
2 cups flour
1 teaspoon baking powder
½ teaspoon salt
Powdered sugar to dredge cakes or sprinkle on top after
    baking

A deep fryer is best, but if you don't have one, use a heavy, deep pan. Pour oil to a depth of 2 inches and let it get very hot, but not so overheated that it smokes or burns.

After you mix the batter, pour it through a funnel into the hot oil, moving it in a circular motion, then in a crisscross one, until you have made a cake about the size of a large doughnut. The little cakes cook quickly, so watch them carefully.

When lightly browned, remove them from the oil and drain on paper towels. While hot, dredge them in the powdered sugar, or if you prefer, sprinkle it over the tops of the cakes. (You can use a large-holed kitchen saltshaker or shake the sugar through a sieve.)

COLD OVEN CAKE

Many readers shared this recipe with me. It gets its name from being started in a cold oven, then baked as usual.

¼ pound (1 stick) butter or margarine
1 cup shortening
3 cups sugar
5 eggs
3¾ cups flour
¼ teaspoon salt
½ teaspoon baking powder
1 teaspoon vanilla
1 teaspoon lemon extract
1 cup, plus 1 tablespoon milk

Cream butter, shortening, and sugar. Add eggs, one at time, beating well. Sift dry ingredients and add to creamed mixture. Fold in vanilla, lemon extract, and milk.

Pour batter into greased and floured tube pan and place in a *cold* oven. Turn oven on to 325°F and bake for approximately 1½ to 2 hours.

The basic ingredients for this cake are those of a pound cake, and recipes sent to me used a variety of flavorings (rum, butter, butternut, coconut) which you could substitute for the lemon flavoring according to your own taste.

WAR CAKE

This old recipe was developed around 1918 during World War I to compensate for shortages of milk, butter and eggs— it's milkless, butterless and eggless. What a treat for someone allergic to dairy products or eggs! And one of the best parts of this dark, heavy cake is that you mix it all in one pan—no fuss and hardly anything to wash.

2 cups brown sugar
2 cups hot water
2 teaspoons shortening
½ to ¾ cup raisins
1 teaspoon each of salt, cinnamon, and cloves
3 cups flour
1 teaspoon baking soda, dissolved in hot water
Couple of teaspoons hot water for dissolving baking soda

Mix brown sugar, 2 cups of hot water, and shortening in a medium-size saucepan. Add raisins and salt, cinnamon, and cloves. Mix and boil for 5 minutes after it first bubbles. Remove from stove. Let cool completely (very important!).

After cooling, add flour and baking soda. Mix well. Pour into a greased tube pan and bake for 1 hour at 350°F to 375°F.

FRIENDSHIP CAKE AND BRANDIED FRUIT STARTER

My thanks to Grandma Lant for sharing the cake recipe with me and starting me on the search for the starter, which is a brandied fruit recipe. I found it at an electric company's Home Service Department. This is indeed a recipe for someone who likes to "play" in the kitchen.

Starter (Brandied Fruit) Recipe:

Step One:
1 cup cubed canned pineapple
1 cup sugar
2 tablespoons brandy

Combine the above ingredients in a 1-gallon jar and let them sit for 2 weeks, stirring daily.

Step Two:

After 2 weeks, add the following and let sit another 2 weeks, stirring daily:

1 cup maraschino cherries and juice from cherries
1 cup sugar
2 tablespoons brandy

Step Three:

On the fourth week, add the following and allow mixture to sit 2 more weeks, stirring daily:

1 cup sliced, canned peaches and juice from peaches
1 cup sugar
2 tablespoons brandy

Step Four:

Separate the liquid from the fruit. The liquid is your starter, and you can use the fruit on ice cream or cake. Do *not* refrigerate the starter liquid.

Step Five:

To prepare fruit for the cakes, put the following into a 1-gallon jar or container:

1½ cups starter
2½ cups sugar
1 (28-ounce) can sliced peaches

Mix well and cover the jar with a paper towel. Do not refrigerate jar or screw a lid on it. Stir *every day* for 10 days.

Step Six:

Add the following ingredients, let sit, and stir daily for 10 days:

2½ cups sugar
1 (16-ounce) can crushed pineapple

Step Seven:

Add the following ingredients and stir daily for 10 days:

2½ cups sugar
1 (16-ounce) can fruit cocktail
1 (10-ounce) jar of maraschino cherries, sliced, and juice

Step Eight:

On baking day, drain the fruit and divide it into 4 equal parts. Save the juice and use it for starter for friends who want to make this treat. You'll have enough for 5 two-cup starters. You can save this fruit mixture by refrigerating the remaining part, but we recommend using it as soon as possible. Do not refrigerate the liquid, because it will stop the fermenting action and you want to give this starter to friends for their cakes.

For the cake:
1 box cake mix
1 small box instant pudding mix
⅜ cup cooking oil
4 eggs
1 cup chopped nuts
1 portion (2 cups) brandied fruit starter

To each cake mix, add the pudding mix, oil, and eggs. Beat until smooth. Fold in nuts and fruit starter. The batter will be thick. Pour mixture into a greased tube pan, then bake at 350°F for 50 to 60 minutes. Turn out while hot.

The cake freezes very well. The choice of which flavored cake mixes and pudding mixes to use is yours. You can use white or yellow or fruit-flavored cake mixes as well as any of the fruit-flavored pudding mixes. Coconut may be substituted for the nuts.

NO-MIX CHERRY-PINEAPPLE NUT CAKE

This is the easiest cake recipe I've ever seen for the holidays or any other time when you have too little time. You make it in the pan—no messy mixing bowls! I have also seen this recipe called the Better Than Sex Cake.

1 (20-ounce) can of crushed pineapple in heavy syrup
1 (21-ounce) can of cherry pie filling
1 package (2-layer size) yellow cake mix
1 (3-ounce) can pecans (1 cup), chopped
½ cup (1 stick) butter or margarine

Preheat oven to 350°F. Grease a 9- by 13-inch baking pan. Spread pineapple with its syrup evenly in the pan. Spoon pie filling evenly over pineapple. Sprinkle dry cake mix evenly over mixture, then the chopped nuts over all. Slice the chilled butter or margarine in thin slices, then put strips evenly over other ingredients. Bake for 50 minutes or until golden. Serve warm.

❋ *Makes 12 servings*

ICE CREAM TRICKS AND TOPPINGS

If you keep ice cream on hand, you have instant easy dessert because you can serve it plain as is, with or without cake, with or without toppings. It always pleases and will look elegant served in crystal stemware. While vanilla or chocolate ice creams will be good with most toppings, experiment with other combinations of ice creams and sherbets. For example, orange sherbet with orange liqueur drizzled on top; cherry ice cream with chocolate sauce; or lemon sherbet with strawberries on top.

Chocolate Cherry: Mix maraschino cherries with chocolate ice cream.

Crunch Toppings: Sprinkle ice cream with crushed peppermint candies, peanut brittle, bits of sweet chocolate, flaked coconut, chopped nuts, or crunchy cereal.

Fruity Frappé: Add unsweetened, flavored powdered drink mix to vanilla ice cream, mix well, and you'll have a fruity frappé. The amount of powder to add depends on the amount of the ice cream to be flavored. Usually, it's about ½ teaspoon powder to 1 average portion of ice cream.

NOTE: Unsweetened mix works best for this recipe because it doesn't make the ice cream too sweet.

Fruity Topping: Top ice cream with sliced peaches, strawberries, blueberries, or other in-season fruit.

Gelatin Confetti: Make a pan of fruit gelatin about 1-inch thick, and after it's jelled, cut it into cube shapes and serve with ice cream for a confetti-looking dessert.

Liquor Topping: Drizzle crème de menthe, coffee-flavored, chocolate, apricot, or other fruit-flavored liqueurs over ice cream served plain or on a piece of angel food or pound cake.

Maple or Fruit Syrup: Heat maple or fruit-flavored syrup and drizzle it on ice cream.

Pineapple-Marshmallow Treat: Spoon canned, crushed pineapple on ice cream and top with melted marshmallows.

Swirls: Instead of drizzling toppings on the ice cream, swirl hot fudge, butterscotch, or other syrups through the ice cream with a twist of a table knife or spoon.

HEALTHY PIE CRUST

Source: University of Texas Lifetime Health Letter

1½ cups sifted flour
½ teaspoon salt
1 teaspoon vanilla extract
⅓ cup canola oil
¼ cup (or less) ice water

Combine all ingredients except water with a fork, pastry blender, or in a food processor with a steel blade. Add enough water to work mixture into a ball. Refrigerate for 1 hour or more before rolling out on a well-floured board. Place in a 9-inch pie tin; trim the edges and flute the crust. If you need a baked shell, prick with a fork and bake for 10 to 15 minutes at 425°F.

JELLIES

Homemade jellies are good gifts for people who have everything, and they are comfort foods, too, because they say "I cared enough to use my time making something for you!"

MY FAVORITE LOW-CAL GRAPE JELLY

You can substitute any flavor juice, just as long as it's unsweetened, so that you can save those calories. Try serving this recipe at brunch or coffee time with biscuits.

2 cups unsweetened grape juice
1 cup water
½ cup tapioca
Artificial sweetener equal to 3 cups sugar

Mix grape juice, water, tapioca, and artificial sweetener in pot. Allow ingredients to sit for 5 minutes, to allow tapioca to soften. Bring mixture to boil, and boil for 1 minute. Skim off any foam, pour into sterilized jars, and seal.

APPLE JELLY

A reader who cooks for a diabetic husband came up with this recipe. It still has natural sugar in it, so diabetics must be sure to figure this into the carbo/calorie count of their special diets.

1 quart apple juice
4 tablespoons artificial sweetener
2 tablespoons lemon juice
2 packages unflavored gelatin

Mix all ingredients in pot and boil gently for 5 minutes. Let cool, pour into containers, and refrigerate.

❀ **Substitute Recipes** ❀

Even the best planning can go awry and leave you with missing ingredients on party day. If you have no time to run to the store, substitute! Sometimes your substitutions of homemade spice mixes will be tastier than store-bought ones.

SWEETENED CONDENSED MILK

This recipe is quick and easy.

1 cup powdered milk
⅓ cup boiling water
⅔ cup granulated sugar
3 tablespoons butter

Mix together milk, water, sugar and butter in a blender until smooth. This recipe is equal to 1 can of sweetened condensed milk.

NO-SALT SPICE SUBSTITUTE

This salt substitute will help you avoid salt in your diet and still enjoy flavorful foods. Use it on meats or vegetables. Please note that it uses onion and garlic powders, not salts.

5 teaspoons onion powder
1 tablespoon garlic powder
1 tablespoon paprika
1 tablespoon dry mustard
1 teaspoon thyme
½ teaspoon white pepper
½ teaspoon celery seeds

Mix all ingredients and store in a tightly covered container in a cool, dark place. Never store spices near the stove, even if it is convenient—they lose their zip.

SEASONED SALT WITH SALT

This substitutes for commercial seasoning salts. Aside from saving money, making your own spice mixtures lets you add spices you like and leave out those you don't like.

1 cup salt
2 tablespoons onion powder
1 teaspoon garlic powder
1 tablespoon celery seed, well ground
2 teaspoons paprika
1 teaspoon chili powder
½ teaspoon cayenne pepper
1 teaspoon dried parsley flakes, well ground

Mix all ingredients together well. Store in any jar with a lid. You can use a saltshaker for table use.

"PRIVATE BLEND" HERB COMBINATIONS

Make these as gifts or for your own kitchen use, from dried garden herbs or from store-bought ones.

NOTE AND CAUTION: When you cook herb-flavored dishes and include bay leaf or whole peppers, put them in a mesh or perforated metal tea ball so that they can be removed easily, to prevent anyone from biting into a pepper ball or choking on a piece of bay leaf.

The following herb combinations are mixed in equal parts except when noted in parentheses.

Barbecue Blend: Cumin, garlic powder/salt, hot pepper, oregano.

Bouquet Garni: Bay leaf, parsley (2 parts), and thyme. Herbs may be wrapped in cheesecloth, or you can wrap the parsley around the thyme and bay leaf.

Homemade "Fines Herbes": Parsley, chervil, chives, French tarragon. (You can also add a small amount of basil, fennel, oregano, sage or saffron.)

Egg Blend: Basil, dill weed (leaves), garlic, parsley.

Fish Blend: Basil, bay leaf (crumbled), French tarragon, lemon, thyme, parsley. (Options include fennel, sage, or savory.)

Italian Blend: Basil, marjoram, oregano, rosemary, sage, savory, thyme.

Poultry Blend: Lovage, marjoram (2 parts), sage (3 parts).

Tomato Sauce Blend: Basil (2 parts), bay leaf, marjoram, oregano, parsley. (Options are cloves or dried celery leaves.)

Salad Herbs: Basil, lovage, parsley, French tarragon.

Veggie Blend (Enhances Vegetable Flavors): Basil, parsley, savory.

NOTE: If you like the taste of garlic but don't like to eat the cloves, try sticking a toothpick through the garlic bud before adding it to food or sauces. Then you can easily remove it before serving.

NOTE: If you have a garden or garden in containers, plant garlic buds and then cook with the chives that will sprout from them. The chives can be cut several times before the clove quits producing. The bonus is that these garlic chives when grown outdoors in flower beds form a border and are said to discourage aphids in roses.

❀ Miscellaneous ❀ Party Recipes

FESTIVE TRI-COLOR POPCORN

Make this recipe for gifts or for parties.

24 cups popped popcorn
¾ cup butter or margarine
9 tablespoons light corn syrup
1½ cups packed light brown or granulated sugar
3 packages (4-serving size) gelatin in different colors

Place 8 cups of popcorn in large bowl. Heat ¼ cup butter or margarine and 3 tablespoons syrup in a small saucepan over low heat. Stir in ½ cup sugar and 1 package gelatin; bring to a boil over medium heat, then lower heat and gently simmer for 5 minutes. Pour syrup immediately over popcorn; toss to coat well. Preheat the oven to 300°F. Spread the coated popcorn on a shallow, foil-lined baking tray (15 by 10 inches), using two forks to make an even layer, and bake for 10 minutes. Allow to cool, remove from tray, and break into small pieces.

Repeat this twice more, using the different gelatin flavors (for example, cherry, lemon, and lime). Make layers using half of each color in two 3-quart bowls. If this is too much to use at once, serve only one bowl and save the remainder for another time.

❀ *Makes 6 quarts*

POPCORN VARIATIONS

Popcorn Edible Cups: Instead of paper party treat containers, make edible party cups to fill with nuts or small candies. Make a recipe of popcorn ball using a mix sold for that purpose, and instead of forming balls, shape popcorn ball mix over the bottoms and sides of glasses that have been well greased with margarine. After the mixture hardens, remove the "cups" from the glasses and fill.

Gourmet Flavored Popcorn: Sprinkle popcorn with seasoned salts, salt-free herb blends, dry salad-dressing mixes, taco or chili seasoning mixes, or grated hard cheses, such as Parmesan, Romano, and/or cheddar. You can take the powdered cheddar from macaroni-and-cheese dinners for this if you can't find powdered cheddar. Save the noodles for a casserole.

Tooth Saver Hint:

Put popcorn into resealable plastic bags after it's cooled. Cut a small hole in the corner of the bag and give the whole thing a good shake so that unpopped kernels fall out of the hole.

CAUTION: Never substitute brown paper bags for commercial microwave popcorn packs. They can catch fire! Either buy a microwave-safe popcorn popper or pop-in-the-bag commercial popcorn designed for microwave popping.

PICO DE GALLO

*Best made fresh and eaten the same day, this can be refriger-
ated for a day or two. Serve with grilled meats or as an
appetizer dip for tortilla chips.*

1 cup coarsely chopped tomato
¼ cup coarsely chopped onion
1 tablespoon fresh cilantro, finely chopped
2 or 3 fresh serrano peppers, minced
½ teaspoon salt

Stir together onion, tomato, cilantro, and peppers. Add salt and
mix well.

❋ *Yields 1½ to 2 cups*

SONIA'S SEVEN-LAYER DIP

*This colorful dip is easily taken to bring-a-dish parties and is
almost a meal by itself. You need to use a glass pan, preferably 13 by 9, so that people can see that they should dip to
scoop some of the bottom layer.*

1 can pinto beans, smashed
2 or 3 avocados, mashed (Add a teaspoon of vinegar or
    lemon juice while mashing to prevent discoloration.)
1 small container of sour cream
Diced green onions
1 small bottle of mild picante sauce
Grated cheese (Longhorn cheddar is good.)
Cubed fresh tomatoes

Spread beans on the bottom of the pan. Spread the mashed
avocados onto the bean layer. Spread sour cream on top of avocados. Sprinkle a layer of diced green onions. Spread a layer of

picante sauce. Sprinkle a layer of grated cheese. Sprinkle cubed tomatoes on top as a garnish.

NOTE: To garnish even more, stab triangular-shaped taco chips into the dip in a design that goes around the pan, or in different places at random. Serve with more taco chips for dipping.

NOTE: You can substitute a can of refried beans, already mashed, for the pinto beans. You can also substitute ready-made guacamole dip for the mashed avocados.

APRIL FOOL "MYSTERY" FOODS

Published as an April Fool menu of surprises in the March 29, 1979, *San Antonio Light*'s Living Today section.

BARBARA MCGEE'S SAUERKRAUT HORS D'OEUVRE LOAF

When this loaf was sampled by people who did not know that sauerkraut was in it, some of whom said they disliked sauerkraut, many thought it was a crab dip or loaf.

1 can sauerkraut
2 cups sharp cheddar cheese, grated
2 tablespoons onion, chopped
2 tablespoons pimiento, chopped
3 tablespoons green pepper, chopped
1 hard-cooked egg, chopped
¼ cup mayonnaise
½ teaspoon salt
½ cup corn flakes or bread crumbs
1 (8-ounce) package cream cheese

Drain and chop sauerkraut, squeeze as dry as possible. Mix all ingredients except cream cheese and shape into a a large loaf pan or several small molds. Chill overnight. Remove from mold and ice with cream cheese which has been softened to spreading consistency. Garnish with olives and or pimiento and serve with crackers.

COLA CHICKEN

1 fryer, cut into serving pieces
1 cup cola soft drink
1 cup ketchup

Season chicken well. Cover with mixture of cola and ketchup. Bake at 350°F for 1 to 1½ hours or until soft and browned.

ANN LINDSAY GREER'S MYSTERY MASHED POTATOES

(As reprinted in the San Antonio Light)
The secret is that they're not all potatoes!

4 to 5 baking potatoes
1 cup lima beans (cooked)
6 slices bacon, fried crisp, broken into chunks
3 tablespoons milk
1 tablespoon butter
1 teaspoon salt
½ teaspoon pepper
1 teaspoon fresh minced parsley
1 teaspoon freeze-dried chives
1 tablespoon mayonnaise
4 ounces cheese, grated (optional)

299

Bake the potatoes and cook the lima beans. Fry the bacon. Remove the "meat" from each potato, keeping the skins to contain the stuffing.

Put the potato chunks in the processor bowl with the beans and process with steel blade. Mince and combine. Heat the milk and butter together. Add the seasonings, mayonnaise and bacon to the bowl, then add the milk and butter through the feeder tube with the machine running. Process briefly.

Stuff the puree into the potato skins and top with cheese. Bake 15 minutes until the cheese is melted and/or the potatoes are heated through.

MRS. CHESTER BARROW'S WATERGATE SALAD

A pretty salad that requires only a minimum effort.

1 (9-ounce) container whipped topping
1 small box pistachio-flavored instant pudding
1 (1-pound) can crushed pineapple and juice
1 cup miniature marshmallows
½ cup chopped nuts

Fold dry pudding mix into whipped topping. Add pineapple and juice. Add marshmallows and nuts. Refrigerate. Serve on a bed of lettuce.

TEXAS COWBELLS BEEF BROWNIES

A recipe that makes dessert sort of a meal.

3 eggs
1 cup sugar
½ teaspoon salt
1 teaspoon vanilla
½ cup butter or margarine
2 squares unsweetened chocolate

½ cup finely ground cooked beef
¾ cup flour
½ teaspoon baking powder
½ cup chopped nut meats
Confectioners' sugar

Beat eggs, sugar, salt, and vanilla until fluffy. Melt butter and chocolate, cool and add to mixture. Add cooked ground beef and mix well. Sift flour and baking powder together and stir into mixture. Add nuts. Spread in an 8- × 8-inch pan lined with wax paper. Bake at 350°F for 35 minutes. Cool, then sprinkle with confectioners' sugar.

MOCK PECAN PIE

1 cup pinto beans, uncooked or canned, unseasoned
1½ to 2 cups sugar
4 ounces butter or margarine
4 eggs
2 tablespoons molasses or dark corn syrup
3 teaspoons vanilla
½ teaspoon salt
Unbaked (9-inch) pastry pie shell
½ cup chopped pecans

If using uncooked beans, cook unseasoned in water until well done. Drain and mash cooked or canned beans thoroughly. In a medium bowl, cream the sugar and butter. Add well-beaten eggs, molasses, vanilla, and salt. Mix in the well-mashed beans.

Pour into an unbaked pie shell and sprinkle chopped pecans on top. Bake at 350°F for 45 to 60 minutes, until firm or a knife inserted into the center comes out clean. Serve with whipped cream or nondairy whipped topping.

❀ *Serves 8*

❁ Shortcut "Quickie" Foods and ❁ Beverages to Serve Unexpected Guests

A reader wrote that sometimes her mom would have supper prepared and ready to serve and then unexpected guests would drop in. When she wasn't sure that there would be enough food to go around, Mom would tell the family, "F H B," which was the family code for "Family Hold Back." Then the family wouldn't take too much food and would leave plenty for the guests to feel welcome.

This story reminds me of an Irish table blessing that one of my editors saw on the wall of an old cottage while touring in Ireland: "May the Lord bless us and keep us alive, for we've seven for dinner and food for only five."

Baby Food: So you didn't plan for a baby guest? You know you can puree most fruits, vegetables, or meat in the blender, but did you know that you can make baby or instant oatmeal from regular oats in the blender, too? Put the dry, uncooked, old-fashioned or three-minute oats into the blender and blend for a few seconds, until they look like baby or instant oatmeal. Mix with formula or milk, as appropriate.

Banana Pops (Easy "Kid-Food" Treat): Poke frozen treat sticks or plastic spoon handles into bananas and freeze for a half day or less. Have some handy at a birthday party for the child who can't eat dairy or cake.

Cheese Cake (Shortcut, No Bake): Mix 1 package of vanilla pudding according to directions. Add an 8-ounce package of softened cream cheese and mix until well blended. Pour the mixture into a ready-made graham-cracker pie crust and refrigerate until set. Top with your favorite canned pie filling and serve. Keep leftovers in the refrigerator.

Cherry-Chocolate Dessert (Shortcut, No Cooking): One reader combines equal parts of cherry pie filling and chocolate pudding for a quick dessert—a sort of Black Forest pudding or parfait.

Chicken and Dumplings (Quick Lunch, "Comfort Food" for Two): Heat 1 can chicken noodle soup or chicken broth to a boil. Combine 2 cups baking mix with ⅔ cup milk and blend well (or use your favorite dumpling recipe). Spoon dough into boiling soup; cover lightly and reduce heat to a simmer. Cook for 12 to 15 minutes.

NOTE: When you are spooning dough into the boiling soup, dip the spoon into the hot broth after each spoonful to prevent the dough from sticking to the spoon.

Cinnamon Butter or "Sin Butter" (My Favorite): Combine ½ pound of margarine, 3 tablespoons of cinnamon, and ½ pound of confectioners' sugar and mix well with an electric mixer. This recipe yields about 20 ounces of delicious and delightful "sin butter" to spread on toast or rolls at brunch or lunch. Store it in an airtight plastic container and keep refrigerated.

Coffee (Shortcut Chocolate Gourmet): To 1 cup of coffee, add drops of chocolate extract to taste. For 8 cups, add ½ teaspoon extract to the pot. For 24 cups, add about 1½ teaspoons extract.

Deviled Eggs (Shortcut): Add canned deviled ham to the yolk mix for a different flavor in deviled eggs.

Grapes: Try some of these great grape tricks:

1. Freeze grapes and substitute them for ice cubes in drinks.
2. Make a grape-kabob drink garnish by alternating different colored grapes on a stick.
3. Decorate cakes with grapes or use grapes as an edible centerpiece or edible decoration on a cheeseboard.
4. Add seeded, halved grapes to chicken or tuna salad.
5. Add grapes to your favorite gelatin for a surprise texture.

Ice Cream Dessert (Shortcut): Drizzle Kahlua, crème de menthe, chocolate liqueur, or other suitable liqueurs over a scoop of vanilla ice cream that you've placed in a glass serving bowl. You'll have instant dessert. You can also put a slice of pound cake or angel food cake beneath or beside the ice cream if you have some.

Iced Tea: You'll always be ready to offer full-flavored, delicious iced tea to a drop-in guest if you make iced-tea cubes. Pour tea (sweetened or not) into ice cube trays and freeze. If you need the trays, you can remove the tea cubes after they are frozen and store them in a zipper plastic bag. When you want iced tea, put the cubes in the glass and pour in freshly made tea; it won't get diluted as the ice begins to melt.

Lemonade: When you have lemons and/or limes and a juicer, you can make lemon or lime juice ice cubes to store in freezer trays or in zipper bags. One cube in water makes a glass of lemonade or limeade; sweeten to taste.

Mint Tea: If you grow mint in your garden, pick a handful of mint leaves, drop them into a quart of boiling water, steep for 10 minutes, strain, and serve.

Rice Cereal Treats: Need some "kid food" in a hurry? Instead of making rice cereal treats the conventional way by melting miniature marshmallows and butter and so forth, try this no-cook-at-all recipe. Mix rice cereal (even generic works) with marshmallow cream—no butter necessary except to grease the pan and your hands so you can press the mixture into the pan.

NOTE: For a no-mess method, instead of greasing your hands, you can put a sheet of plastic wrap over the top of the mixture after you put it into the pan and then press away.

Taco Casserole (Shortcut Quick Dish) (Also please see Sonia's Seven-Layer Dip): Grease (or spray with nonstick spray) a casserole dish, put a bit of salsa on the bottom, then add torn-up tacos or taco chips and layer with leftover taco meat and/or beans, cheese, peppers, and more salsa. Bake until hot, then cover with sour cream, olives, and chopped lettuce before serving. This is one of those "non-recipes" we all keep in our heads—there's no set amount or even set number of ingredients, only what you have on hand as leftovers or in cans in the cupboard.

LETTER OF LAUGHTER: A reader who makes "non-recipes" when she cleans leftovers out of the fridge and freezer wrote that when her children were eating a particularly delicious "creative" casserole, one of them said, "This is really good, but it's one of those things she makes up . . . Too bad we'll never have it again."

Tomato Soup: Cook 1 quart of peeled tomatoes, fresh or canned, in a saucepan over medium heat until they are soft. After cooking, strain off seeds and mash remaining lumps. Then bring the tomatoes to a boil and add a pinch of baking soda. Then add 1 quart of hot boiled milk, then salt and pepper to taste. Last, add 3 tablespoons of butter and rolled cracker crumbs (optional). Heat through and serve. *Bon appetit!*

NOTE: You can "cheat" and just start with a large can of tomato juice. The whole fresh or canned tomatoes taste better, but the canned juice is faster because it bypasses the first cooking and mashing steps.

Yogurt Tricks: Stir fruit cocktail into vanilla yogurt for a nutricious and delicious fruit salad or dessert. Or make a yogurt parfait in a wineglass by layering vanilla yogurt with any of the following: small chocolate chips, crunch cereal, jelly or jam, fresh or canned fruit pieces.

❀ Make-Ahead and ❀ Take-Along Recipes

While many of the recipes in the Recipe Section are good for taking to potluck events and many can be made ahead of a party, at least partially, so that you don't have so much to do on the day of the party, the following recipes are especially good for these situations.

TWO EDAM CHEESE SPREADS

These two spreads are delicious, can be made ahead, and are served in their own "bowl," which is the red wax shell in which the cheese is sold. Nobody will have to return a container to you if you take them to a potluck event.

EDAM CHEESE SPREAD WITH WINE

1 large Edam cheese (at room temperature)
1 teaspoon parsley
1 teaspoon pimiento
2 teaspoons sherry wine
2 teaspoons minced onion
1 tablespoon mayonnaise
1 teaspoon Worcestershire sauce

Carefully slice the top from the cheese approximately 1 inch from the top. Scoop out the cheese up to ½ inch from the rind. Combine cheese and other ingredients in a large bowl. Blend well with a mixer and return mixture to shell.

Refrigerate for several hours or overnight. Serve as an hors d'oeuvre with breads, crackers, or water biscuits.

EDAM CHEESE SPREAD WITH BEER

1 large Edam cheese (at room temperature)
1 cup beer
¼ cup butter
1 teaspoon caraway seeds
1 teaspoon dry mustard
½ teaspoon celery salt

Prepare cheese as above. Combine scooped-out cheese with beer, then blend in the other ingredients. Return to shell, refrigerate, and serve as above.

FAST SHRIMP SPREAD

8 ounces cream cheese, softened
½ cup mayonnaise
4 ounces tiny cocktail shrimp, drained and rinsed
   (preferably fresh or frozen)
2 tablespoons seafood cocktail sauce
½ cup onion, finely chopped
⅛ teaspoon garlic salt

Thoroughly mix cream cheese and mayonnaise until well blended. Mash or chop shrimp and add to mixture; stir in remaining ingredients. Refrigerate until needed. Serve at room temperature.

❀ *Makes about 2 cups*

CHICKEN TAMALE

From Make It Now—Bake It Later

3 tamales, cut into bite-size pieces
1 cup canned tomato pulp (drain solid pack canned
   tomatoes well)
1 small can whole kernel corn
1 cup ripe olives, chopped or sliced
½ cup chili sauce
1 tablespoon olive or salad oil
1 tablespoon Worcestershire sauce
2 cups cooked chicken (equal to 1 large stewing hen), cut
   into good-size chunks
1 cup grated cheese

Mix all of the ingredients but the cheese and store in a casserole
in the refrigerator. When you are ready to bake it, cover the top
with grated cheese and bake for 1 hour at 350°F.

❀ *Serves 6–8*

NOODLES AND MUSHROOMS

From Make It Now—Bake It Later

1 green pepper, diced
1 white onion, diced
½ cup salad oil
1 box medium-wide noodles
½ can cream-style corn
1 can tomato soup
1 small can chopped or sliced ripe olives
1 small can mushrooms, drained
Grated cheese

Fry diced pepper and onions slowly in oil until glossy. Boil noodles for 9 minutes. Mix all ingredients together, except cheese. Place in a casserole and refrigerate. When ready to bake, cover top with grated cheese. Place casserole in pan containing a small amount of warm water and bake at 350°F for 1 hour.

NOTE: This recipe can be a side dish with ham or a roast, or if you want to serve it for a main dish, brown 1 pound of ground round or chuck and add it to the casserole.

PARSLEY DRESSING FOR FRESH TOMATOES

From Make It Now—Bake It Later

2 cups fresh parsley
½ cup chopped chives
1 cup sweet pickles, drained
2 cloves garlic
Salt and pepper to taste

Cut chives very fine (scissors work best). Put all ingredients through the food grinder or processor twice, using the small blade. Save any juices that escape. Then add:

½ cup olive oil
½ cup red wine vinegar
¼ cup tarragon vinegar
Juice left over from grinding

Mix all well and keep in a covered jar at room temperature for 24 hours, then refrigerate. This dressing will keep in the refrigerator for 2 weeks, so it can really be made ahead. Serve ice cold on a platter of chilled, peeled, sliced tomatoes.

CASSEROLES

Everyone has a favorite take-a-long lasagna recipe. The following casseroles are a delicious change in flavors and, best of all, can be ways to use up leftover turkey or ham from holiday meals. This makes them good next-day luncheon casseroles when you've had overnight houseguests for the main holiday meal.

TASTY TURKEY TETRAZZINI

⅔ cup mayonnaise
⅓ cup flour
½ teaspoon celery salt
Dash pepper
2 cups milk
7 ounces spaghetti, broken into thirds, cooked and drained
2 cups cooked turkey, chopped
3 ounces Parmesan cheese, grated
1 (4-ounce) can mushrooms, drained
2 tablespoons pimiento, chopped
2 cups fresh bread cubes
3 tablespoons margarine, melted

Mix mayonnaise, flour, and seasonings in a medium saucepan and gradually add milk. Stir constantly over low heat until thickened. Add spaghetti, turkey, 2 ounces of cheese, and all of the mushrooms and pimiento and mix gently.

Pour the mixture into a 2-quart casserole dish. Toss the bread cubes with margarine and the remaining cheese, then sprinkle over the casserole for topping. Bake at 350°F for 30 minutes or until lightly browned.

❅ *Serves 6*

HAM PIE WITH CHEESE BISCUIT TOP

The Filling
3 tablespoons onion, minced
4 tablespoons green pepper, chopped
4 tablespoons butter or margarine
6 tablespoons flour
1 (10½-ounce) can condensed chicken soup
1⅓ cups milk
1⅓ cups diced ham
1 tablespoon lemon juice

Place onion and green pepper in a medium or large saucepan. Soften over medium heat in butter or margarine. Do not brown.

Add flour and blend until frothy. Then stir in soup and milk until thick and smooth. Add ham and lemon juice, remove from heat, and pour into buttered casserole.

Cheese Biscuit Top
1½ cups prepared biscuit mix
½ cup grated cheese
6 tablespoons milk

Combine biscuit mix, cheese, and milk to make a medium-soft dough. Place dough on a floured board and roll into a thick layer. Cut into biscuits with biscuit or doughnut cutter.

Arrange biscuits on top of the ham/vegetable mixture as a pie crust and bake in a 450°F oven for 20 minutes or until biscuits are golden brown.

❄ *Serves 4–6*

DESSERTS

ANGEL FOOD CAKE AND ICE CREAM

A make-ahead and keep-on-hand-in-the-freezer dessert.

1 angel food cake, baked from mix or store-bought
1 gallon of ice cream, any flavor
Chocolate syrup, liqueur of a flavor to complement the ice
     cream, or fresh fruit

Slice the angel food cake into three layers with a thread (it works more neatly than a knife). Let ice cream soften a bit. Now, working as quickly as you can, scoop or slice ice cream so that you can layer about ½ to 1 inch of ice cream between the cake layers as you stack them and also on the top of the cake. "Frost" the sides of the cake with the remaining ice cream. It may be very soft by now, so you may have to use your hands to press slabs of ice cream to the sides of the cake.

Wrap the cake with plastic wrap and rush it to the freezer to get solid. Then add an extra wrap of aluminum foil. The cake will keep several weeks in the freezer.

At serving time, allow to soften for about 5 to 10 minutes to make slicing it easier. Serve as is or with chocolate syrup or a liqueur drizzled over it or drizzled in a design on the plate before you place the cake on it. Some combinations are vanilla ice cream cake with crème de menthe, or chocolate ice cream cake with Kahlua. Or use fresh fruit: strawberry ice cream cake garnished with fresh strawberries, and so on.

CRANBERRY FLUFF

A quick and pretty holiday dessert!

1½ cups raw cranberries, finely chopped
1 cup miniature marshmallows
¼ cup sugar
½ cup mayonnaise
1½ cups apple, finely chopped
¼ cup chopped walnuts
⅛ teaspoon ground cinnamon

Combine the cranberries, miniature marshmallows, and sugar and stir lightly. Cover and chill before gently mixing in the remaining ingredients.

❉ *Serves 6*

RASPBERRY FLUFF

1 (3-ounce) packet raspberry-flavor gelatin
1 cup boiling water
1 (12-ounce) package frozen raspberries
1 pint raspberry sherbet
1 cup whipped cream or nondairy whipped topping, thawed

Pour gelatin mix into a large glass or metal bowl. Stir in boiling water until gelatin is dissolved. Put frozen raspberries into hot gelatin and separate with a fork. Add sherbet and blend. Put in refrigerator and allow to cool and solidify for approximately 1 hour. Fold in whipped cream or nondairy topping and mix well. Chill for several hours or overnight.

CHRISTMAS RAINBOW POKE CAKE

This favorite isn't just for Christmas but can be enjoyed any time you want a pretty dessert. There's no rule that says you can't substitute different but compatible gelatin flavors to get different colors.

1 package (double-layer) white cake mix
1 (3-ounce) packet raspberry-flavor gelatin
1 (3-ounce) packet lime-flavor gelatin
2 cups boiling water
8 ounces nondairy whipped topping, thawed
Green and red gumdrops

Prepare cake mix as directed on package. Pour batter into 2 round pans (9 by 1½ inches) and bake as directed. Cool about 10 minutes in the pans before removing and allowing to cool on a wire rack. Clean the pans.

Place cake layers, top-sides up, back into the clean pans, and prick each layer with a wooden-handled utility fork at ½-inch intervals. Dissolve the raspberry-flavor gelatin in 1 cup of boiling water in a bowl and spoon over 1 cake layer. Repeat with lime-flavor gelatin over the other cake layer.

Refrigerate both layers for 3 to 4 hours. Remove pans by dipping in warm water for 10 seconds, then invert them over a plate and shake gently to loosen.

Sandwich layers together using one cup of the whipped topping. Frost the cake with the remaining topping and refrigerate. Decorate with flattened gumdrops cut into holly leaf and berry shapes if it's for Christmas.

Index

Index

Index

Dough, 51, 280
Doughnuts, easiest ever delicious, 282
Drain cleaner, 83
Dressing, corn bread, Heloise's, 222
Drink mixers, 12–13
Dumplings
  and chicken soup, 303
  matzo balls, 268
Dusting, 83, 84, 87, 90
Easter, 165–167
Eggnog, lower-calorie, Heloise's, 216
Eggplant, grilled, 242
Eggs
  boiling, 42–43
  deviled, 303
  egg drop chicken soup, 259
  floor spill, 104–105
  green, 193
  herb blends for, 294
  salad, 196
  salmonella in, 22
  substitute, 59
Elderly, gifts for, 114, 117, 119
Elephant ears, 281
Entertainment, party, 148

Fajitas, 238–239
Family history, 185
Family reunions, 138
Father's Day, 169–170
Fats
  burning, 104
  disposal of, 43
  spattering, 104
Favors, party, 71, 134–135
February celebrations, 186–191
Fireplace, 70–71, 83
Fish
  doneness, 23
  herb blends for, 294
  salmonettes, 230
  swordfish, grilled, with mustard sauce, 223
  tuna salad, 243, 303
Floor
  scuff marks, 85
  spills, 104–105, 106
Flour, 17, 59–60
Flowers
  arranging, 71
  centerpiece, 69, 72
  gifts, 115–116
  transporting, 71
Food
  African/African American, 164
  amounts per serving, 15–16
  French, 193
  gifts, 115, 116–118, 126, 295
  handling, 22–26

menu planning, 5–7
nonperishable, 11
perishable, 11, 19, 20, 22, 26, 117
poisoning, 22, 30, 117
portable, 64–65, 143
repair tips, 31–34
service needs, 7
storage, 27–31
substitutions, 56–63
Football bowl games, 182
Frappé, fruity, 288
Friendship cake and brandied fruit starter,
  285–287
Frosting, substitute, 57–58
Frozen foods
  hamburger patties, 45
  inventory list, 29–30
  pre-chopped, 30–31
  thawing, 23
  treat sticks, 44, 302
Fruit
  brandied starter, and friendship cake, 285–
    287
  candied, 17
  candied, citrus, simple, 276–277
  dried, 30
  frappé, 288
  ice cream topping, 288–289
  peel, 17, 44, 47
  salad, 39
  soups, 271–272
  stains, 43
Fudge
  cookies, no-bake, Lorraine's, 277
  Heloise, 275
Funerals, 143
Funnel cakes, 282–283
Furniture care/repair, 94–99, 111

Garbage disposal
  cleaning, 84
  odors, 44, 83–84
  unsticking, 105
Garlic
  bacterial problems, 22, 30
  chives, 295
  crushing, 61
  in oil, 30
  removing from cooked foods, 294–295
  shrimp, 223
Gazpacho, 269
Gelatin
  confetti, on ice cream, 288–289
  fruit juice in, 61
  grapes in, 303
  scooping, 44
  shapes, 44
Gift cards, 127–131

318